Here was a smiling country
Winning the heart at sight
—Owen Wister

THE SMILING COUNTRY

A HISTORY OF THE METHOW VALLEY

Sally Portman

Published by Sun Mountain Resorts Inc.
Winthrop WA 98862

Cover: "Spring Awakening Methow Valley" by Laurie Fry.

Book design and production by
Pack & Paddle Publishing, Inc.
Port Orchard, Washington

ISBN 0-9636921-3-5

 This book is produced in the USA
with recycled paper.

TABLE OF CONTENTS

PREFACE

I asked Sally Portman, a resident of the Methow Valley who has a deep appreciation for this area, to write this book. It is designed to preserve some of the wonderful memories my family has for this special place. Since 1973 our family has made annual visits to the Methow. For many years we traveled into the mountains on horseback with packer Jack Wilson.

Because we love the Methow and its unspoiled beauty we want to make an effort to help preserve it. Thus, a portion of the price you have paid for this book goes to the Elizabeth Haub Foundation which is dedicated to protecting the environment. This foundation was formed in memory of my husband's mother, who in the early 1960s recognized the problems facing our planet. During her lifetime, she actively promoted the preservation of our environment, a matter very important to her and to me.

The foundation, headquartered in Washington D.C., is creating a library of publications which support the legal protection of the environment. It also actively supports international treaties designed to guard against the destruction of the environment.

All over the world we see the destruction of total landscapes, particularly forests and wetlands. Daily, animal species are being declared extinct. Many irreversible things are done today without concern for the future of our planet. I believe strongly that we should not delegate the responsibility for an intact environment only to the government. Every one of us should be involved.

I believe the fact that you are reading this book is evidence that you share my concern over our responsibility to ensure that we leave to our children and grandchildren "Nature" intact, as we have experienced it.

Thank you for being involved.

Helga Haub

INTRODUCTION

Here was a smiling country
Winning the heart at sight
—Owen Wister

These were author Owen Wister's words when he visited the Methow Valley. It's the theme that reappears again and again in the Methow's history and in this book—the beauty of the valley and how its beauty affects our lives. When I drove into the Methow for the first time, it won my heart at sight just as it did Wister's. The same could be said for the pioneers. The hardships they faced here in an unsettled land were balanced by the joys of living in such a lovely place.

Soon after I became Winthrop librarian, I became aware of the need for a book on Methow Valley history. Newcomers wanted to learn about the Methow's heritage. Tourists requested information on the pioneers and miners, the cowboys and Indians of the area. They wanted to know all about Sun Mountain Lodge, the unique Methow mountaintop resort, who built it and how it was constructed in this remote place. My own interest in learning about the Methow's origins had always been strong and as librarian I found it became stronger.

True, pioneers, journalists, and researchers had already written about the valley's past—the *Okanogan County Heritage*, *Methow Valley News* and two dozen or more books and publications featured the valley's history—but it needed to be brought together in one book. When possible funding for publishing a local history became available through Erivan and Helga Haub, I knew I would try to write the Methow's memoirs.

Before I began this project I visualized a short book and a year's investment of time. As I began my research I immediately realized that to do the valley and its people justice, the book could not be brief; the information was too extensive, the biographies too interesting, the photos too irresistible.

A summer's project turned into a three-year saga. Even so, I left out lots of history. Out of all the pioneer stories, I chose only a few. I limited my topics and my interviews. This doesn't mean the people and events left out weren't worthy subjects to include. I simply had to limit my research at some point. (I hope the final product tells a story complete enough to satisfy pioneers and their descendants, the people whose roots are in the valley.)

For the rest of the readers, I hope this chronicle brings both a new meaning to familiar names and places in the valley and sparks a continuing interest in learning about and preserving the heritage of this unique and still-unspoiled place.

Instead of writing a strictly chronological history, I've chosen to organize the book by subject. Each chapter focuses on a different aspect of history that often took place at the same time as events and trends described in other sections of the book. Thus, each chapter paints another layer of history within a limited time frame.

Although the chapters follow a logical sequence, every chapter can stand on its own. Choose a chapter at random and it will make sense without having to read all that comes before it.

Acknowledgements

I'd like to thank the following people who helped me produce this book:

—my mother, my editor, Taffy Larcom, retired professional journalist and journalism professor, whose gentle corrections, wise suggestions and appreciative comments, all penned in her fresh and lively writing style, improved the form and substance of the text, boosted my spirits and gave me confidence in my work;

—my husband, Don, my primary and constant advisor, who at any time of the day always received my interruptions, questions and requests for his opinion with unfailing thoughtfulness and love;

—Barbara Duffy, the Methow Valley's acclaimed historian, for helping me with her remarkable memory of names, places and events and for offering to me the use of her own history notes and personal sources of information;

—Ken White and Dick Chavey with whom I spent many enlightening hours tramping over the Methow landscape on history-discovery field trips (Ken always shared with me the poetry he found in history);

—generous Dick Webb, Twisp photographer, who, because he believes historical photos are the property of the whole Methow Valley community, made it possible for me to include many great pictures which otherwise I could not have afforded;

—Isabelle Spohn, who wrote extensively and so fluently about her volunteer work for MVCC;

—Mary and Frank Kenney for their advice, encouragement and patience; Mary, especially for her professional proof-reading job;

—Marjory White, whose writing expertise got me started on the editing process of this book;

—Mary Thompson, owner of the Trail's End Bookstore, for her expert advice on typeface and book cover appeal;

—Henry Van Baalen for his support of this project from the start and his enthusiasm for the book after reading the manuscript;

—John Barline for his helpful advice and assistance in publishing the book;

—North Central Regional Library, the Shafer Museum, the Okanogan County Museum, the Washington State Historical Society staffs and employees in the Special Collections Division Library at the University of Washington for their assistance in research and in providing photographs;

—Erivan and Helga Haub for their financial support of this project and for their love of the Methow Valley which inspired their support;

—and journalist Diana Hottell for having the interest and insight and energy to interview so many Methow pioneers in the 1970s and early 1980s when they were still with us.

Sally Portman
Winthrop, Washington
December 2001

14

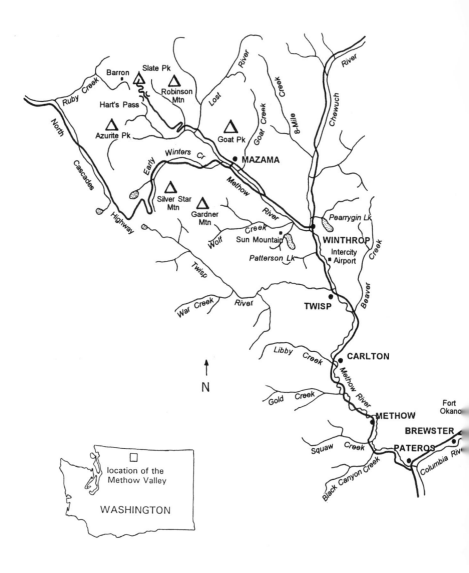

The Methow Valley:
from the Cascade Crest to the Columbia River

Chapter 1

METHOW GEOLOGY

Measuring the Methow Valley

The Methow Valley lies cradled in a mountain fortress. It's bordered on the north, south and west by the Cascade Mountains, while gentler slopes rise in the east. Twenty or more summits over 8,000 feet frame the Methow. Gardner Mountain at 9,000 feet dominates the upper end of the valley. The rugged profile of 9,000-foot Silver Star Mountain pierces the western sky. Robinson Mountain, Last Chance Point and Goat Peak ring the head of the valley, while Big Craggy, Isabella Ridge and Tiffany Mountain rise in the northern sky. Foothills flanking the valley reach as high as 5,000 feet in elevation.

The Methow River begins in the North Cascades and ends at the Columbia River. It weaves down the 70-mile-long Methow Valley, calmly at first, gaining turbulence as it descends. Flowing through the lower Black Canyon, south of the town of Methow, the river is a frothy mass of waves.

Where it meets the Columbia River the Methow Valley sits at 775 feet above sea level. The town of Twisp lies at 1,619 feet, Winthrop at 1,765 feet and Mazama at 2,150 feet. Perched at 3,000 feet, Sun Mountain Lodge overlooks the entire valley.

North of Carlton the valley opens into broad plains in some places two miles wide, while south of Gold Creek it squeezes down to a narrow width of one-eighth mile. The average width is just under a mile.

Plate Tectonics Create the Methow

The Pacific Northwest coast once lay somewhat east, not *west*, of Okanogan County. Over millions of years the coast moved west as geological forces added new land to North America.

According to the theory of plate tectonics, huge continents of land (plates) floating on a hot layer of the earth's crust began to ooze toward the original coastline. The Pacific Ocean lying between the migrating islands and coastal shores was consumed in a deep ocean trench. As the sea floor sank into the trench, it tugged the island continents with it toward the North American coast. Like putty, one plate after another was plastered to the coast.

About 100 million years ago what geologists call the Okanogan subcontinent sailed into North America to become the new coastline. The western margin of the new shoreline ran where the Okanogan River now flows.

The Methow at this time was Pacific Ocean floor. It lay submerged between the old North America plate and new plates sliding toward the coast. An abundance of shellfish lived in the shallow sea covering the Methow, and their fossil remains accumulated in Methow sediments. Fossil hunters have unearthed mollusks, ammonites and belemnites (the hard part of squids) in many areas of the valley. Sun Mountain Lodge sits on top of a *Trigonia* genus clam bed dating to the Upper Cretaceous geologic time 70 to 130 million years ago. When contractors excavated rock for the lodge swimming pool, they exposed a treasure chest of buried marine fossils, mostly clams and oysters.

While a submerged Methow played host to a trove of marine fauna, another floating land mass approached the coast. Dinosaurs living in the Okanogan highlands must have witnessed the appearance of foreign terrain on the horizon. They saw the ocean become a narrow gulf between the coast and the migrating island. Just as the dinosaurs vanished from the earth, the Cascade subcontinent collided with North America.

Once the new subcontinent hit the coast it continued traveling in a northeasterly direction, breaking the land it slid past into huge faults trending north to south. Two parallel faults formed the boundaries of the Methow. The land between the faults sank relative to the adjacent terrain, and the Methow for the first time assumed the shape of a valley.

Glacial Sculptures

When the last ice sheet began grinding its tortured path down from Canada, the Methow was already a valley drainage. The original valley floor, however, lay near the top of Goat Wall— 1,000 to 1,500 feet higher than today. Hanging valleys seen along the summit of Goat Wall mark the level of the first Methow Valley. The last continental glacier scooped the valley to a depth of 1,500 feet lower than today—then refilled the basin with sediment up to its present elevation.

The last major ice flow started about 100,000 years ago and melted out by 13,000 years ago. During these eons the glacier advanced and retreated, stagnated for a while, then melted away.

If one could have flown over the Methow in glacial times it would have looked like Greenland. A sea of ice 4,500 feet to a mile thick encapsulated the area as far south as the mouth of the Methow River near Pateros. The jagged tops of the highest local mountains stuck out like islands in the frozen ocean. The glacier rounded, smoothed and polished all the terrain lying below the highest summits.

In the wake of glaciation lay a Methow Valley completely changed. The glacier had carved the Methow drainage into a steep-sided, broad-bottomed U-shaped valley. The rock of Goat

Glacier-carved Methow Valley. Photo by Don Portman.

18

Staircase-like kame terraces. Photo by Don Portman.

Wall had been sliced vertical by the river of ice. As it cruised over the summit of Goat Peak, the glacier scored a pattern of striations in the rock face.

When the temperature rose, meltwaters began to flow between the glacier and the valley wall. Heavy with sediment, these streams deposited their overload of gravel and sand in horizontal terraces of varying widths. Because of the stop-and-go nature of the melting process, the terraces formed at different elevations. Midvalley, these so-called kame terraces create a gentle, giant staircase from the valley floor up to the mountains. Glacial meltwaters created the stair-step topography on Patterson Mountain southwest of Winthrop, and on Studhorse Mountain directly east of Winthrop. Some of the widest platforms in the Methow and Chewuch valleys serve as high dryland hay fields.

Many of the Methow's side canyons formed when the valley became overwhelmed with glacial meltwater. Pipestone Canyon, Davis Lake, Pearrygin Lake, Patterson Lake and Elbow Coulee were all dredged out by meltwaters from the ice sheet seeking the path of least resistance. The main Methow Valley was plugged by a huge ribbon of ice which acted like a dam. Since the meltwaters couldn't descend to the plugged central valley, they squeezed out and gouged side channels. Later, when more of the main valley glacier melted, the flow could return to the Methow River basin. One meltwater torrent had first been forced out Elbow Coulee to the Twisp Valley. Eventually this glacial river returned to the main valley by way of the Thompson Creek drainage, carving the Moccasin Lake Ranch area in the process.

The Methow's Twin Lakes, considered classic kettle lakes by geologists, formed as two gigantic blocks of glacial ice melted and left deep depressions in the terrain. Since the holes were below the water table, they filled up and became lakes. There are also several deep cone-shaped pits resembling amphitheaters located in the Twin Lakes area. These too must have been formed from melting cubes of glacial ice.

During its southward journey, the Canadian-derived ice sheet picked up and carried along a phenomenal load of rock and soil. Thus, wherever the glacier melted, it left an untidy trail of debris. On road cuts one still sees unsorted glacial till. The entire Twin Lakes area is a rumpled, lumpy, glacial rock and gravel dump. Scattered about the Methow are also large boulders different in composition than the bedrock on which they rest. These boulders, called erratics, are foreign imports that hitchhiked on the ice sheet and were dropped off once the glacier melted. A good place to see these souvenirs of the last ice age is on the Ridge Trail at Sun Mountain.

Bibliography

Alt, David. *Roadside Geology*. Mountain Press Publishing Company, Missoula, Montana, 1984.

Barksdale, Julian. "A Strange Love Affair: a Geologic History of Western Okanogan County, Washington." *Okanogan County Heritage*, Spring 1983.

Barksdale, Tucker. Phone interview. Winthrop, Washington, fall 1991.

Rohn, Thomas Jesse. Introduction to "Guy Waring and the Methow Trading Company, 1891-1936." University of Washington Master's Thesis, 1973.

Wilson, Bruce. *The Late Frontier: A History of Okanogan County, Washington*. Okanogan County Historical Society, 1990.

Infant on cradleboard (1900-1910). This effectively designed cradleboard snugged the baby inside a buckskin pouch with a protective board above its head. This baby is probably a girl since the cradleboard is fully beaded. Usually for boys only the edge was decorated. Photo by Latham, from Special Collections Division, University of Washington Libraries, negative NA1026.

Chapter 2

THE METHOW INDIANS

When Indians Were Year-Round Residents

The first Methow Valley inhabitants arrived 8,000 to 10,000 years ago, say anthropologists. These early immigrants lived much like Indians the white explorers and settlers met here during the late 1800s and early 1900s. In one important way, however, their lifestyles differed. The more recent Methow Indians were seasonal residents, while researchers believe the original natives stayed in the valley year-round. Thus, the Stone Age settlers, unlike their descendants, faced the problem of winter survival.

To protect themselves during the Methow's cold, snowy season, the aborigines observed the wise ways of other species and burrowed into the ground. Large circular, square, or rectangular depressions which archaeologists believe to be pit house foundations have been found at 18 sites in the Methow including the mouth of the Methow River, the mouth of Wolf Creek, and near the mouth of Early Winters Creek. The Indians excavated these permanent shelters some time before A.D. 1600. (A researcher found a 300-plus-year-old tree growing in one pit house.)

The Indian pit houses resembled basements with conical roofs over the tops. The builder dug a pit about 5 feet deep, then used grass mats, willow branches or poles for roofing materials.

Within these larger depressions, scientists discovered smaller talus-filled holes dug in the earth, containing thick deposits of wood ash, charred pine cones and layers of rock. Researchers say these conglomerates are ancient earth ovens. Smoke from the pit-house fire escaped through a hole in the roof.

During the long hours of winter darkness, the Stone Age people created tools and utensils. Weapons, such as arrowheads, spearheads and tomahawks, have been discovered in pit shelters as well as earthenware mortars and pestles. At the Shafer Museum in Winthrop, Indian antiques on display include arrowheads, bottle-shaped mallets, paint pots, pestles worn smooth from grinding roots, seeds and grains, plus a ceremonial tube smoking pipe.

The earliest Methow dwellers established temporary seasonal camps as well as permanent winter villages. Many Indians camped at the mouth of Beaver Creek and continued to set up tepees there after white settlers homesteaded the area.

From the beginning Indians frequented a campsite at the mouth of the Twisp River. Now the Twisp City Park, this scenic shoreline offered the natives flat terrain perfect for setting up tepees as well as a strategic spot for trapping salmon.

Indians had no written language, but they still preserved their stories on stone. They concocted paint from "red stone" (iron oxide) mixed with tallow (an animal fat) and painted indelible pictographs on boulders. Historians believe young natives in training revealed their hopes and dreams in the rock paintings or they related events which occurred during their training for adulthood.

Pictographs on the Chewuch Road. Photo courtesy Forest Service.

Ancient Indians painted scenes at sites throughout the Methow Valley. Indian artwork appears near the base of Grizzly Mountain northwest of Winthrop and also at several sites along the Chewuch River. One can view a fairly well-preserved Indian pictograph on a huge granite boulder about one-half mile before Falls Creek on the West Chewuch Road. Cross the 20-mile bridge over the Chewuch, then go north a little more than one mile to find another massive pictograph rock. "Unidentified Indian Objects" could be the title of this second portrayal. The composition is very old, for slow-growing lichen (average growth rate is .0004 inch to .23 inch per year) covers part of the artist's work.

Like most of the 100 or more tribes of Washington state, the Methows spoke a Salish dialect. But since dialects differed, they communicated mostly by sign language when trading with tribes from out of the area. "Bella Coola" jade found here indicates the Methows traded with tribes as far away as the coast of British Columbia, Canada.

After whites came to the valley, the Indians developed a universal language called "Chinook," which contained Salish words as well as English, Spanish and French words. Many pioneers conversed with Indians in Chinook.

Long ago local Indians logged huge cedars in the Lost River area to carve canoes for themselves and neighboring tribes. US Forest Service workers accidentally came upon cut stumps in this vicinity they estimate to be 500 years old. Even then, these massive trees were rare; hence, they were hoarded by generations of Indian canoe-builders.

The lifestyle of local Indians probably remained unchanged for 6,000 years. Then suddenly a revolution occurred which completely transformed the Indians' world. Indians acquired horses and became equestrians.

Horses arrived in the Okanogan territory in the mid- to late 1700s. They came first from the plains east of the Rocky Mountains, then later from California. By the early 1800s Methow Indians rode horses more than they walked. This efficient new vehicle of transport doubled the speed and the distance Indians could travel. Horses became a source of wealth and a measure of worth. The creatures brought pleasure and offered endless sport. When the pioneers arrived in the Methow, they marveled at the grace and dexterity of Indian riders.

When Indians acquired horses their lifestyle changed radically. Photo from the Okanogan County Historical Society, negative 1882.

The introduction of horsepower not only revolutionized Indian transportation, it radically changed their seasonal migration patterns. Before horses, the Methow tribe hunkered down in the valley during the winter months. But their new charges couldn't feed once deep snow covered the valley. To solve this problem the tribe vacationed with their horses in warmer, snow-free climes where their herd could graze through the entire winter.

How Indians Made a Living

For Indians, making a living meant simply supplying themselves with a continual source of food. In spring, summer and fall a cycle of food gathering, fishing, hunting and preserving went on in temporary Indian camps. By snowfall, enough provisions had to be stored to last the winter. During the coldest months, only an occasional hunting trip to provide fresh meat was necessary.

Ownership of land was an unfamiliar concept to Methows, though they recognized traditional "homelands"—grasslands, rivers, creeks, lakes and hills where they hunted, fished and gathered plant food. The homeland for the Methow tribe was the Methow Valley. Within the valley, the local tribe migrated with the seasons, traveling the most during spring and summer when they chased the richest plant food sources.

Tepees were the perfect abode for these nomads because they could be erected or torn down in minutes. To construct their tepees, most early Indians used tule—a form of bulrush harvested from lakes or swamps, then dried and sewn together with hemp thread to make mats 3 to 4 feet wide. First the home-builder set up a cone-shaped pole structure. He or she next laid tule mats on top of this frame, then placed a second set of poles over the mats to keep them from blowing away. Indians found tule a practical construction fabric since it became swollen when moist, thus keeping rain out, and it shrank

Tule was harvested from marshy areas, dried, sewed into mats, then placed over a framework of tepee poles. Photo by Latham, from the Special Collections Division, University of Washington Libraries, negative NA964.

26

*Huckleberry harvester. Photo by Bertelson, from the Special Collections
Division, University of Washington Libraries, negative NA1637.*

in dry heat to allow air flow.

After white people came, the Indians began covering their tepee frames with old discarded sails they bought from seamen.
Indians in the Okanogan country called their tepees "sail-
houses" when talking to white men, recalled Ulrick Fries in his
autobiography.

With the first hint of spring, Indians began hunting for bears.
The hunters hoped the sleepy hibernators still had fat on them,
for the Indians were lean from eating light winter fare. Usually
a bear hunt required only a day trip.

Local Indians traveled extensively to gather roots. A month
might be spent on the trail journeying to fresh fields where
they'd collect a year's worth of nutritious root vegetables.
Wild carrot (*Lomatium macrocarpum*), one of the first harbin-
gers of the Methow spring, was an Indian staple as well as
wild onion (*Allium spp.*), Indian potato (*Claytonia lanceolata*),
and bitterroot or rock rose (*Lewisia rediviva*), which all grow
abundantly in the valley to this day. Hills on both sides of the
Methow River between Twisp and Winthrop were renowned for
being good bitterroot and wild carrot gathering places.

Before settlers introduced pastries, Indian palates were unspoiled by the ultra-sweetness of sugary desserts. To them,

wild berries were ambrosia. All summer and fall they'd eat the fruit fresh, plus preserve it for winter.

As summer progressed, different delectable fruits would ripen to a juicy perfection. In June, July and August, Indians collected the serviceable serviceberry. Women wore coiled cedar-root baskets tied to their waists in front which kept their hands free to pick and nibble the seedy but tasty fruit. They sun-dried and stored a large part of the harvest in hemp bags. Later, they'd use the sweet berry to flavor many bitter foods. One Indian recipe called for fresh berries cooked with bitterroots or salmon eggs.

Natives savored currants and raspberries in June and July, while strawberries, thimbleberries, huckleberries, chokecherries and gooseberries ripened in July and August. In the fall Indians relished the tart, blue elderberry. Hills west of Twisp were Indian huckleberry haunts and, as any local hiker knows, the scrumptious blue-black berries are prolific on trails leading into the Sawtooth and North Cascade mountains.

Many Methow pioneers praised the Indians' fishing skills. Natives got plenty of practice catching fish for it was their main source of winter protein. Steelhead trout ran from March to July, chinook salmon from June to September, and silver salmon from June through August. Indians caught them all, feasted on fresh fish and preserved the rest.

When Indians were the Methow's sole inhabitants, the valley's rivers and streams were an enormous fish factory. Most years Indians had all they could eat and store. Indian fishing technology was sophisticated. They set their weirs (fish-retaining fences) at prescribed spots, with traps often placed at

Indian weirs. Photo from the Okanogan County Historical Society, negative 2061, by Frank Matsura.

the center of the weirs. They built platforms and dug channels as fishing aids. They used seines, spears and basket traps to catch fish. Only men fished. Women processed the catch.

Early Methow resident Ellis Peters once observed a successful Indian fishing strategy in Mazama. One man rode his horse into the river until he arrived at the upriver side of a deep pool. Indians on foot waded out to the lower end of the pool, then threw rocks to scare the fish toward the man on horseback "sitting like a stone poised with his spear raised," recounted Ellis. An Indian spear never missed its mark, Ellis testified. The natives caught lunkers, he said, citing as evidence, "Those fish were so big, when they tied them onto the backs of their saddles, their tailfins practically dragged the ground."

Deer ranked second only to salmon as a source of winter sustenance. Indians hunted them during every season, but fall was best, for then the deer were fattest, their hides had the longest hair, and the animals herded together at that time of the year.

Every autumn, hunting parties returned to the same hunting grounds, sometimes traveling 30 miles a day. After setting up a base camp in the hills, they hunted intensively.

Local Indians often organized deer drives. First, a group of boys would form a barrier across a small valley below an area where deer had been sighted. The young hunters would then ascend the valley shouting their loudest, waving their arms and appearing very threatening. Their dogs scurried about barking furiously to add to the tumult. As predicted, the frightened deer would flee up the valley right into an ambush where adult hunters waited in hiding places with their bows and arrows readied.

Another proven Indian hunting tactic was to hang well-used moccasins from trees or rocks in a large area. Hunters would flush out deer in the vicinity, then scare them into heading toward the moccasins. As soon as the animals sniffed the human-scented footwear, they'd stop in their tracks, at which time the hunters entered the scene.

Deer hunting had a religious significance for local Indians; prayers and charms had the power to make a hunt successful. Before an expedition a hunter cleansed himself and meditated on the forthcoming event. In the sweathouse he sang a song for good fortune, sometimes adding his own unique verse. One Indian chant went as follows: "I'll be traveling around, not looking for a deer, then a huge deer will appear just in front of me.

Indian women decorated their dresses with beads, bells and dentalium shells. Photo by Latham, from the Special Collections Division, University of Washington Libraries, negative NA 984.

Sweathouse, help me to easily capture the deer." (Curtis, *North American Indian*, quoted from the *Okanogan County Heritage*, March, 1966.) To make his bow infallible a hunter would shake a power stick while chanting.

Indian Culture, Myth and Legend

To ensure winter survival an Indian family needed to preserve enough fish to fill 10 tule sacks, each sack containing some 20 salmon, plus an equal amount of deer meat. Famed local Indian Chiliwhist Jim said a winter's worth of food made a pile 6 feet tall. If a band's bounty reached this height, members could anticipate a relaxed indoor season of sewing, crafts, tool making and talking. During the long, dark Methow nights of midwinter, the Indians told legends, performed sacred dances and rituals, played games, and gambled. Winter was a time to re-establish social and cultural bonds.

Within the shelter of their earth-bermed pit homes, Indians spent endless hours decorating the tanned buckskin clothing they wore in cold weather. They ornamented their garments with porcupine quills, shells, bone beads, animal teeth and feather quills. They embroidered their clothing with horsehair and accented their creations with paint. They sewed moccasins out of animal skins or woven hemp.

While the women wove baskets of cedar root strips, sweetgrass or beargrass, storytellers wove tales of the tribe's origin and history. Their legends taught ethics and religion. Indians believed a Great Spirit had a hand in creating the earth and all things in it. Their God watched over creation and caused events according to his mood. An angry Great Spirit sent storms and floods.

A lesser deity, but one of equal importance, was an individual's guardian spirit. Upon reaching adolescence, a young adult ventured into the hills alone hoping to discover a lifelong spiritual guide. Patiently, the youth awaited a vision that would give the seeker special powers to excel at hunting, gathering, craft making, healing or some other valued work. An individual might receive a unique song or dance during the journey. After the youth returned, the mystical experience remained a secret.

The animal people were main characters in many Indian legends. These creatures lived on earth before humans and paved the way for man's arrival. Of the animal folk, Coyote was the Indians' favorite. Coyote was the smartest and most capable among his associates, but what really won the clever canine popularity was his weakness for pretty maidens, his mischief and his trickery—in short, his irresistible human shortcomings.

One Coyote tale revealed how all the rivers in this region received the gift of salmon. After visiting many other streams in North Central Washington, Coyote arrived with his school of salmon attendants at the mouth of the Methow River. He pow-wowed with the animal people he met in the valley, offering a bargain. "If you give me your prettiest daughters, I'll leave some salmon in this stream. If you don't, I'll build a dam here and take my salmon with me," threatened the rascal. The Methow animal people gladly traded some lovely girls for some silver swimmers.

Pleased with the arrangement, Coyote replied, "I'll take the salmon right up to the head of your river." But it was not to be. Nearing the source, Coyote called a halt to the migration. "It's too rough up ahead. If you go past here, you'll die," he warned his disciples. And that is why forever after, salmon spawned in the Methow River but never traveled to the river's source.

Dick Webb once heard another local Indian myth. According to the legend of Pearrygin Lake, long ago the "Fish Eaters," or Indians of the coast, fought with the "Real People" of the interior. Over time, many battles took place. Once a huge feud ensued in Wenatchee. The interior Indians sent a single ambassador west to prevent a war. Along the way the man passed Pearrygin Lake and heard the mellifluous voice of a maiden calling him from the bottom of the lake. The love-smitten brave was lured to the siren's lair. Negotiations between the quarreling tribes never took place. War broke out and many lives were lost. From then on it was taboo for an Indian to go to Pearrygin Lake. Dick Webb said he never saw an Indian there.

Indians of this locale had a democratic system of government. The head of a village functioned as an administrator rather than a dictator, receiving authority by consensus rather than inheritance. The hefty responsibility of the health and welfare of the tribe rested on the leader's shoulders. He made certain the tribe had enough food, acted as judge in disputes and kept a watchful eye on his followers' affairs.

The shaman or medicine man exerted as much authority as the secular leader, for he possessed the power to heal. The shaman knew how to extract healing forces from each of the Methow's 50 medicinal plants. He knew what root, bulb, leaf, flower or stem cured a disease or eased pain. To heal wounds he prescribed yarrow. Mullein leaves and Oregon grape root relieved a variety of ailments. Some medicine men also possessed magic powers strong enough to make an enemy become ill and even die.

When Indians felt the need to purify themselves, they'd visit the sweathouse. Often this was done to enhance chances for success at an upcoming event such as a hunt, a fishing trip or possibly a reunion with one's beloved. The spiritual or temporal supplicant entered a 4-foot-high dome structure usually formed of saplings stuck in the ground and covered with buckskin, grass, bark and/or soil. On a fire outside, Indians heated rocks until red hot, then rolled them into a pit within the sweat-lodge. The bather entered naked, closed the door and poured water on the hot rocks, creating the Indian version of a Finnish sauna. Lying in the cleansing steam, one became purged of toxins and mental turpitude. After about 10 minutes, when the heat grew unbearable, the bather plunged into the nearest cold creek.

Local resident Enid Milner discovered Methow Indians used an alternative type of sweathouse. While exploring Early Winters Creek, this pioneer found caves dug into hillsides where Indians once took sweat baths.

To treat smallpox, Indians sat in the sweat-house then jumped into an icy creek. For this white man's plague, the Indian remedy proved inadequate, for many, many Methow natives died of the dread disease.

Recreation

The stick game was an Indian tradition as old as the sweathouse bath, and like the Indian sauna, it was rooted in spiritual beliefs. Luck was not just a matter of chance and probability, but proof of an individual's power and enlightenment. Indians believed a lucky player possessed a sacred attribute. In the earliest times only specially designated men played the game. Behind the chosen players hovered Indian medicine men, who observed the actions closely and controlled the flow of the game.

Skilled stick game players were quick with their hands and had to be good actors as well. The object of the game was to guess which of your opponent's hands held a certain deer bone. Two teams faced each other kneeling behind parallel posts set on the ground. A member of one team shuffled two small bones (usually one unmarked and one striped) from hand to hand attempting to confuse the opposite team. Teammates of the bone-handler created distractions by singing, chanting and pounding short sticks on a log in front of them. The turbulent actions of the team in possession of the bones grew more and more intense. Onlookers became spellbound. Finally, when the chanting and drumming reached a crescendo, a member of the opposing team guessed which hand held the unmarked bone.

A correct guess meant the bones must be handed to the guesser's team. If the watching team guessed wrong, they lost one of the sticks used to keep score. Each side started with 10 sticks. To win, a team needed to accumulate all the sticks.

What appears to be merely an amusing game could also be a serious form of gambling: a great deal of valuable loot might be lost or gained during an evening's entertainment. Furs, jewelry, baskets and other booty were tantalizingly placed between the competitors. When the stakes were high, a lucky team might take home a horse, one of the Indians' most prized possessions. The prospect of winning or losing such treasures heightened the excitement of the contest and long nights passed quickly when Indians played the stick game.

The Rise and Fall of Indian Reservations

Without forewarning, the US Congress in 1871 proclaimed they no longer recognized Indian tribes as independent nations. The Indians had no say in this new mandate which eliminated their right to negotiate and sign treaties affecting their ancestral lands and their own lives. From that point on, presidential executive order created reservations.

The same year this mandate passed, President Ulysses S. Grant established the Colville Reservation from the Columbia River east to the Pend Oreille River and from the 49th parallel south to the Spokane River. The government intended the reservation to be the new home for diverse tribes of the area including the Methows, Okanogans, San Poils, Nespelems, Lakes, Colvilles, Calispels, Spokanes, and Coeur d'Alenes. The decision ousted some Indians from their traditional homelands, lumped all the tribes together and forced them to share one area.

White settlers and miners already living in the newly created reservation reacted to the executive order with outrage. To them a new reservation encompassing their land was unacceptable. Back to the drawing board for President Grant and his cabinet.

The first Colville Reservation returned so fast to the public domain, the Indians hardly had time to pack up their tepees. The government soon created another smaller reservation, bounded by the Columbia River to the east and south, the Okanogan River to the west, and the 49th parallel to the north.

Now the Indians felt resentful, especially the Methows, who were ordered to abandon their treasured valley. Descendants of the original Methow tribe now live on the Colville Reservation, but when the territory was first set aside, few were willing to pull up their roots and leave the lands that had nurtured them.

Next, the US government focused its attention on Chief Moses and the four tribes under his leadership—the Columbias, Wenatchees, Entiats and Chelans, who originally lived in areas now forming Grant and Douglas counties.

Born where the Wenatchee River joins the Columbia in about 1829, Chief Moses was a large, powerful man with a commanding presence. Revered as a statesman and spellbinding speaker, he also was legendary for his love of rich food, strong drink and gambling.

Chief Moses was no rebel. In fact, because of this man's wisdom and foresight, arrangements between whites and Indians in the area went peaceably, if not equitably. The wise chief perceived the strength of the white authorities. To explain this to a follower he asked the individual to count the grains of sand. "There are too many," said the man. "It is the same with whites," said Moses. "There are too many."

When Moses traveled to Washington D.C. at the request of the US government, he was prepared for disappointment. His tribe rejected the alternative of living on the Yakama Indian Reservation, yet he believed his followers would never be allowed to return to their ancestral hunting and gathering lands on the Columbia Plateau. Dejected, but realizing objection was futile, Moses accepted in 1879 the boundaries of a US-government-created reservation for his people. Named the Columbia Reservation, but known more commonly as the Moses Reservation, it extended from the Cascade crest to the Okanogan River, north to the Canadian border and eventually included the Methow Valley and south to Lake Chelan.

The pattern of events succeeding the establishment of the Moses Reservation was reminiscent of the aftermath of the Colville Reservation designation. Vocal opposition of ranchers and miners living in a northern portion of the reservation con-

---

Chief Moses, about 1890-1898. Photo by Latham, from the Special Collections Division, University of Washington Libraries, negative NA948.

vinced Washington to return a 15-mile upper strip of the reserve to the public domain.

All of the tribes affected by the formation of the Moses Reserve were unhappy. In particular, the Methow tribe resented the idea of Moses and his followers usurping land stolen from the Methows by the whites. As it turned out, the Methows' indignation was moot, for Moses and his people never moved to the new reservation.

After the government sliced off the top 15-mile strip to pacify miners and settlers, Moses worried that the rest of the land was insecure, so he moved back to the Big Bend area for food gathering, then wintered on the Colville Reservation. This compromise lifestyle proved unsatisfying to Moses' people who felt like drifters without firm roots.

When miners discovered mineral riches in the Methow and

Twisp river drainages plus other areas within the Moses Reserve, once again the government ordered Chief Moses back to Washington D.C. This time Chiefs Sarsopkin and Tonasket accompanied him. "Your tribe hasn't been living on the reservation," the US legislators pointed out, which gave the government a perfect excuse to reclaim the entire reservation, unlocking the door for miners and extending an open invitation to homesteaders.

Moses agreed to relinquish the Methow Valley and all the lands within his own reservation and move to the Colville Reservation as the new law dictated, but he bargained for some compensation. Each member of his tribe should receive two cows, insisted Moses. Each adult male should be given farming implements, and a sawmill and gristmill must be built for his followers. Moses also asked the government to contribute $1,000 toward the new house the Chief planned to build, plus pay Moses a yearly pension of $1,000 for the rest of his life.

Congress accepted most of Moses' demands—and no wonder! In exchange for a small yearly stipend for the chief, some buildings and tools, the US government returned 6,963 square miles of grassland, forests, rivers, lakes, fish, wildlife and mineral wealth to the public domain.

Four years earlier, Secretary of the Interior Carl Schurz had promised the Moses Reservation would last "as long as the Cascade Mountains." But in 1883, the US government erased the entire Indian reserve from the maps. Three years later, on May 1, 1886, President Cleveland officially proclaimed the Moses Reservation open to white settlement.

Most of the Indians involved were dissatisfied with the final arrangements. Their choice was to either receive square-mile allotments west of the Okanogan River or live on the Colville Reservation. The original Colville owners were forced to share their lands with Moses, yet they received no compensation for the loss. Adding insult to injury, the federal government unilaterally appointed Moses to be head chief over the entire reservation. Traditionally, each tribe chose its own chief; an outside authority placing Moses in charge had no precedent in any treaty. For his part, Moses felt humiliated being sent to a reservation where he was not welcome.

Chief Moses received a final concession from the government which further infuriated the original Colvilles. He requested that his friend Chief Joseph and Joseph's band of Nez Perce survivors be invited to live on the Colville lands as well. At the time the remnants of Joseph's band were languishing on an Oklahoma reservation where they had been imprisoned. Moses was grateful when the government agreed to his wish. However, the San Poils living on the Colville were livid, since Chief Joseph had once led expeditions against the tribe. The only people pleased with the government's negotiations were miners and homesteaders.

Samuel Rodman's Moses Reservation Reconnaissance

What was the Methow like at the moment it was opened to white settlement? Could the smoke from Indian tepees still be seen down the length of the valley? Did Methow mountains echo the voices of Indian hunters and the hoofbeats of pinto ponies? According to Samuel Rodman, who explored the enormous Moses Reservation in 1883, the Methow was, in fact, a quiet place, where only the voices of his own explorers could be heard.

The lack of Indian habitation in the Methow surprised Rodman. In his journal he wrote:

> It would seem that such a beautiful valley as
> this would be sought by Indians for their homes.
> The grass is very good, the soil rich and to all ap-
> pearances the site would seem more favorable than
> that of its sister stream the warm and sluggish
> Okanogan.
> —*Okanogan County Heritage*, Spring 1976.

After visiting numerous burial sites in the valley which appeared to have been hastily made, Rodman suddenly realized why he had met so few Indians here.

In the 1800s, smallpox had struck local tribes causing epidemic illnesses and unfathomable suffering. An estimated one-third to one-half of all Okanogan Indians perished. Methow Indians had not been spared.

The grave sites Rodman saw were surrounded by rude log fences. A stick of wood served as a headstone. Rodman learned that deaths had been so numerous and rapid that separate burials were impossible, hence each site contained 10 to 20 victims. While the plague raged, the Methows abandoned their ancestral home hoping to escape an infection to which they had

By 1883 white culture had influenced native dress. Photo from the Carolyn Hotchkiss collection.

no resistance.

Rodman guessed correctly that cold temperatures and 6-foot snow drifts had chased many Indians out of the valley in wintertime even before smallpox hit. Those who had survived contagious diseases, however, still spent summers in the Methow, so it's strange that Rodman encountered so few Indians while he was here.

Rodman failed to meet Methow Indians in their home valley. But while traveling through other parts of the Moses Reserve, he enjoyed lively encounters with Indians who either were Methows or were closely related to the tribe. All local tribes communicated with each other. They spoke similar Salish dialects and all shared a universal sign language. Their lifestyles were alike, thus Rodman's description of the Indians he met on his trip serves as a fairly accurate portrayal of the original Methow residents.

The white man's influence on the Moses Reserve Indians was already apparent, for while the natives readily agreed to work for the explorers, they demanded good pay. To be ferried across the Columbia in dugouts, Indian guides charged 50 cents each way. Rodman's group never complained about prices which they deemed fair considering the expertise of the Indian paddlers, who safely transported the men and their cargo through rapids with boats dangerously loaded to the brim.

When Rodman arrived in July, he found the Indians busily preserving their winter food supply. Salmon and venison hung from racks, while women spread berries on the ground to dry. Some men were trapping salmon in a network of sticks placed across a stream; others were spearing the fish with long poles.

The Indian women fried fresh salmon and baked bread made with yeast powder for Rodman's company. At every one of Rodman's camping spots Indians visited them, bearing vegetables and fruits. An Indian "clootchman" (woman) brought a bag of "fine, large potatoes, for which we gladly paid her a dollar," said Samuel.

By this time, white culture had altered native dress. All Indians still wore moccasins, but the women sported colorful calico skirts sometimes accented by a shawl at the waist and scarf over the head. Men wore flannel shirts and buckskin or cloth trousers.

Rodman found the natives attractive:

> Their features are frequently very regular and with long, black hair, straight and coarse, and sinewy, well-developed figures, they are sometimes handsome and at all events strikingly picturesque.
>
> —*Ibid.*

It seemed the Indians inspected the white explorers as much as Rodman's crew observed them. As Rodman related, "They are curious but reserved: will look at and carefully scrutinize you, but rarely ask any questions." Apparently, it wasn't Indian nature to be garrulous or share their knowledge before it was requested. When asked for information, however, "they were civil and intelligent in their answers," Rodman wrote. When he needed directions, the Indians drew an accurate map on the ground. The natives did not speak of distance, but rather time needed to travel from one point to another.

> I [Rodman] asked my guide one day how far it was to a certain place. He pointed to the sun and pointing to a position it would occupy later on, said: "Sun leah-wa mi-ka klap o-cook il a-he," meaning, "When the sun is there you will reach that place." His reckoning was correct, time and rate of travel being his basis of estimating distance.
>
> —*Ibid.*

Indians in the post-Moses Reservation era always treated Rodman kindly and courteously. If the natives felt bitter regarding the fickle nature of Washington D.C. arbitrators, they did not reveal their animosity to Rodman's group. With few exceptions, the Indians also treated the soon-to-arrive white settlers with friendliness, or at least acceptance.

How Settlers Viewed the Indians

After the federal government eliminated the Moses Reservation, Indians still migrated to the Methow each spring. Nothing in the new rules forbade them from gathering food in their original homelands, so they carried on time-honored customs as long as they could. As late as the 1940s, Twisp residents knew Indians who lived in traditional tepees and made moccasins and buckskin garments the traditional Indian way.

Some early pioneers only observed Indians from a distance; others made friends with them. All were intrigued by the native people who ventured into the valley at certain seasons of the year.

In the early 1900s Virgil Webb watched spellbound as day after day a steady stream of hundreds of Indians headed to the upper valley in search of wild vegetables and fruits. Feeling at home with the Indians, Virgil soon formed strong attachments to them.

> Ninety percent of my friends at that time were
> Indians. I learned their language and I knew Long

Cul-Cul-a-Weela, a wealthy and influential local Indian in ceremonial dress, 1900-1905. Photo from the Special Collections Division, University of Washington Libraries, negative NA1040.

Indian camp on the Methow River. Photo from the Dick Webb collection.

Jim; he was a big man and rode fine horses. I also
met Chief Joseph.
　　　　　—*Methow Valley News,* October 13, 1977.

Pioneer Perry Clark felt an immediate kinship with the Indians. When 10-year-old Perry arrived in the Methow in 1900,
he saw more Indians than whites here in the summer. One time
Perry counted 32 tepees near Lake Creek (north of Winthrop).
"We boys took a liking to those Indians," Perry said. He
learned the Chinook language so he could communicate with
his native friends and he spear fished for salmon with two
famous Indians—Methow George and Chiliwhist Jim.

A lively sense of humor helped Mazama pioneer Ellis Peters
form friendships with local Indians. Ellis relished meals shared
with his native neighbors until one memorable evening when a
pal passed a brown, dry, silver-dollar-sized dessert. The Indian
dish tasted intriguing to Ellis, so he kept popping the sweet-
sour morsels into his mouth ... until he discovered the recipe.
The treats turned out to be ants collected in honey-filled jars,
then pressed compactly together.

Most contact between whites and Methow Indians involved
food. The Indians wanted to buy food, sell food, trade for food,
or protect a food source. The latter became an issue with
Deke Smith's family living on Libby Creek. Every summer
Indians camped at a favorite site near Deke's parents' farm, so
Deke got to watch them hunt deer, pick berries and fish near
his home.

One of the last moccasin makers, Catherine Antwyne Joseph, Colville Reservation, 1947. Photo from the Special Collections Division, University of Washington Libraries, negative NA1638.

One year, Deke's dad put a fish trap in Libby Creek right up by their house. "Oh, the salmon would just be a-boiling in there," said Deke. The Indians, who had their own Libby Creek salmon trap, resented the Smiths' invasion of their territory. As a compromise, Deke's father offered to share his trap with the Indians. They accepted, and everyone ended up satisfied.

Indian women stopped at many valley homesteads to trade for food during the early 1900s. Evelyn Emery said her mother gave them milk, eggs, bread and sometimes meat and vegetables. Several years, the Indians traded salmon they'd caught for pork.

Evelyn enjoyed watching squaws dig roots in the spring and harvest sunflower seeds when they ripened. To collect the seeds, women carried woven willow baskets lined with cloth along with a tool that resembled a ping pong paddle. When gatherers bent the seed-heads over the basket and gently patted them with a paddle, the tasty tidbits were released.

When Ruth Davis, born in 1894, was a child, Indians camped on the flat below her dad's store in Heckendorn near Winthrop. Since they were frequent customers at the Davis' general merchandise shop, Ruth got to know them well.

> We kids used to look forward to their coming
> and had fun playing with the Indian kids. They
> taught us some Chinook and we taught them some
> English so we were able to understand each other.
> —*Okanogan County Heritage*, Fall 1974.

Pioneer patriarch Mason Thurlow found Indians to be friendly and honest. They always repaid small loans, he said. When Mason left his house unattended and unlocked his one rule was, "Please close the cabin when you leave." Though Indians visited in his absence, nothing was ever stolen.

Mason's son Frank said the Thurlows paid the Indians a dollar for washing the family's laundry or traded apples, pears and prunes fresh from the family orchard in exchange for the Indians' services.

Some pioneers recalled their Indian encounters with more fear than fondness. Alice Rader, born in 1887, believed Indians weren't always friendly and that they resented the intrusion of white people. If Indians looked threatening when they visited the Rader homestead, her mother would order Alice and her siblings to quickly hide in the woodpile. Once, Indians pounded on her door demanding flour and her family refused to share since they barely had enough to feed themselves. Later, the Raders felt afraid when they heard a "warwhoop" and watched Indians congregating outside their home. They weren't harmed, but the next year, Alice claimed, Indians set fire to their hay and burned it all.

The Indian habit of entering homes without knocking didn't help their reputation. When asked about their boldness, an Indian replied, "Well, you can't knock on a tent, so we don't." Dick Webb shed further light on this innocent form of trespassing. Indians made camp right by the Webbs' property on the Twisp River and the family soon became immune to the unannounced appearance of Indians in their home. Indians would saunter in without even a tap on the door, say nothing, snoop around, take nothing, then leave, related Dick.

Dick's mother, who had a relaxed attitude, told her children, "It's okay; just let them come in and look." And she was right. Indians had a different concept of personal property and privacy. Their unusual habit just caused a little culture clash.

Dick Webb claimed a time warp existed in the Methow; history happened later here. When he watched Indians set up their tepees near his home in the 1930s and early 1940s, it could just as well have been the 1880s. Indian men played the stick game and women picked berries as if time had stood still. While in grade school, Dick still traded deer skins to Indians for gloves and moccasins.

A head woman ran the Indian community, Dick recalled. After the tribe arrived, the matriarch always called on his mother and they'd converse as best they could. One year his mother happened to be six to eight weeks pregnant, though she was mum on the subject during her friend's visit. The Indian leader must have had a sixth sense for on her next visit she brought a pair of baby moccasins.

Some whites thought the Indians possessed special senses which helped them forecast the weather. At the rodeo grounds one day, Bill Robler quizzed a couple of Indian companions about the upcoming season. "I've heard you are good at predicting how the weather is going to be. What's it going to be like this winter?" asked Bill.

One Indian said, "Oh, it's going to be a hard one, very hard." The other Indian countered, "No, it's going to be an easy winter."

Bill scratched his head, "Well, what is this? One of you says it's going to be hard and the other says it's not." One Indian answered, "Oh, I got hay to sell and he got no hay to sell." (*Methow Valley News*, Summer 1977.) The Indians' powers of prediction might be disputed but certainly not their sense of humor.

Methow George

Many of the earliest settlers met Methow George. He was a chieftain's son and the only Indian to settle on a homestead in the Methow Valley, at least until the government finally got around to surveying Okanogan territory. As soon as surveyors established official boundaries on homesteads, the government levied taxes, and these George refused to pay. "Why should I pay taxes when other Indians get free allotments on the reservation?" wondered George. He gave up his valley homestead reluctantly, for George considered himself a "Boston Man," or brother to the white settlers.

Pioneers still enjoyed George's company every summer when he came to hunt and fish, while his wife gathered roots, herbs and berries. His aged father, Chief Methow, and his mother remained in camp where they dried produce, cured herbs and made venison jerky. George's camp should have been overflowing with children, for George and his wife produced 14 offspring, but unfortunately all died from diseases, mostly tuberculosis.

Sometimes George visited in the winter to pick up deer hides the settlers would save for him, recalled centenarian Walter

Nickell. From the prized hides, George fashioned moccasins, coats, gloves and shirts. First George soaked the hides to make them more pliable, then stretched the skins in all directions over a frame. After George had scraped all the hair from the hides, they

Methow George—who reportedly lived to 104—and wife Jennie, about 1910. Photo from the Wenatchee Valley Museum & Cultural Center.

were smoked. Finally George and his clan sewed the tanned hides into clothing then decorated the articles with fringe and beading.

In his book, *From Copenhagen to Okanogan*, Ulrick E. Fries recalled his visits with Methow George, who became the author's friend in the late 1800s when Fries carried the mail from Malott in the Okanogan Valley to the Silver and Winthrop post offices. Fries described George as "an exceptional Indian—honest, upright and friendly."

During a terrible blizzard in the winter of 1893, George accompanied Fries from the Loup Loup summit to the Methow Valley, helping the mail carrier to break trail in the shin-deep snow and intercepting Fries' packhorse when it took fright and tried to head for home. During the rough trip, George talked a lot about his childhood in an interesting fashion, remembered Fries, which made the time pass quickly.

When they reached George's cabin on Benson Creek, Fries accepted George's invitation to come to dinner. Here is Fries' description of his first Indian meal:

> From a gunny sack, she [George's wife, Jennie] took a double handful of dried serviceberries, and a handful of rock rose roots. From the ceiling there hung some smoked deer fat which had come from around the intestines of the deer and she took some of this and put it into a kettle along with the berries and roots and some sugar.
>
> I dished out a few berries but they were too greasy to tempt my appetite. I was careful not to try the smoked fat. The rock rose roots were the best part of the meal, tender and flavored something like a parsnip. Tea had been made in the coffeepot before the coffee was put in and the tea leaves had not been removed. I cannot recommend the fifty-fifty flavor that resulted.
>
> —*From Copenhagen to Okanogan*

Fries found Jennie's camas-flour biscuits more to his liking after he succeeded, "with a great deal of determination," in wrenching off a bite of the hard roll. Once chewed, however, the pastry, which "had a distinct flavor, yet not a strong one," melted in his mouth. Before white men brought wheat flour, Indians relied on camas bulbs for their bread making, related Fries.

Fries appreciated George and Jennie's generosity though he remarked he would have enjoyed the food much more if it had been seasoned with salt. "The Indians apparently never used salt," said Fries.

Matilda Wapato

Matilda Wapato, born in 1865, was perhaps the most famous of all Methow Indians. Her father, called Dr. Jim because he practiced medicine, came from the Yakama tribe. Agnes, her mother, was a Wenatchee Indian. Matilda lived on 160 acres of land at the north end of Wapato Lake near Lake Chelan.

Matilda's lifestyle was a blend of traditional Indian ways and white culture. Eating bacon on Fridays was forbidden for Matilda, a strict Catholic. At the same time, she rejected

Matilda Wapato. Photo from the Okanogan County Historical Society, negative 2599.

the settled life of white homesteaders. According to her Methow friend, Mary Thurlow Kerr, "Wise old Matildy refused to be shaped into the mold of the white man's and woman's civilization."

Summer, spring and autumn found Matilda gathering roots and berries to store or trade for other winter provisions. She'd exchange fresh, wild berries for keeper potatoes the settlers grew. Once, during a root-collecting expedition, a pregnant Matilda suddenly went into labor. As Indian women have always done in the past, Matilda bore her baby by herself. Calmly, she dropped out of the group to give birth alone along the trail. Afterward, she rejoined the group hugging her new-born wrapped in a blanket.

Matilda had a comfortable home in Chelan and owned a big Cadillac, but she chose to drive an old-fashioned rig when calling on Methow friends. Mary Kerr recalled, "My mother always looked forward to a visit from her friend Matilda Wapato. Matilda drove her crazy old buggy into mother's yard, pitched a tent, and paid a visit to her white sister." (*Okanogan County Heritage*, September 1969.)

Mary's mother, Grace Thurlow, and Matilda Wapato shared a genuine and affectionate friendship. Over leisurely cups of coffee, the women talked about their children. Grace knew some Chinook, Matilda knew some English, and the two would talk and laugh for hours.

Grace, who taught at the Beaver Creek School, wanted her children to learn the Indian language to broaden their education. Daughter Nedra said she did acquire some indispensable Chinook vocabulary as a result; for example: "skookum" meant good, and "hi yu skookum" very good; "klatawa" meant scram and "cultus" bad.

Although Matilda pursued many traditional Indian ways, her sons chose a different path, fitting themselves into the white man's system. Son Paul became a reporter and feature writer for *The Wenatchee World* and *Spokane Chronicle*. Later, he turned evangelist and preached in different parts of the United States.

Matilda's other son, Paschal Sherman, began his career as an attorney for the Veterans Administration. Later, he became Chairman of the American Indian Civil Liberties Trust.

Paschal related a story about his mother's extrasensory perception, a gift which she possessed for about 10 years during her early married life. Perhaps Matilda inherited her unusual sensitivity from her father, Dr. Jim, who, like Matilda, could foretell the future and locate hidden items.

One time Matilda took her baby son on a Columbia River steamer trip. "It was a cold day so she wrapped me well and laid me near the smokestack," said Paschal. "Suddenly some-thing told her to pick me up. Shortly thereafter, the boiler and stack blew up. I would surely have been killed if she hadn't moved me." (*Ibid.*)

Matilda later moved to a place near Okanogan where she spent her last years. She still came to the Methow to catch salmon, not so much out of necessity, but for an excuse to visit old haunts and good friends.

The Indian Scare of 1891

Early in 1891, local settlers heard that 500 Indians, then converging on the Chiliwhist Trail, planned an attack on whites in the Methow Valley. Pioneers quickly built a stockade and fled there for protection. All night men molded bullets and cleaned firearms, while women furiously packed survival supplies. Whites were still feverishly preparing for battle when a group of Indian women rode down the Chiliwhist Trail bearing an olive branch. "There is nothing to fear," the women promised.

The anxiety felt by whites in this case cannot be dismissed as mere paranoia. Indians of the area had reason to feel outraged and had motivation to threaten whites. Recently, the US gov-ernment had opened the Moses, or Columbia, Reservation to white settlement. Also, a northern portion of the Colville Reser-vation had been unceremoniously sliced off in deference to white miners and pioneers. The coup de grace came when a mob of vigilantes lynched a young and probably innocent In-dian boy named Stephen.

Stephen's story is a sad saga of misunderstanding and mob mentality. During the early 1890s, a crowd of infamously rowdy men mined in the Ruby-Conconully district. One day a freight carrier from this mining district, S. S. Cole, was shot and killed on his way to Ruby. No one witnessed the murder, but an Indian woman reported that Stephen confessed the crime to her. The boy's motive was supposedly revenge for Cole's ridiculing Stephen's Indian companion, John, for trying to grow a mustache. John had sworn retaliation after the freighter in-sulted him.

When the Cole murder was reported, two deputies set out to capture the suspects. One deputy found and killed John. Stephen surrendered on condition that he be released on bail after a preliminary hearing. The justice in Conconully, however, refused bail and sent Stephen to jail.

On a cold morning early in January a group of vigilantes wrenched Stephen from his cell and incarcerated his jailer. A half-mile from Conconully, the assassins hung 16-year-old Stephen from a tree. According to Bruce Wilson in his book, *Late Frontier*, Stephen was regarded more as a witness than a suspect. "Not a shred of evidence suggested he was Cole's slayer," reported Wilson.

Local Indians, already angered by Stephen's death, became enraged when the white man delivering the boy's body to the reservation arrived sitting on top of the pine casket, an action which showed disrespect.

The mourning and dancing at Stephen's funeral alarmed local whites, who interpreted the ceremonies as an Indian call to arms. Rumors were rampant. A military party commanded by General A. P. Curry marched into the area, bearing 180 guns and 3,000 rounds of ammunition for distribution to settlers.

General Curry met with the Indian leaders. He insisted the intimidating dances end and ruled the Indians could carry guns only when hunting. In return, the US Army would leave in peace rather than annihilate the tribes, which, he warned, they could easily do.

In the Methow, people resumed their daily activities, but remained vigilant long after this period of Indian unrest.

Perhaps the Indian scare of 1891 has been blown out of proportion. Did the Indians seriously consider an attack on Methow settlers? There is no proof that they did. Nevertheless, the anxiety and fear experienced by local pioneers was very real.

Bibliography

Davis, Ruth. "Mining Lured McLean to the Methow." *Okanogan County Heritage*, Fall 1974.

Duffy, Barbara. Notes from Wenatchee Valley College Class on Methow Valley History. Winthrop, Washington.

———. "Pioneer Girl." *Okanogan County Heritage*, Winter 1976.

Dutton, Michael. "Museum Corner," Parts 1 and 2 on the Indian Scare of 1891. *Methow Valley News*, May 12, 1988, and May 19, 1988.

Emert, Frank. "Indian Sweat Houses." A short article.

Featherstone, Rene. "Still Popular After 10 Thousand Years." *Methow Valley News*, October 1990.

51

"Foods of the Okanogan Indians (The Sinkaietk or Southern Okanogan of Washington)". Laboratory of Anthropology, Sante Fe, New Mexico. Study conducted in 1930. Reprinted in the *Okanogan County Heritage*, March 1966.

Fries, Ulrick E. *From Copenhagen to Okanogan*. Caxton Printers, Caldwell, Idaho, 1949.

Fulkerson, Cathy. *Predictive Locational Modeling of Aboriginal Sites in the Methow River Area, North Central Washington*. Prepared for the Okanogan National Forest by Washington State University, 1988.

Horn, Nedra. Interview. Winthrop, Washington, summer 1990.

Hottell, Diana. "Virgil Webb." *Methow Valley News*, October 13, 1977.

———. "Perry Clark." *Methow Valley News*, Souvenir Issue, summer 1977.

———. "Ellis and Martha Peters: A Mazama Story." *Methow Valley News*, December 14, 1978.

———. "Evelyn Emory Speaks Out." *Methow Valley News*, January 1, 1981.

———. "Frank Thurlow: Four Generations in the Methow Valley." *Methow Valley News*, Souvenir Issue, summer 1977.

———. "Bertie Lehman: She's Been Here Longer than Anyone." *Methow Valley News*, Souvenir Issue, summer 1977.

———. "Bill Robler: Announcing Rodeos and Calling Square Dances." *Methow Valley News*, Souvenir Issue, summer 1977.

———. "Enid Milner: Memories Strong and Sustaining." *Methow Valley News*, July 5, 1979.

Kenady, Mary. Research notes on Methow Indians. US Forest Service.

Kenney, Frank. "Indian Relics." *Methow Valley News*, March 31, 1988.

Kerr, Mary Thurlow. "Matilda Wapato: An Indian Woman's Life." *Okanogan County Heritage*, September 1969.

———. "I Remember." *Okanogan County Heritage*, June 1963.

Nickell, Walter. *The Way It Was*. Naples, Florida, June 1990.

———. *Methow Valley News*. May 10, 1990.

Pidcock, Emma Rader. "Pioneer Life in the Methow Valley." *Okanogan County Heritage*, June 1969.

Rodman, Samuel, Jr. "Moses Reservation Reconnaissance." *Okanogan County Heritage*, spring 1976.

Smith, Steven. "Chief Joseph Loved River Birthplace." *The Wenatchee World*. May 11, 1992.

Strickland, Ron. *River Pigs and Cayuses: Oral Histories From the Pacific Northwest*. Lexikos, San Francisco 1984.

Thompson, Laura. "Laura Thompson Came to Stay." *Okanogan County Heritage*, March 1967.

White, Ken. Field Trip to see Indian Pictographs, summer 1990.

Wilson, Bruce. *The Late Frontier*. Okanogan County Historical Society, 1990.

Woody, Ozro H. "Mason Thurlow." *Glimpses of Pioneer Life of Okanogan County*, Washington, 1983.

Alfred Downing's woodcut shows the ascent of Lt. Henry Pierce's expedition to a blind pass near War Creek. A mule and pony are falling down the cliff on the left. Downing has drawn himself (lower right) sketching. Photo from the Washington State Historical Society, Tacoma, Washington.

Chapter 3

FUR TRADERS, TRAPPERS AND METHOW MOUNTAIN EXPLORERS

What Led Trappers and Traders to the Methow Valley
The wealth to be found in beaver fur lured the first trappers to the Methow Valley. Chinese mandarins paid premium prices for the pelts which they wore in full-length coats or used to decorate their silk gowns. When beaver hats became the rage for well-heeled Englishmen in the early 1800s, demand for beaver fur rose so high, trading companies headed west in search of new suppliers. Thus began a race between traders to establish new trade routes in Washington state.

The pelt competition eventually drove trappers to the Methow Valley. Here they found the Pasayten country to be the most fertile trapping grounds, especially the Thirty Mile area, Hidden Lakes and the headwaters of the Methow River. While beavers drew the first wave of trappers to the valley, martens, lynx, weasels, minks, bobcats and cougars enticed later fur seekers.

Early Okanogan area fur traders built trading posts on well-travelled routes, then waited for independent trappers to come to them with the pelts rather than send their own men on extended trapping trips. Indians supplied a large percentage of the beaver pelts to the trading posts. Hudson's Bay Company employees taught the natives how to use traps and told them the types of furs they wanted. The Indians then travelled to familiar areas searching for furs to trade for merchandise.

Both the traders and Indian trappers benefitted from this business relationship and it appears the whites got along well with the native people who trapped for them. Instructions to Hudson's Bay officers in 1823 urged them "to obtain the good will and confidence of the natives ... particularly in the Columbia. Every assurance should be given them that our object is confined to carrying on a trade which must be beneficial to them, and that we have no desire to possess or cultivate their lands beyond the little garden at the trading houses." (Preliminary Report, *Pasayten Wilderness History Project,* October 1, 1980.) The company's policy of noninterference undoubtedly helped promote friendly relations between traders and Indians.

Fur Traders Searching for Markets

With high expectations, David Thompson launched his boat July 11, 1811, and began his descent of the Columbia River from Kettle Falls, Washington. His mission was "to explore this river (the Columbia) and open out a passage for the interior trade with the Pacific Ocean," Thompson wrote in his journal. The North West Fur Company, an English firm, was financing Thompson's expedition in hope of gaining a competitive edge over their American rival, the Pacific Fur Company, run by one of the wealthiest men in the US, New Yorker John Jacob Astor.

Three days into his river odyssey, Thompson met an encampment of natives, whom he called the "Smeethhowe" Indians, at the mouth of the Methow River. Due to his parley with this local tribe, Thompson has earned his place in history as the first non-Indian to visit the Methow.

Thompson was a good ambassador and an adept salesman as well. He was courteous to his hosts, and gladly partook of the Indian smoking ritual which the native people employed to establish a congenial atmosphere for conversation. Thompson's crew and the "Smeethhowe" tribe exchanged pleasantries and presents. The Indians offered three roasted salmon and half a bushel of arrowwood berries to the traders, who in return presented the Indians with tobacco, hawk bells and two awls.

Once a friendly ambience was created, Thompson explained his goal of securing a trade route on the Columbia River from Eastern Washington all the way to the sea which would include conveying merchandise to Indian settlements along the way.

Methow fur trapper with pelts. Photo from the Methow Valley News.

Pleased by the prospect of future trade with the white explorers, the chief thanked Thompson and wished him a safe journey. The Indians helped transport the voyagers safely around the Methow rapids and described the navigational problems they'd encounter en route to the next native camp. "At noon we left these friendly people," wrote Thompson in his journal.

Meanwhile, Thompson's competitors, the Pacific Fur Company, had left Astoria about two weeks after Thompson left Kettle Falls. The Astorians traveled Thompson's route in reverse, but had the same goal in mind—to forge a lucrative Columbia River trade route before their rivals beat them to it.

Coincidentally the Astorian group met the same neighborly tribesmen at the mouth of the Methow River near Pateros that Thompson and company had called on earlier. Once again, the Indians seemed delighted to see the foreigners and this time the natives took the initiative by suggesting the Astorians trade with the "Smeethhowes" through the winter. The Astor group declined and continued on to the Okanogan River where they set up shop one-half mile upstream from the Columbia, establishing the first Fort Okanogan on a flat between the Okanogan and Columbia rivers.

The new "fort" built by John Jacob Astor's Pacific Fur Company in the fall of 1811 might better have been called a small fur-trading post, for it was an unpretentious 16- by 20-

foot cabin made of driftwood. Despite its unimposing appearance, the post instantly generated a flurry of trade activity. Beaver pelts piled up and sold for profit. The local Indians proved so friendly, the company needed only one man to run the show in the wintertime.

Astor relinquished his thriving trade center to the British North West Company in 1816. The new stewards built the first *official* Fort Okanogan at the site of the original cabin. Later, the powerful Hudson's Bay Company absorbed the North West Company and built still another Fort Okanogan.

By the mid-1830s not only was the fur trade proving less profitable, but the Hudson's Bay Company could foresee that the US, rather than Great Britain, would eventually inherit the territory surrounding Fort Okanogan. When the US boundary was set at the 49th parallel, the Bay Company bid farewell to their financial holdings in the area and sought new trade centers elsewhere.

The fur traders at Fort Okanogan had run a prosperous business venture for more than 25 years. They had received millions of dollars worth of beaver furs from Indian trappers including Methow tribesmen. Part of their success was probably due to their noninterference with native cultures. The traders' interests lay in developing a lucrative fur trade rather than homesteading or mining traditional Indian lands.

Alexander Ross' Dangerous and Disagreeable Sojourn in the Methow Valley

Trapper Alexander Ross arrived at Fort Okanogan in 1811 to fill the position of clerk for the Pacific Fur Company. As the single staff person appointed to the post, Ross developed a spectacular business trading with local Indians for beaver pelts.

When the North West Fur Company took over the Okanogan area fur commerce, Ross changed his allegiance and agreed to explore a route from the Okanogan to the Pacific in the hope of discovering fertile fur-trading grounds for his new employers. According to Ross' book, *The Fur Traders of the Far West* (1855), there lay a range of untamed, unexplored mountains west of the Okanogan Valley which, Ross hoped, "held out a good prospect for extending the trade."

From Ross' book, local US Forest Service experts have ascertained that much of the territory he explored now lies in the

Twisp Ranger District. While anonymous others may have preceded him, Ross' journal provides the first written account of a European man investigating routes through the Methow Valley and accomplishing the first crossing of the Cascade Range this far north. Ross himself said, "The undertaking had often been talked of but as often failed to be put into execution. This is the first time it (the trip) had been attempted by white men."

The route Ross followed was well known to Eastern Washington Indians who fostered an extensive system of trade with Western tribes. Treasures offered by natives of Eastern Washington included horses, buffalo robes, dogbane hemp, camas root, beargrass and native tobacco in exchange for the coastal cornucopia of salmon, clams, berries, dentalium shells, wapato roots and artifacts gleaned from west-side European and American traders.

To reach Puget Sound, Methow and other local tribes ascended the lower Methow, Twisp and Stehekin rivers, crossed the fearsome wall of Cascade Pass and descended to the Skagit River. Frequently their trade route followed up War Creek (a large tributary of the Twisp River) to War Creek Pass before dropping to the Stehekin Valley. Alternately, they ascended to Twisp Pass or Copper Pass at the head of the Twisp River Valley, dropped down to Bridge Creek, then headed up the Stehekin River and over Cascade Pass.

There is no written record of Indians crossing the North Cascades by way of the upper Methow River, Washington and Rainy passes to Granite Creek, or Hart's Pass to Slate Creek. Nor did the fur traders, explorers or miners appear to choose these routes. Instead, they wisely enlisted the help of Indian guides and followed well-worn Indian routes whenever possible. This is exactly what Ross planned to do.

Alexander Ross hired an Indian guide and two other natives to accompany him on his planned trans-Cascade tour. From Red Fox, Chief of the Okanogans, he received rather rudimentary directions, then set out on foot carrying a blanket, a kettle, three days' provisions and guns for hunting game. He allotted two months for a trip he estimated to be a distance of 200 miles.

Ross' exploration of the Methow Valley began at the mouth of the Methow River. From that point, his group ascended north of Alta Lake because the banks of the Methow River were too steep to traverse. They trudged in a northwesterly direction, parallel to the Chelan divide, but always a few miles east of it (according to present US Forest Service interpretation).

Clearly Ross' journey was disagreeable from the start. On one cold and rainy day, Ross and his companions passed Hoodoo Peak, oblivious to its beauty (could it have been hidden in the fog and drizzle?) and plunged onward to the West Fork Buttermilk Creek, finally encountering banks of snow along the way which further chilled their bones. The following day's journal entry reflected Ross' discouragement at this point in the trip.

> Country gloomy, forest almost impervious with fallen as well as standing timber. A more difficult route to travel never fell to man's lot ... Rocks and yawning chasms gave to the whole an air of solemn gloom and undisturbed silence.
>
> —*Okanogan County Heritage*. December 1964.

From here, according to Ross' compass readings, the guide bypassed the popular Indian War Creek Pass route choosing instead to travel up the main Twisp River and ascend Copper or Twisp Pass.

At about this time during his trip, Ross began to experience difficulties with his comrades. First, his guide fell ill. Ross decided to leave one native to nurse the guide while he forged ahead with his other companion. Then on the west side of the Cascade divide, Ross ran into a hurricane and his Indian escort became paralyzed with fear.

> The crash of falling trees, the dark and heavy clouds, like a volume of condensed smoke concealed from us at the time its destructive efforts ... (It) leveled everything in its way to dust. The very grass was beaten down to the earth for nearly a quarter of a mile in breadth leaving a hollow track behind it.
>
> —*Ibid.*

"Thunderstruck with superstitions," Ross' companion refused to go farther, and escaped in the night. Thus, at a place somewhere near Sedro Woolley, Ross had reached "Point Turn About," according to his journal, a location which his guide later figured lay four days from the ocean.

Retracing his steps, the trader returned to his ailing guide, the latter now accompanied by the colleague who had deserted Ross. Neither Ross nor his erstwhile Indian companion were in the best of humor after their stormy engagement, but eventually the original foursome made their way home to the Okanogan. It was "a perilous and disagreeable journey of 30 days," concluded Ross.

After his trip, Ross wrote a pessimistic report on the potential for a trans-North Cascades fur-trading business. There weren't enough pelts for sale, he said, nor enough Indian traders in the vicinity. Most important, he concluded, no feasible route existed from Okanogan through the Methow Valley to Puget Sound.

Ross' bosses found his report convincing and the fur traders and trappers of the North West and Hudson's Bay companies mostly ignored the North Cascades after his abortive exploration.

Prospectors Explore the Methow Passes

Hart's Pass might well have been named McGee Pass since it was prospector A.M. McGee who ascended the Methow Valley in the mid-1870s and first discovered the 6,198-foot pass. Many fabulous finds such as McGee's discovery of Hart's Pass will never be known, since few miners kept journals and journalists seldom kept up with miners' exploits. At least McGee's exploration of the Methow was published in *The Northern Star*, a Snohomish paper, in July 1877. The publication reported:

> On the Methow River is a valley unoccupied by
> whites which he (McGee) regards as the finest
> seen for stock or grain. This river (Methow) as-
> cends to the summit (Hart's Pass) from the south-
> east by an easy grade ... it would form the best
> pass in the Cascade Range for wagon or railroad.
> —*Northwest Discovery*. June 1983.

Indians had told McGee the pass was previously unknown to whites, so the prospector knew his discovery was significant.

Six miners in search of an alleged gold placer on a branch of the Methow River made the second confirmed crossing of the North Cascades by white men (the first being Alexander Ross' epic trip more than 60 years earlier). In the summer of 1877, miners Otto Klement, Charles Von Pressentin, Jack Rowley, Frank Scott, John Duncan, John Sutter and their Indian guide, Joseph Seaam, came to the Methow from the west side of the Cascades. Their route took them up the Skagit and Cascade rivers over Cascade Pass and down the Stehekin River to Lake Chelan. Then, most likely, they hiked by way of War Creek to the Twisp River. More successful at finding mountain routes than riches, the six miners failed to locate the rumored source of gold. Giving up hope, the men retraced their steps to the Skagit River.

Most early miners/explorers came from the west side of the Cascades but Dick Miller was an exception. Miller left Spokane around 1880 to seek his fortune in the Ruby Creek gold fields. He navigated the Chiliwhist Trail to the Methow, then wandered up the valley to Early Winters Creek. Along the way, Miller marveled at the Methow's natural resources. He had never seen such a heavy growth of grass and as for game, Dick proclaimed the Methow to be a regular hunter's paradise, abounding in deer, bears, mountain goats and grouse.

Dick went on to say that his brothers and a companion encountered some game they didn't care for in the area. One day a huge grizzly loomed up in front of them near Early Winters Creek. The grizzly gave one roaring growl and rushed at them with slashing paws fanning the air. They proved to be the faster runners, and left the grizzly far behind.

Soon afterward Dick enjoyed a friendlier meeting with two men engaged in building a trail up Robinson Creek. With the goal of getting to gold country quicker, Miller helped the pair in their pursuit.

While exploring the region, Dick Miller almost reached the summit of Hart's Pass. He at least made it to the fabled "fields of gold," staking a claim somewhere near Ruby Creek, but soon left disappointed and discouraged.

The Robinson Brothers Search for Fur in the Methow

The Robinson brothers weren't the first trappers in the Methow, but they were very likely the most literate of their profession, for the two left an extensive diary describing their activities in the valley.

Tom and Jim Robinson were originally Michigan men. In 1886, the orphaned brothers found themselves in Ellensburg,

Washington, with a total of 85 cents between them. When they heard of beavers in the Methow Valley so numerous they were attacking settlers, the pair hastily traded a trunk for a couple of old guns and some cash, then set out for the area with packer and guide Narcisse, chief of the Methow Indians. Traveling by foot in rubber boots, it took them two weeks to get there.

At the mouth of Beaver Creek, the group met John W. Stone and Jack Forrester, who were camped at the site of the future town of Silver. The Robinsons claimed in their diary only nine men lived in the Methow in 1886-87.

The beaver business proved unproductive at Beaver Creek, despite the encouraging name of the drainage. Hearing of beaver abundance near Winthrop, the Robinsons headed up the Methow and camped at the site that is now Winthrop's baseball diamond. The 14- by 14-foot shelter they fashioned there of cottonwood poles, cattails and bulrushes often felt colder inside than outside. (The brothers couldn't chink the cracks in the walls since they'd neglected to bring along a shovel.) While camping at the ball field, Tom and Jim received a guest destined to gain future fame.

Alfred L. (Parson) Smith strolled into the Robinsons' camp bearing the heaviest pack the brothers had ever seen, over 200 pounds, they estimated. Smith had just tramped across the Pasayten Wilderness after an unprofitable prospecting sojourn in Hope, B.C. Like the Robinsons, he planned to do some winter trapping in the Methow.

On his southbound hike from B.C., on a lodgepole pine 19 feet this side of the Canadian border, mountain man Alfred Smith proved he had a poet's heart when he carved the following verse:

> I've roamed in many foreign parts, my boys,
> And many lands have seen
> But Columbia is my idol yet
> Of all lands she is queen
> —Parson Smith. June 1886.

In the fall of 1887, the Robinsons returned to their Winthrop camp to discover a large band of Indians had settled in. Preferring to avoid a dispute over real estate, Tom and Jim went up to Robinson Creek (later named after them) and set up two camps in the area. "Camp Troublesome" was the name they gave to their base of operations and "Camp Hasty" became the name of their second home. All winter they trapped beavers, fishers, martens and wolverines in the upper Methow Valley, never meeting with much success. "We went to our traps today but found them as usual empty," wrote Jim in his diary.

When trapping was bad, food and recreation became the brothers' consolation. They played endless games of checkers for diversion, while dining on broiled goat meat, venison, apple pie baked in a skillet, and sourdough doughnuts fried in bear grease.

The brothers finally became convinced that most of the beavers had been trapped out by the Hudson's Bay Company years before. Tom traded in his trapper's trappings for a miner's pick and Jim became one of the valley's first orchardists.

Lieutenant Henry Pierce: An Officer and a Poet

Lieutenant Henry Hubbard Pierce's 1882 army expedition across the crest of the North Cascades duplicated much of Alexander Ross' 1814 route from the Methow Valley to the Skagit River. Pierce's report of the journey, however, is a lyrical counterpoint to Ross' depressing story.

Pierce's Cascade crusade was fired by fear of Indian hostilities; his mission was to find a workable military route through the range. The expedition, which was the third recorded crossing of the North Cascades, failed to find a feasible passage through the mountains, but other facets of the trip were a crowning success. Following his journey, Pierce, along with artist and topographer Alfred Downing, produced the first extensive geographic description of the Twisp River drainage. Pierce precisely recorded details of the Methow landscape crossed by the party. Downing not only mapped the terrain, but made numerous delightful sketches of their camping spots and of scenic vistas he saw along the way.

With an Indian guide, the expedition traveled from the Okanogan Valley over the Chiliwhist Trail. Pleased with his guide's leadership, Pierce described the normally tortuous passage from Okanogan to the Methow in glowing terms:

> The Indian trail from the Okanogan River was
> free from obstructions, broad, well defined and
> shorter by 50 miles than that traced on maps, was

Parson Smith's famous poem carved in a Pasayten Wilderness tree. Photo from the Okanogan County Historical Society.

far better and more direct than anticipated, striking the Methow some five miles below the mouth
of the "Twitsp."

—*Northwest Discovery.* May 1982.

The soldiers followed Benson Creek for four miles, traipsing
over foothills covered with bunchgrass and scattered pines.
Beaver Creek provided a hospitable place to camp, "with abun-
dant wood and rich pasturage for the herd," related Pierce.
Later, traveling on good Indian trails, the army came to the
Twisp River and headed up to War Creek.

Pierce was constantly astonished by the beauty of the Twisp
River Valley and wrote many romantic passages describing the
scenery he admired along his route. Here's Pierce's description
of a well-known view, part way up the Twisp drainage:

> While leisurely riding with my guide over a fine
> grassy plateau, a glance revealed (up Poorman
> Creek) a picture of such startling effect as to call
> forth an exclamation of surprise; two friendly
> peaks, 30 miles away—the one shaped like the
> point of an egg (Hoodoo Peak), the other like a
> pyramid (Spirit Mountain) lifted their snow-clad
> summits to the sky. The blue of the distance
> framed in the green and gold of the foreground,
> completing a landscape worthy of the highest ef-
> forts of the painter.

                                                    —*Ibid.*

Near War Creek, the expedition suffered a setback when the
guide chose a bad route. A pony and a mule both lost their
footing on the hazardous ascent, falling 500 feet to their
deaths. Undaunted by the dangerous detour, the Pierce party
finally found War Creek Pass, descended to Juanita Lake,
climbed to the summit of Purple Pass, stumbled down to Lake
Chelan, scrambled over Cascade Pass to the Skagit River and
then hiked all the way to Mount Vernon.

In Pierce's final report on the expedition, one poetic passage
summed up his observations of the Methow Valley environment:

> Outside its charms, the Methow Valley offers
> great attractions as a place of abode ... The soil is
> fertile and the climate, as claimed by our Indian
> guide, is remarkably genial, snow rarely falling to
> a greater depth than 12 inches. In many instances

A view from the Twisp River up Poorman Creek, 1882. Sketch by Alfred Downing from the Mike Lynch collection.

the foothills terminate in broad, level benches,
rich in bunchgrass. The streams where beaver
dams are frequent throng with splendid trout (no
less than 200 having been caught during our stay)
and their banks with tufted grouse, while thousands of deer are said to roam the fruitful uplands.
—*Ibid.*

When Pierce traveled through the Methow Valley in the early
1880s, the landscape looked to him like a utopia. Over 120
years later, the Methow terrain is now trammeled; noxious
weeds have invaded areas where bunchgrass once grew and
houses dot the hillsides. But the beauty remains, and in many
ways it is still the utopia Pierce described.

Bibliography

Duffy, Barbara. Notes from Wenatchee Valley College Class on Methow Valley History. Winthrop, Washington.

——. and Jessie Schmidt. "Poetic Tree." *Okanogan County Heritage*, December 1964.

Kenady, Mary. Preliminary Report, Pasayten Wilderness History Project, USFS. October 1, 1980.

Mansfield, R.H. "When David Thompson Passed By." *Okanogan County Heritage*, March 1967.

Pierce, Henry. "An Army Expedition Across the North Cascades in August 1882." *Northwest Discovery*, Harry M. Majors, ed. May 1982.

Robinson, Tom and Jim. *Robinson Brothers' Diary*, written in the 1880s. Barbara Duffy's History Notes. Winthrop, Washington.

Roe, JoAnn. *The North Cascadians*. Madrona Publishers, Seattle, 1980.

Ross, Alexander. "The First Crossing of the North Cascades." *Northwest Discovery*, Harry M. Majors, ed. August 1980.

——. "A Perilous and Disagreeable Journey: Alexander Ross Seeks a Way West." *Okanogan County Heritage*, December 1964.

Wilson, Bruce. *The Late Frontier: A History of Okanogan County Washington*. Okanogan County Historical Society, 1990.

Chapter 4

GOLD DREAMERS AND SEEKERS IN THE METHOW VALLEY

Before 1900 and for many years after, a huge number of miners swarmed up the Methow and Twisp rivers and their tributaries, climbed over the perilous passes and burrowed deep into the most remote and inaccessible mountains surrounding the Methow Valley. Fearless, bewitched by the prospect of quick riches, the miners came to Squaw Creek, Gilbert and the Slate Creek District, working at hazardous jobs for a pittance. It was dirty, dangerous work, done in the dark, deep in the earth, but ... always a miner could hear a whispering in his ear—"gold!" The search for gold and the mining life was addictive.

Speaking on prospecting as a lifelong occupation, Frank Heath, who mined in the valley in the late 1800s and early 1900s, claimed:

> There will be ups and downs, hopes and disappointments and sometimes loneliness lurking on every trail that the prospector travels. One last warning: Do not highgrade the samples you take for assaying, for if you do, you will only be fooling yourself.
> —*Okanogan County Heritage*, Fall 1972.

"Highgrade" has several related meanings. In this case, Frank was probably warning prospectors to resist the temptation to take *only* the richest ore that they mined to the assayer. It seems during the Methow gold rush, miners "highgraded" their hopes even more than the ore they milled, for there was much more excitement generated here than profitable production.

Placer Versus Hard-Rock Mining

Placer mining (gold panning in creeks and rivers) came first to the Methow. Around 1858, when most miners headed north in the hope of hitting a mother lode during the first Cariboo gold strike, Chinese immigrants with more modest goals began placer mining at the mouth of the Methow River. The patient and industrious Chinese constructed a ditch from the Methow River to a spot along the Columbia to run their placer operations. The sand bar at the Methow's mouth was rich, the Chinese reported (but keep in mind these miners were satisfied with as little as 75 cents per day).

It was hard-rock mining, not the gentler, safer, placer method, that built the Methow mining boom. Hard-rock miners tapped mother lodes secreted deep in the rocky interiors of mountains. They drilled tunnels and went underground. Beyond the extraction of the ore, concentrating mills were needed to reduce the ore volume for shipping to smelters. Power was needed to run the mills. It was altogether a backbreaking, energy-consuming and environment-devouring operation.

Methow hard-rock mining broke many a miner's heart as well as his back. Methow ore was rich enough to ignite interest and enlist investment but too low grade to last. The scrambled nature of North Cascade geology created a dilemma for local mining investors.

Eureka! ... miners would discover a good seam, money would be invested, then the vein would peter out before large profits accrued. Engineers could never predict if the ore vein would be rediscovered by drilling a bit farther or if the lost vein had been crushed so deeply into the earth's crust by mountain building, it was beyond extraction. In this terrain no one could depend on a nice solid deposit passing all the way through a mountain. Investors could invest more dollars in search of the illusive seam or simply give up.

Even when miners made a substantial strike, smelters and money markets were so distant, profits might be eaten up just in transporting the ore. Train transportation from the Methow might have saved the day, but tracks were never laid in the valley.

The First Discovery of Methow Gold

According to some sources, the first gold rush was launched by an old Methow Indian, Captain Joe White, who was a guide for a US government exploration party. The expedition camped at the headwaters of War Creek, a tributary to the Twisp River. One morning in 1886 while out hunting horses, Captain Joe stumbled across a big gold ledge. Smart Joe broke off a piece and showed his prize to one of the officers, Colonel F.S. Sherwood. Later, when the group retraced Joe's steps, they couldn't find the same ledge. Nevertheless, Sherwood unveiled the ore in Portland and inspired a mining exodus to the Methow Valley.

Squaw Creek and the Town of Methow

Squaw Creek, a lower valley Methow River tributary, was the site of some of the earliest hard-rock mining in the valley. Miners swarmed to the Methow when quartz showing free gold was discovered in the vicinity of Squaw Creek. An article from the *Big Bend Empire*, published in Waterville, reflected the excitement generated by this 1890s mining find:

> Now just to reflect and think back a few years
> ago this camp was as desolate and wild as the
> jungles of Africa ... Nothing but the dismal howl
> of the mountain lion and smoke of the Indian
> campfire. Now we hear merry voices of miners
> coming in for supplies and going out to their
> claims with a baked apple smile as they meditate
> on the great expectations in store for them.
> —*Okanogan County Heritage*, Spring 1968.

Every day, several families and many single prospectors joined the mining camp on the north bank of Squaw Creek. One of the great founding fathers of the Methow, W.A. Bolinger, came to the little settlement around 1889; he observed the frenzied activity, saw a need, and started a general merchandise store. Then came a blacksmith shop, a barber shop, an assay office run by the LaMotte brothers, Bill and Pete, and a schoolhouse, all within one year. This little town, named Squaw Creek, was located one mile up its namesake stream.

Accomplished carpenter and contractor Mr. Buckner, along with his wife and four daughters, moved to Squaw Creek during the gold rush, and built most of the little houses in the mining town. Frank Heath claimed a very good hotel opened in Squaw Creek and described the settlement in glowing terms:

> Squaw Creek was unlike most gold stampedes in that no vice came to town. For amusement there were dances with music from the Highland Mine on the violin. The schoolhouse doubled as a dance hall.
>
> —*Okanogan County Heritage*, Summer 1972.

The *Big Bend Empire* seemed to corroborate Heath's rosy portrayal in the following excerpt on the Squaw Creek District:

> Harmony prevails with the exception of one little dispute, over a fraction on the Ocean Wave Mine. The result was one man received a broken arm, another a black eye. Such is life in the wild and woolly west.
>
> —*Okanogan County Heritage*, Spring 1975.

Pretty tame stuff for an argument involving gold!

This mini-mining metropolis eventually harbored four general stores, two hotels, a restaurant, saloon, livery stable, meat market, a blacksmith's shop and a sawmill. A five-stamp mill (a machine that crushed ore using five iron blocks) stood on the banks of Squaw Creek and in 1892, two arrastras (rock crushers) operated between town and the stamp mill.

In the early 1890s the *Big Bend Empire* had only good news

The Bolinger house made of granite in the town of Methow. Photo by Don Portman.

to report on the Squaw Creek boom. A double shift was required at the sawmill to supply the Ocean Wave Mine; the Excelsior "showed up wonderful" at a 30-foot depth, claimed the paper, and the Paymaster looked promising 16 feet down. "Second to none" was the Philadelphia Mine where a well-defined vein of "rock fairly glistens with fine gold." The *Big Bend* reporter insisted, "The above mines are the best properties in the camp, but there are hundreds of others presumably as good; all they require is development." (*Ibid.*)

The Squaw Creek gold rush ended as fast as it was born. Having read the writing on the wall, W.A. Bolinger decided to homestead three miles up the Methow River from the mouth of Squaw Creek, and moved his store and post office there. He built a unique house entirely of granite collected from a rock slide one mile north of the present town of Methow. Drive through Methow today and you can view this sturdy landmark. With his prodigious energy, Bolinger worked to establish orchards, irrigation ditches, and roads in the valley.

After Bolinger moved, the hotel followed and then the school. People christened the new town Methow after the Methow River. In 1894 the Methow Post Office opened and the little town expanded to three stores and a restaurant. A weekly stage line ran to Chelan.

Squaw Creek meanwhile turned into a ghost town. Most of the miners drifted northward in their quest for gold. Gold Creek saw some activity when the North Star Mine located on the north fork of this Methow River tributary. Other miners headed farther north to the Twisp District, Mazama, Goat Creek and on up to the Slate Creek District on the Cascade crest.

The Town of Silver and the Red Shirt Mine

Simultaneous with the Squaw Creek rush, a small mining boom occurred five miles south of Twisp near an area that became the town of Silver.

John Chickamun Stone had made the first strikes within the valley on Polepick Mountain between Benson and Beaver creeks near Twisp. Stone received the nickname "Chickamun," which meant "money" in the local Indian language, possibly because of his mining luck, but more probably as a result of his bartering finesse at an early trading post.

Stone sold his mine as well as squatter's right to his land to

72

The steamer City of Ellensburg *transported ore to Wenatchee. Photo from the Okanogan County Historical Society, negative 2558.*

James Byrnes for the bargain-basement price of a red shirt and a bottle of whiskey, a legend that seems to place doubt on the aptness of Chickamun's Indian alias. After that sale the Polepick site became known as the Red Shirt Mine. Whether the story was true or false, Byrnes appeared pleased with his purchase, especially when a second strike nearby opened up a ledge of quartz and crystallized limestone that held profitable amounts of gold and silver.

Byrnes continued to run Chickamun's original pioneer trading post. He established a post office and in 1890 became the first postmaster of one of the first towns in the county—Silver—so named because of the silver ore deposits found in the Red Shirt Mine alongside the iron, copper and gold.

For a time the mine buzzed with activity, producing 35 tons of ore daily at a 20-stamp mill and employing 55 men. Miners earned $2.75 per day while support workers received $2.25. Out of this amount workers paid 75 cents per day for their board. Here's how the *Big Bend Empire* summed up the mine's success in May 1897:

No doubt as to the quality of ore—low grade—

but it concentrates readily and repeated shipments
demonstrate its value as a money-maker.
—*Okanogan County Heritage*, September 1968.

Beyond the problem of low-grade ore, there was the problem
of long-distance shipment. First the ore traveled more than two
miles by wagon road from mine to mill. After treatment at the
mill, freighters transported the rock concentrates by wagon to
Central Ferry on the Columbia. Once it reached the Columbia
(which must have taken days, considering the deplorable state
of roads and lack of direct routes) the steamer *City of Ellensburg* bore the ore to Wenatchee, from whence it journeyed by
way of the Great Northern Railroad to the Everett smelter.

A year later the *Big Bend* changed its tune somewhat on the
Red Shirt's success story when it reported in July 1898: "On
the Methow a great deal of assessment work is in progress but
little development. That section awaits capital to make it profitable." Jack Stewart and his company purchased the Red Shirt
Mine but suddenly dropped it for more golden fields up north
at Goat Creek in Mazama.

Despite the bust of the mining boom that created Silver, the
little town continued to bustle with a life of its own. It was a
natural site for a town, near where the Chiliwhist Indian Trail/
pioneer road entered the Methow Valley, and where Beaver
Creek empties into the Methow River. Indians always camped
at the hospitable spot, and had established a racetrack on the
flat by the river. Prospectors frequented the campsite as well.
Eventually some of the richest Methow farms flourished in the
area near Silver. Mr. and Mrs. Harvey Nickell and their four
children were the first family to settle permanently near Silver,
homesteading an area near the mouth of Beaver Creek.

In 1894, the Methow River began to rise and continued to
rise, finally overflowing its banks and undermining the buildings
in Silver which were built on the river's floodplain. The flood
of 1894 scoured out Silver like food fragments in a frying pan.
Young Frances Pryzylowiez, the niece of Mrs. James Byrnes,
went down to the river for a pail of water while the river was
rising dangerously high. The bank gave way, poor Frances fell
into the frothy torrent and drowned. Six miles downriver, at the
mouth of Libby Creek, rescuers recovered her body.

Wild flood waters changed the course of the Methow River
which has flowed in a different channel ever since. This ex-

plains why the historical marker for Silver appears not along-side the river, but by the highway with the river not even in sight.

Following the flood, the store proprietor erected a new build-ing on a bench 25 feet higher than the old location. Towns-people held dances and entertainment in the hall above the store. A saloon, blacksmith shop, three houses and some out-buildings completed the reconstructed town of Silver.

In 16 years Silver saw nine postmasters. P.L. Filer carried the first mail from Silver to Ruby about 50 miles away. People in Silver pooled their resources and paid the postman $6.25 for the round trip he made once a week by horseback. Filer was a busy letter-bearer, as Guy Waring up in Winthrop also hired him to deliver mail, paying a premium $12 price for the round trip.

For a while Silver was a freight destination, not only for ore but for household goods and supplies of all sorts. A freight team traveled three days from Silver to Brewster and back to Silver, traversing the Bald Knob Mountain Road, a rough, un-graded route the pioneers scraped out by trial and error.

As neighboring towns of Twisp and Carlton grew, Silver faded. Only 15 to 25 people still lived in Silver by 1904 with about 40 families residing in the immediate vicinity. Twenty students attended the school. Burke Brothers' Store was the sole remaining business enterprise.

Even while fading, Silver remained the site of festive gather-ings. Since it was conveniently located between Carlton and Twisp, young people regularly rendezvoused there to have a "hi yu" time. Jesse Schmidt claimed when enough people got "foot stomping" on the floor of the upstairs dance hall, and re-ally "hoed it down" to the tune of the fiddle, organ and mouth harps, the top story of the building actually swayed.

The town of Silver captured many "firsts" in the valley. It was the Methow's first town. Pioneers built the first trading post, first post office and first department store in Silver. Samuel Metcalf's home served as the first school in 1891, where Mrs. Metcalf taught the valley's first 12 students. Silver hosted the Methow's first moving picture shows, which audi-ences screened in the hoedown hall. Unfortunately, Silver also gained fame as the first bona fide ghost town in the valley.

In 1907, Silver closed its pioneer post office and the first Methow town passed out of existence. The Burke brothers, who last owned the post office and Silver store, moved to Twisp. Farmland covers the site of the second Silver up on the bench. Today the highway to Pateros runs right by Silver but not a rock or foundation remains to mark the spot, only an historical marker.

Mining Up the Twisp River

At the same time men unearthed mineral riches from Squaw Creek and the Red Shirt Mine, Methow miners also began cracking rocks to expose buried treasure in the Twisp Mining District. Gold was first discovered near the headwaters of the Twisp River about 1885. But serious prospecting didn't begin until later discoveries were made in 1892. Soon more than 200 mining claims dappled the North and South Creek areas and up the Twisp River to Twisp Pass. The plot of claims between the Twisp River and Cascade Pass grew together until they resembled a modern subdivision, according to JoAnn Roe in *The North Cascadians*.

Near North Creek and the Twisp River, the town of Gilbert grew up in the mid-1890s as mining development in the area went into high gear. Both the settlement and nearby mountain where miners worked were named after P. Gilbert, who filed the original pioneer claim on the site.

One lucky day Gilbert excavated a large chunk of high-grade ore which he lugged out from this remote point and sold for a large sum. He used this money to build a road from Gilbert to Twisp. (Poor access plagued the Gilbert area as it did all the other Methow mining districts.)

Later, on a less lucky day, while Gilbert hunted for gold in the same tunnel, he blew his fingers off one hand. Companions took him by wagon then train to Coulee City and Gilbert survived, but he never returned to the place of his accident again.

Gilbert (the mining camp) consisted of a half-dozen buildings. Most miners only lived there in the summer since no services were available except possibly a blacksmith shop.

In the early 1900s, the hotel owner in Twisp, Paul Shonefelt, located the Wolverine Claims high up on Gilbert Mountain. Miners and supplies traveled a wagon road up the Twisp River to Gilbert by that time, but from Gilbert to the camp on the mountainside, horses had to pack provisions up a perilous trail. Once a horse bearing supplies up the steep route slipped into the abyss. No one could possibly retrieve the poor beast from the cliffs below, so both animal and provisions were lost.

Local lifelong miner Frank Heath worked the Wolverine Claims for a spell in the early days. He first arrived at the rugged outpost in November. A tunnel driven into the mountain for 60 or 70 feet served as a "cozy" bedroom for Frank and his co-drillers. Miners slept in cots strung out the whole length of the tunnel—a veritable bunkhouse, except this one was solid rock, pitch black, and probably dripping cold water to boot!

Heath's second adventure at Gilbert began around 1912 in the more clement month of May. This time he moved with his wife. All was pretty quiet in camp as the first big gold rush had petered out several years before. A few diehard prospectors with better claims hung on but Camp Gilbert was a de facto ghost town. Some farmers from Winnipeg, Canada, with money and a Pollyanna outlook, had meanwhile purchased the main claims in the Gilbert area, which then became known as the Crescent Mining Claims.

The Crescent Mine manager installed a water-powered sawmill on the banks of the Twisp River. The new owners also built a power plant with insulated wire running from the electric plant to the mine. The Canadian firm hired Heath to build a road ascending from the plant to the mine.

With only eight men Heath accomplished this formidable task. Later, an electric power drill became available in the camp, but while Heath was engaged in his road-construction project he'd been stuck with all hand drills and hammers, called single and double jacks. Men drilled in pairs; one team member held the drill while the other struck the drill with a gargantuan hammer. With a single jack, one man labored alone with a 4-pound hammer. "This was very slow," admitted Heath.

A depression struck both the US and Canada the second year Heath worked on his road, and the source of money for the Crescent Mine development dried up. After a few years, the Canadian consortium abandoned the site. According to Heath, the camp seemed to have a black eye after the work force quit, and no one showed a glimmer of interest in developing it further.

Willing to take risks and itching for adventure, veteran Methow miner John Klinkert leased some claims from the Gil-

John Klinkert, Twisp miner. Photo by Bill Hottell. Courtesy Susan Klinkert.

bert Mountain mines in 1940. Klinkert had recently married and the newlyweds spent their honeymoon in an 1895-vintage cabin in the abandoned mining town of Gilbert.

A season's drilling proved fruitful and in the autumn of that year, John, along with partners Clyde "Ole" Scott and Vivian Buckmaster, became the first people to actually ship gold from Gilbert to a smelter. By packhorse and truck the trio transported nearly three tons of gold and silver over the Cascade Mountains to the Tacoma smelter. A few weeks after delivery of the ore, John received a check for his efforts. After deducting shipping fees, the check came to a total of $2.21.

Still optimistic about the area's gold-bearing potential, Klinkert began reconstruction of the North Creek Trail at the head of the Twisp Valley in order to extract ore and transport it from a mountain basin at the trail's end. In 1983 REKS Inc. located 280 claims on Abernathy Mountain and Gerald Henderson of Oroville, Washington, blanketed the Gilbert area with 375 Jolly claims in 1984, though little development work had been done by 1991.

Two old mining cabins still stand in Gilbert. Some foundations and depressions in the ground identify where additional structures once stood. It's a pleasant, peaceful spot in the woods, not a bad place for a miner to reside. It's when you look up, up, up at steep-sided Gilbert Mountain that you realize what a tough venture these gold seekers undertook and what hazardous lives they led.

The Alder: A Million Dollar Mine

The history of the Alder Mine near Twisp lacks the legends, lore and lively remembrances associated with Squaw Creek, the Red Shirt and Gilbert claims. Yet the Alder has been one of the most productive metallic mines in Okanogan County, yielding $1 million in zinc, silver, copper and gold.

In 1896, while panning near the mouth of Alder Creek, T. H. Culbertson found traces of gold. Excited by this tantalizing ore sample, Culbertson kept working up the creek until he came to an outcropping rich in minerals. Later this site became the Alder Mine.

Culbertson, however, soon ran into difficulties at Alder Creek with poor health and poor drilling equipment hampering him from developing his claims. Later owners built a large mill near the mouth of Alder Creek and the mine and mill have operated sporadically over the years.

When the price of zinc rose after World War II, the Alder Mine ran successfully for a short time. While zinc was the main product of the mine, it also yielded quite a bit of gold and some copper. Once a week a truck hauled the zinc concentrate from the mine to a smelter in Trail, British Columbia.

For five or six years Winthrop miner Slug Davis worked as head assayer at the Alder Mine. He was one of the first men hired when the mine reopened in the 1950s and one of the last to leave when the price of zinc fell and the mine shut down.

Slug remembered 20 to 30 men were employed at the mine site during that time. A crusher and millwright worked at the mill and local miner Glenn Parker assisted Slug with the assaying. Most of the miners lived in a little village located in a pleasant meadow about two miles from the mine site. A sawmill in the village supplied lumber for the mine.

Slug loved working at the Alder Mine—loved the chemistry of assaying. His job was to take samples of mineral concentrate and test them for their value. For example, he would place a gold bead (a little nugget of gold the size of a pinhead) in a tiny pan, then put this on a gold balance to measure the weight of the speck of ore. Slug claimed the weighing device was so precise, if you took the pan out of its glass case and blew on it, then replaced it in the container, the scale would register the weight of your breath.

Slug also assayed tailing samples to see how much ore was getting lost. At home he keeps a collection of zinc and gold concentrate samples he tested at the Alder Mine.

In the evenings at the Alder, Slug moonlighted with the superintendent of the mine, Allen Shafer. Slug gladly helped Shafer after hours because "Shafer himself was always willing

The Alder Mine. Photo from the Okanogan County Historical Society, negative 2808.

to lend a hand when others needed help." So at night Allen took Slug to the mine tunnel where the two would shoot "bootlegs" which were live dynamite charges that didn't go off properly.

Here's how the job worked: Just before the mine drillers left the site in the evening, they'd set off charges to break up rock for the next day's work. Slug and Allen found the bad "bootlegs," fixed their fuses, hooked on longer wires to connect to the blasting machine then ... BOOM! The rogue charges would explode, thus eliminating the possibility of having powder detonate in a miner's face the following morning when he began to drill. "That evening job was pretty interesting," said Slug, who refused to admit the task had a dangerous side.

Bibliography

Duffy, Barbara. Notes from Wenatchee Valley College Class on Methow Valley History. Winthrop, Washington.

Esvelt, John P. "Upper Columbia Chinese Placering." *Okanogan County Heritage*, Summer 1977.

Heath, Frank. "Gold." *Okanogan County Heritage*, Summer 1972.

Hottell, Diana. "John Klinkert, Miner." *Methow Valley News*, Souvenir Issue, Summer 1977.

Laughlive, Mrs. Olive. "Silver and Its Colorful History Pioneer Story." *Okanogan County Heritage*, Spring 1990.

"Mining Boom," *Big Bend Empire. Okanogan County Heritage*, September 1968.

Roe, JoAnn. *The North Cascadians.* Madrona Publishers, Seattle, 1980.

———. North Cascade Institute Class. Sun Mountain Lodge, Winthrop, Washington, fall 1991.

Schmidt, Jesse. "First Town in the Methow." *Okanogan County Heritage*, June 1964.

"Squaw Creek Boom," *Big Bend Empire. Okanogan County Heritage*, Spring 1975.

Steele, Richard F. *History of North Washington.* Western Historical Publishing Co., Spokane, 1904.

Chapter 5

THE LEGENDARY
SLATE CREEK DISTRICT

Gold-Dust Hustlers

A man named Rowley made the original mineral discoveries in the Slate Creek area in about 1880 according to the 1897 book, *Mining Progress in the Pacific Northwest*, by Lawrence K. Hodges. Placer gold, found in glacial or alluvial deposits of gravel or sand, attracted the earliest miners. Hodges estimated around 2,500 men panned Slate Creek in the first season culling $100,000 worth of gold dust from this rugged, mountainous region at the headwaters of the Methow River.

Because transport of ore and supplies proved impossible, prospectors abandoned the remote area. Over a decade later, when miners reappeared at Slate Creek, placer gold was no longer their goal. Now they sought solid ledges of the precious metal.

Alex Barron and the Mine in the Sky

Alex Barron was a husky bull of a man, made rough and tough from years spent working outdoors carrying a 100-pound pack on his broad back. That heavy pack held all he needed to survive in the mountains—a frying pan, a bedroll, groceries and the tools of his trade: a short-handled shovel and a miner's pick.

One day in the year 1893, Barron was sweating hard while panning his way up the west side of Hart's Pass, when he lost trace of the gold trail he'd been tracking. "Eureka!" he ex-

Alex Barron (left) and Guy Waring rest on a narrow-gauge wagon used to haul freight up to the Hart's Pass mines. Photo from the Dick Webb collection.

claimed, as he realized the rich source of the gold nuggets he panned had to be just ahead in the hill above him.

With visions of a bonanza, the burly miner urgently sank a series of 2- by 6-foot exploratory holes now called the "graveyard." There is evidence he panned an area near the top of a hill, repeatedly bearing quantities of water on his back up 1,000 feet in elevation from the creek below. Finally, Lady Luck smiled on Barron, who struck gold right near the surface. Later, a mining town mushroomed at the site of the claim about three miles from the Cascade summit. The rough and tumble refuge for miners was named Barron after the original Glory Hole discoverer.

Where Miners Find A Home

Overnight, Barron became a western boom town sprouting multiple saloons, stores and assorted shelters to serve the 2,500 miners employed in the district. Dance hall girls kicked up their high heels doing the cancan at the Barron Hotel, while miners kicked up their heels to lively dance tunes. Most workers had some discretionary money and as a result, gambling was rampant. These miners were mostly middle-aged men, according to

Frank Heath, and they enjoyed adult amusements while at Barron, far from the constraints of the law and "proper" ladies.

During its short, hectic tenure in the Slate Creek District, the town of Barron had far-reaching effects. Hard-working miners exhibit huge appetites and this trait proved to be a financial boon for towns like Winthrop. George Witte, a butcher during the heyday at Barron, drove cattle right up to the town and slaughtered them on site, so the miners could feast on fresh steak. He and others brought up fresh vegetables and fruits to hundreds of hungry men.

Because Barron was located so far from Winthrop, the nearest settlement and trade center, small way-stations grew up along the road leading to the area mines. Some large camps harbored several buildings and lots of mining equipment. Sawmills and flumes were a common sight.

Robinson Creek, 22 miles from Winthrop, was the end of the road and the point of departure for the Slate Creek miners in the late 1800s. The town of Robinson sprang up after the earlier tent town of Ventura, two miles lower on the road, had died, the latter town losing its usefulness once the road was extended.

For a while, Robinson ranked as a lively little settlement. A

The town of Barron showing the Methow Trading Company at right. Photo from the Okanogan County Historical Society.

*Where miners find a home. Photo from the D. Kinsey Collection,
Whatcom Museum of History and Art, Bellingham, Washington.*

hotel and barn sprouted at the mouth of Robinson Creek along
with a freight depot, all to serve the miners. Twice a week in
the summer and weekly in the winter, a stagecoach connected
Robinson to the rest of the world. Scattered through the woods
in the area was a Methow Trading Company store, a post office, a blacksmith shop and the obligatory saloon.

Around 1910, 16-year-old local Ruth McLean and her family
visited the ghost town of Barron so her dad, C.R. McLean,
could check on a mine he'd located in the area. They camped
in one of the old mining buildings, where Ruth and her sister
uncovered a different type of gold mine. The two sleuths dove

into some old boxes left in haste by former dance hall girls and delightedly lifted out fancy-lady dresses. Said Ruth, "My 10-year-old sister, Florence, put on one and started running as fast as she could up the path. When asked why she was running away, Florence answered, 'I heard this dress belonged to a fast woman and I'll bet I'm just as fast as any of them.'" (*Okanogan County Heritage*, Fall 1974.)

Why did the "sporting" ladies leave their fancy clothes? When in 1907 the mines in the area failed to produce promised riches, apparently the inhabitants of Barron became panic-stricken. Within weeks, everyone deserted the town. In their haste, Barronites left tools, blacksmith shop equipment, wagons, bedding, cooking utensils, and clothing carelessly scattered everywhere. Mice and pack rats inherited the food stock in the general store.

Despite the mining, drilling, dust, and dirt all around Barron, the environs must have been stunning only a short distance from "downtown." Ruth (McLean) Davis described the utopia she found there as a young girl. "What a summer, climbing around the mountains enjoying the beautiful flowers and wildlife, picking wild berries and fishing the streams." (*Ibid.*) Surely miners living in Barron must have stolen a moment or two now and then to relish the spectacular scenery so near the dark recesses where they spent most of their time.

The Fate of Barron's Fortune

Alex Barron was a prospector, not a developer, and money in the pocket interested him more than long-term investments, so he promptly sold his claim to Colonel Thomas Hart for about $50,000-$80,000, a fortune considering it was the mid-1890s. In the wink of an eye, Barron spent his entire fortune carousing on the coast, so the story goes. He returned penniless, but with the same energy and gold-digger's gleam in his eye, to the site where he'd made his first strike.

The wheels of fortune favored Barron a second time in the Slate Creek District. Just three miles from the original Glory Hole, he discovered the Beck Claims which earned Alex another $75,000 to $100,000. Who knows how the maverick miner spent his second windfall? He was not one to settle down and the riches rumored to be made in the Klondike Region of Alaska coaxed him northward.

trail over Hart's Pass at Dead Horse Point before work
ne by the U.S. Government and the Azurite Gold Co. in 1931.

The trail over Hart's Pass at Dead Horse Point before 1931. Photo from the Dick Webb collection.

Colonel Hart and the Road to Gold

In 1895, two years after Alex Barron made his golden strike, a pair of hands shaped very differently from Barron's began to mold the destiny of the Slate Creek Mining District. Colonel W. Thomas Hart, a mining man and a promoter, an agent for Montana interests with financial backing, arrived on the scene. He was a tall, broad-shouldered man who dressed to impress. A fine mustache and military bearing helped to instill confidence and respect in his staff. The Copper King of Montana, Marcus Daly, was his boss.

Representing the Granite Mining Company and Methow Syndicate, Hart arrived in the Methow in 1895 and took options on the Squaw Creek and Slate Creek districts. The first option never panned out, but Hart really "set things a-humming" on the Slate Creek District, according to miner Frank Heath, launching a second gold rush there called the Hart Boom.

Hart hoped to ship 100 tons of ore per day from Slate Creek—first down the Methow Valley, then west over the Cascades to smelters on the coast. He budgeted $100,000 for this undertaking. Obviously the pack trail between Robinson Creek and Slate Creek needed to be improved before ore could be transported. Hence began Hart's road-building extravaganza.

The smartest thing Hart did was hire Charles Ballard, mineral surveyor, assayer, and civil engineer, to survey the road designated to follow the north side of the upper Methow Valley to what is now called Hart's Pass. The route was insanely hazardous by any standards. But the mining men involved in the project had a high fear threshold!

It is no exaggeration to report that at one spot the "road" engineered by Ballard dangled on the side of a sheer cliff where for 18 feet planks rested on iron pins hammered into the face of the rock. From this toehold, the mountainside dropped a thousand feet to the canyon below. Not long after the road's inauguration, a packhorse slipped at this precipitous promontory. Within seconds the lead horse had pulled the pack train to the brink and the entire entourage plunged into the abyss below. After the tragedy, Dead Horse Point became the permanent name of this heart-stopping bend in the Hart's Pass Road.

Building the road continued to be a battle for Ballard's men. One day his 65-man crew killed 130 rattlesnakes. Higher up, things drew to a standstill when workers encountered 6 feet of hard-packed snow. Then suddenly, after only two weeks of road construction, Colonel Hart paid his men and abruptly departed. Apparently Hart's backers had lost faith and fired him citing "extravagant and unnecessary use of money," according to the *Leavenworth Times*.

For two years Hart had managed the Eureka Mine near the Glory Hole where the first ore discoveries in the area had been made. It proved to be a large deposit rich in gold. However, after miners reached a certain depth, the value of the deposit decreased. Under Hart the Eureka Mine produced $120,000 in gold, not too thrilling when you consider the original price paid to Alex Barron, whose strategy of discover-then-sell-out was perhaps the more financially astute.

On Beyond the Glory Hole

The old Glory Hole at Hart's Pass still bore some gold after Colonel Thomas Hart left for greener pastures. John A. Stewart, Mazama (who earlier owned the Red Shirt Mine claims near Twisp), gained title to the Eureka site in 1905 and gave it a fresh new name—the Bonita Mine.

While superintendent of the mine, Stewart employed 15

88

The Eureka Mine and tram line, 1901. Photo from the D. Kinsey Collection, Whatcom Museum of History and Art, Bellingham, Washington.

workers during the miserable winter months of 1906. A stamp mill crushed raw rock and a small cyanide plant separated ore at the site. The Bonita complex consumed energy, compliments of the Chancellor Gold Mining Company, which had built a power plant in 1906 in the settlement of Chancellor, located at the confluence of Slate Creek and Canyon Creek. Electricity from Chancellor's 240-horsepower generator surged over a 6-mile transmission line to charge Stewart's operation.

The powerhouse had been a costly investment for the Chancellor Gold Mining Company. As a prerequisite, a sawmill needed to be constructed first, then lumber cut to build the powerhouse plus a flume 2 feet wide and 2 miles long. Water swirled down the lengthy flume, generating electricity at the power plant.

Considering the extreme weather in the high Cascades and the length of the Bonita's power transmission, it is not surprising that frequent power failures curtailed work at the site. In fact, the mine had operated only a short time when just after Thanksgiving Day the big dynamo burned out. The lights went dead and the juice turned off at the mine site and mill. Winter was coming fast and most of the men hightailed it out of that cold and lonely place, wading in thigh-deep snow up over avalanche-prone Hart's Pass to the Robinson Creek supply house. Stewart closed down all operations, retaining only a few hardy souls for exploration work on the mine.

After 1907, the Chancellor power plant ceased operation and most of the mines in the area closed about that time.

Many years later, the New Light Gold Mining Company constructed a new mill on Bonita Creek to treat ore from the old Eureka lode, but a government war order closed all gold mining operations in the US in 1942. When restrictions were lifted in 1946 after World War II, Western Gold Mining Inc., which had acquired the Eureka property six years earlier, tested the original Eureka lode—the one that had led to the 1890s gold rush.

By the time Western Gold began evaluating the old Glory

Doctor-on-call; Mrs. George M. Parrish prepares for the rough ride from Lost River up to the mining town of Barron where her husband has been called to care for a sick miner. Photo by Dr. George M. Parrish from The Wenatchee World *files.*

Hole, all the easy access free-milling gold was long gone, and an expensive chemical separation process was required to extract gold. This costly method made mining low-grade ore a doubly dubious venture. Nevertheless, the assays made by Western Gold offered hope. They continued exploration work and waited for the price of gold to go up.

Throwing caution aside, Western Gold financed a spanking new mill in the 1950s at the same spot as the original Barron mill above the ghost town of Barron. To provide energy for the mill, the company bought an Atlas Imperial marine diesel, a behemoth engine weighing umpteen tons that had powered a ferry boat on Oakland Harbor, California, in its former life.

Hauling the prize to its angle of repose on one of the highest mining sites in the Cascade Mountains proved to be a formidable task at best. The first truck and trailer to attempt the job sank three times up to its axles and had to be towed out three times by a Forest Service cat conveniently left on the road nearby. The rig finally groveled over Hart's Pass with the load. However, coming down from the pass, it cornered one switchback at which point the 7-ton Atlas, accompanied by its 5-ton generator, unceremoniously plunked off the trailer. Called to the rescue, local Hank Dammann custom-constructed a road from the felled engine to the mill.

For a while the dinosaur diesel proudly powered Western Gold's entire mining operation. As of 1992, the company still owned about 200 acres of patented land near Barron. There is still gold buried in the area, but any suggestions in regard to revving up the Atlas again have so far been squelched.

The '60s and '70s were quiet times for the Slate Creek mines. Then in the 1980s, Lion Mines, a Canadian group, reopened the Eureka yet again, operated it for three years and even sent some concentrate to Trail, British Columbia, for processing. Just when things were looking up, an avalanche leveled the mill in 1983.

What remains to be seen of the town of Barron, the Glory Hole and its companion mines? Today from the vantage point of the Pacific Crest Trail, one can still view the scarred meadows and pock-marked hillsides left as testament to gold fever. Some foundations and a caved-in saloon and post office are reminders of former lively times at the mining town of Barron.

Although you can't drive to this historical site, you can walk to view the ruins.

Charles Ballard and His Mammoth Proposition

Charles Ballard may be the real unsung hero of the Slate Creek District, for during his mining years in the Methow, Ballard accomplished more than any other man.

Along with his brother, Hazard Ballard, Charles widened the infamous route up to the Slate Creek mines and Hart's Pass, which at 6,200 feet is the highest road in Washington state. Without the Ballards' arterial to Hart's Pass, mining the area would have been impossible.

Ballard also managed the Mammoth Mine for 20 years and promoted the Azurite Mine into the 1930s, the latter being a vital source of employment during the Depression, if not a continuing source of wealth.

Because of his accomplishments, both a mountain and a Forest Service campground were named in Ballard's honor, but he never gained the fame of Colonel Hart or the notoriety of Glory Hole discoverer Alex Barron.

In 1886 Charles Ballard had left Butte, Montana, to create a new life on the Washington frontier. He was a skilled civil engineer and in his early years in North Central Washington, Charles laid out the townsites of Ruby, Conconully and Chelan. During the same period he served as probate judge, surveyed mineral claims, and assayed ore.

One of the samples Ballard assayed from Slate Creek intrigued him. He pursued the rancher who owned the claims containing the ore and bought them outright for $18,000 cash. Ballard's new claims were in the Mammoth vein, discovered in 1895 by G.C. Mathews, and located a mile southeast of the Eureka lode. Just as the assayer hoped, the lode proved lucrative.

Ballard rolled up his sleeves and began production of the Mammoth Mine in earnest. He had a high-tech, steam-powered 5-stamp mill built on the site which both crushed and ground the raw ore. Workers strung several hundred feet of aerial tram to feed ore from the Mammoth lode to the mill.

During its brief productive life, the Mammoth earned about $400,000, though it never made Ballard a rich mining baron.

After the mine closed around 1901 or 1902, Ballard spent several years in Arizona and Nevada, then moved to Alaska.

But the lure of Methow gold still flowed in his blood and when he returned to Washington state in 1915, Ballard bought 31 claims from C.R. McLean, then scrambled back up to the lofty peaks around Hart's Pass to mine.

The Late, Great Azurite
Azurite Mine Vital Statistics:
   Location—32 miles northwest of Winthrop in the Mill Creek
   Valley, three miles northwest from the Cascade divide.
   Began—1915
   Peaked—1936-1939
Slipped into quiescence a few years later.

The Ballards Buy the Azurite
It was named the Azurite Mine because of the azure-blue mineral men bored out of it—a copper carbonate that could be seen in the vein at the surface.

Charles Ballard returned to the Methow with renewed vigor and more money to invest. With financial backing from the East, he formed the Azurite Copper Company of Delaware in 1918 and with brother Hazard obtained a series of claims in the Mill Creek Valley, soon to be known as the Azurite Mine site.

The first summer, using only hand tools, the Ballards drove in a short adit named the Discovery Tunnel to expose the Azurite vein. That fall, Charles proudly walked out of the adit with a gleaming bar of gold.

During the next seven years, the brothers hauled freight by packhorse 24 miles from Lost River to the distant site, threw up a camp and blasted out trenches and pits to better expose the vein.

Expenses were high and coffers were low so Charles reorganized his partnership and changed the name from Azurite Copper to Azurite Gold Company, perhaps hoping the new title would better entice investors. He elected himself president, and sold enough stock to finance further work. By 1929, he'd packed an air compressor, mining equipment, food and fuel to the site. The Hart's Pass Road hadn't improved since the days Ballard surveyed and built the original 24-mile stretch and horses still pulled freight vehicles to the tune of $100 per ton.

The deplorable road access was eating up all the money so

the company decided to improve 17 miles of old narrow-gauge road from Lost River over Hart's Pass then 11 miles more over Cady Pass to the mine site. The new road *did* reduce freight costs, but was passable only five or six months of the year.

In the early '30s, the Azurite Co. erected a smelter and began shipping ore to Tacoma for further refining. However, a 1933 shipment of 15 tons of ore containing $2,344 in gold, $8 in silver, and $29 in copper probably failed to seduce many new investors.

ASARCO Becomes the Main Character at the Azurite

The famous ASARCO (American Smelting and Refining Co.) entered the Azurite mining scene with a proposal to lease 36 lode claims and six mill sites for 25 years, sharing profits 50-50 with Ballard after ASARCO recouped its production investment. Ballard shook hands with the big wheels and the deal was sealed.

Early in 1934, the same year the agreement was struck, the price of gold rose from $20 per ounce to $35 an ounce. Pleased with this turn of events, ASARCO drove down deeper into the ore body and simultaneously developed the whole mining area. Under the steady hand of Mr. H. G. Washburn, general manager, a crew was assembled, gasoline-powered compressors installed, a machine shop, blacksmith shop and sawmill buildings built, plus fuel, mining supplies and food to last an entire winter were freighted to the Azurite site. ASARCO was ready to roll the winter of '35, but the miners hadn't wagered on what mother nature had in store for them.

Surviving the Winter of '35

Even in kinder summer conditions, the rugged alpine terrain of the Azurite Mine region makes access difficult. And even in an *average* winter, heavy snowfall causes slides that pour down every gully forcefully and frequently. The winter of 1935 was like all previous ones, except worse.

The mine itself was located smack in the middle of a slide zone. Wisely, all mine buildings plus the cookhouse, bunkhouse and fuel storage tanks had been built with their roofs the same slope as the mountains above them. When slides roared down, which was often, they all went over the tops of the buildings.

Miners shoveled out tunnels to ensure air circulation.

A letter from Ray Walters to his wife, written January 31, 1935, described conditions at the Azurite that winter.

> It turned warm and started to snow ... seven feet
> fell in two days. It then started to rain and poured
> down for three days. The old snow was packed
> hard and conditions were just right for snow
> slides. They started at once and the hill was pop-
> ping for five days. There was hardly a five-minute
> interval that you couldn't see a slide running in
> the daytime or hear one roar at night.
>
> Our mine building was demolished and had to
> be dug out and rebuilt. The roof of our sawmill
> caved in from the snow load. Our bull cook,
> Charlie Graves, stepped out of the kitchen to fetch
> a pail of water and was buried in a slide ... It took
> 45 minutes of digging by the whole crew to find
> him and get him out. He still had a big chew of
> tobacco in his mouth. He didn't have room to spit
> it out and didn't want to swallow it!
>
> —"The Azurite Mine Story 1915-1942,"
> from ASARCO Records, Feb. 1975.

The miners apparently kept their sense of humor in the midst of grave danger. Some reminiscences of another miner, Richard R. Smith, not only illustrate an unflappable optimism, but a delightful writing style as well. Smith recalled:

In the late 1930s, miners grind their way up to the Azurite Mine on the narrow Hart's Pass Road. Photo from the Dick Webb collection.

> I was glad to get underground at the Azurite
> because of the bad weather (wintertime). It was
> eerie to one who had never been anything deeper
> than a root cellar. The ground overhead talked to
> you constantly with little pops and creaks. That
> made it hard to concentrate on shoveling the
> muck. About the time it would be talking the
> loudest, your carbide light would snap, fizzle and
> go out leaving you in total darkness which didn't
> give your morale any boost at all.
>> —*Coyote Tales*, Spring 1974.

And for the miners' diversion, there were natural wonders to
view as well as audio-visual entertainment, according to Smith.

> The mine being down in a deep canyon on a
> north slope in the dead of winter meant that the
> only time you saw the sun was for 10-15 minutes
> as it peeked through Azurite Pass about noon,
> weather permitting. On a bright day this attrac-
> tion always drew more spectators than the jumpy,
> scratchy movies they were showing inside the
> bunkhouse.
>> —*Ibid.*

And when the place was thoroughly snowed in and even the
antics of mother nature lost their thrill ...

> Everyone became content to listen to his hair
> grow. Some interesting beards, mustaches and
> hairdos began to emerge. Among the better was a
> "General Grant" type and outlaw type.
>> —*Ibid.*

ASARCO Picks Up the Pieces

ASARCO built new structures to replace those destroyed by
slides and repaired the snow-damaged ones. Snow slides
thrashed the area again the next winter but no one was injured.

Early in 1936 the mine was finally slated to start production.
Five months of frenzied work had produced a 100-ton per day
cyanide mill, a new office site, bunkhouse, and cookhouse—all
complete with snowsheds to pass the slides right on by. The
hired crew came mostly from the Methow Valley. The depression had hit and men welcomed the work despite its perils.

Two months after production began a huge snow slide
barreled down the valley, grazed the buildings at the mine
portal, crashed into the ore bin, carried the bin down valley

100 feet and damaged the cable on the aerial tram to the mill beyond repair.

ASARCO mined from November 1936 to February 1939, and during that 28-month period, they produced $972,000 in gold and silver but failed to recoup their original investment. Nevertheless, they had provided employment for 70 men, mostly from the local area, who worked hard during times when it was hard to find work.

The Azurite Dog Team Express

The Azurite Mine in the dead of winter was virtually a prison. Walls of snow, threatening avalanches, mountain weather and a long road to civilization prevented anyone from driving or walking out. Dog teams served as the miners' life line during the snowed-in months from December to May—a canine line of communication and transportation of men and materials for half the entire year!

Hearing the spirited sound of the canine crew in the distance filled the miners with anticipation. Here's how one winter resident remembered it:

> If it was clear and cold you could hear the sled
> dogs barking for hours before they arrived. Their
> noise was a welcome sound. One never knew,
> maybe someone loved you enough to send you an
> epistle of warmth and tenderness.
> —*Coyote Tales*, Spring 1974.

Ed Kikendall and his brother, Chuck, drove the dog team express which supplied the Azurite Mine in the winters of 1936-37 and 1937-38. Before dog teams bore the burden, Ed had packed 1,250 pounds of freight and mail on his own back over Azurite Pass during the winter of 1935-36.

The Kikendalls had the best qualifications for the dangerous hauling job. Both had spent entire winters trapping in the North Cascades. They'd ride into the mountains on decrepit horses, then use the beasts for bait in their traps. They trapped coyotes, weasels, skunks, cougars and black bears. Once the horses had collapsed the two traveled cross-country on skis, often exercising in 30-below to 60-below weather. Their skis got to feel like feet after a while. "I could climb trees on skis," said Ed Kikendall.

Ed's basecamp to service the Azurite was at Robinson Creek.

The Azurite Dog Team Express takes a break on the way up to the mines. Photo from the Dick Webb collection.

At one time, over 25 dogs—a little over three teams—stayed at the camp. The canine pack was composed of crossbreeds: Siberians, malamutes and huskies with some Irish setter blood. Seven pups made a team; the team traveled in pairs with a lead dog. In unison, they pulled about 350 pounds. One team leader was a beautiful pure-white Siberian husky worth more than $1,500. Though he was the least aggressive dog on the team, he scared people because of his strange-looking milky-blue eyes.

Ed had contracted to run four round trips a month which was fine when the journey took its usual time of one day in and one day out. In bad weather, however, a one-way trip could take five days which allowed little time to recover before the next excursion. Unexpected emergency trips occurred when a miner fell ill or was injured. When machinery broke down, Ed and company had to make an impromptu trip to rush repair parts up to the site.

The favored route for the team went up the shorter but steeper Azurite Pass rather than Hart's Pass/Cady Pass. Sometimes, though, the dogs did go by way of Hart's Pass and it was on this route that they nearly spoiled their perfect record of never losing a load. On one fateful day, a big team of 12 dogs had arrived at Dead Horse Point with load in tow, when just at the spot where snow narrowed the already narrow, cliffhanger road, a nanny goat with her kids leaped in front of the pack. Instinct took over and the dogs shot after the goats. Kikendall whistled the command. The trusty lead dog stopped on a dime just saving the squadron from a plunge over the edge. Teetering inches from the cliff was the pack's load of $2,000 worth of precision machinist tools!

By far the most exhausting and stressful trips for Kikendall and his dogs involved miners with appendicitis attacks. Three cases occurred the single winter of 1936-37. Chipped cookware used in the mine's kitchen turned out to be the cause of the attacks.

In January 1937, Fred White, the shift boss in the mill, came down with appendicitis. A doctor was rushed to the mine by dogs, but he decided the patient needed to go to Okanogan for an operation. A "black boomer blizzard" and 20-below temperatures blasted the rescuers while they carried out the sick man. It took the troop 12 hours to evacuate the invalid to Robinson Creek. Sadly, after a 17-hour marathon trip by dog team, then ambulance, to Okanogan, the man died. Fred White was the only recorded fatality involving an employee during the entire life of the mine—an incredible statistic considering the mine's location and dangerous conditions.

Forty-five days after White died, there was a second emergency case of appendicitis. Devastated by the White tragedy, the miners refused to waste a moment in the rescue. They immediately strapped the ailing man to a sled with six workers sent as substitute sled dogs. Things ran smoothly until suddenly the sled escaped and slid over a cliff. Miraculously, the rescuers managed to hold on to connecting ropes. They retrieved the victim, who did not die of fright *or* a ruptured appendix. In fact, he healed and returned to the Azurite for another round of work and adventure.

The last man Ed Kikendall had to rescue the year-of-the-appendectomy was Chris Weppler. This trip tired "Kike" more than any other of his herculean excursions. He had just returned from a two-day round trip to the mine when he got called back up to pick up Weppler.

One story goes that the relief rescue team was indisposed, so Ed had to transport the sick man out by himself. On the lower portion of the route, lack of snow prevented the sled from running so Ed carried Chris piggyback. All the time his ear was cocked hoping to hear the rescue team coming. In total, Ed and his exhausted dogs stayed up for three days and nights—72 hours of continuous labor on the trail.

To most of the miners, Kikendall's dogs were friends and heroes. They were the bearers of news from home, fresh food and all supplies. They were fun to play with—a livelier form of recreation than the weekly movie, pool, cards and reading. The dogs didn't win over everyone, however, as revealed by the following testimony of miner Richard Smith who took the trip out by dog sled following an accident at the Azurite:

> Being my first experience behind dogs, my earliest shock was a smothering wave of foul air that greeted my nostrils. Compared to that, horse aroma is Chanel No. 5. The lead dog on the sled behind mine was "Old Wolf." A more sinister face you have never seen on a dog. His ears were tattered, his jaw drooped, lips torn and he had a light scum over one eye, all from old fighting injuries. Torn lips exposed long yellow fangs in a perpetual snarl and his one good, baleful eye rarely changed expression.
>
> —*Ibid.*

No doubt Richard gave this review with a smile on his face and a twinkle in his eye. After all, the dogs he so maligned were on one of their many missions of mercy.

Azurite Epitaph

Up at the Azurite Mine site, nothing remains except tailings and debris from buildings. All valuable equipment was yanked out years ago. Everything's in ruins, according to Greg Knott, Forest Service minerals expert. "It looks like five acres on the surface of Mars."

Tools of Their Trade:
The Shafer Museum Mining Exhibit

The Shafer Museum in Winthrop is home to one of the best mining displays in the Northwest. Some of the equipment on exhibit is extraordinarily heavy and extremely rare, and the successful effort to disassemble it, lug it down from Hart's Pass and reassemble it at the museum seems miraculous!

Most of the mining equipment came from the town of Barron where early miners used gravity separation methods to obtain the valuable minerals. Their goal was to produce sand by crushing rock, then siphon off the gold. Following are descriptions of some of the machines on exhibit:

100

An *air compressor* on display was used at Barron around
1912. It was hauled to the site on solid rubber wheels and used
to power the miners' drills.

The *air drill* worked like a jackhammer. Air was used instead of gas because the work was done underground and gas
would make fumes. A huge adjacent post supported the long
steel bar with its sharp points which drilled out rock.

Miners would hand-sort the ore and put it on a *mining car*
like the one on display and the *mucker* would highgrade the
ore, meaning separate the valuable ore from the worthless rock.

The *jaw crusher* at the museum was a primary crusher. Two
metal plates smashed together like cymbals to produce gravel.
The gravel traveled to a secondary crusher, either a Chilean
mill or stamp mill.

A huge monstrosity at the exhibit is the *Chilean mill* from
Barron. It's one of the largest ever built and one of two left in
the world. Powered by a steam engine, huge wheels revolved in
a circle around a track, crushing gravel in the track to sand.

From the Mammoth Mine near Barron there's a *stamp mill*

The Chilean mill crushed gravel to sand. Photo by Don Portman.

on display. Stamps were heavy iron blocks that looked like organ pipes but sounded like the percussion section of a hard rock band—very hard rock! They were raised 20 inches then dropped, smashing the ore with an ear-splitting clamor.

Water power ran the stamps by way of the *Pelton wheel* brought from Chancellor, the prime power station for the Mammoth Mine. It looks like a showboat waterwheel with cups that scoop up water on a revolving iron wheel.

The Pelton wheel provided water power to run a stamp mill at Hart's Pass. Photo by Don Portman.

Water flowed down the *shaker table* which worked like a big gold pan. A motor gave the tilted table a rocking motion. Water carried fine material down the table while the heavier gold would separate off.

An example of the *narrow-gauge wagons* used to pull up huge equipment and bring down mountains of ore is on exhibit. Horses in single file could barely hoist the heavy loads so a block and tackle was frequently set up to pull the wagon up tough spots on the trail. Before these custom-built wagons, supplies went by foot, packhorse, skis or dog sled.

From Winthrop's Riverside Avenue, looking up the hill toward the museum, one can see the "Belle of Barron" mill taking shape, compliments of volunteer Dale Tonseth. Pursuing his goal of duplicating a turn-of-the-century gold mill, Dale has imported a steam engine and jaw crusher from the Azurite Mine.

Most equipment at remote mountain mines is simply left to rot over the eons. The Shafer Museum people have brought the gargantuan machinery to town for all to see. One can almost hear the clang of the metal and din of the rock crushers while viewing these antiques.

Bibliography

Bainbridge, Lu. "Glory Hole Claim Lured Men for Decades." *Okanogan County Heritage*, Fall 1977.

Blonk, Hu. *Methow Valley News*. July 6, 1961.

——. "There was Gold in Them Thar Hills." *The Awakening, Methow Valley News*, Aug. 31, 1972.

Davis, Ruth. "Mining Lured McLean to Methow." *Okanogan County Heritage*, Fall 1974.

Heath, Frank. "Gold." *Okanogan County Heritage*, Summer 1972.

——. *Methow Valley News*. Nov. 5, 1981.

Kenady, Mary. Notes on Pasayten Wilderness History. US Forest Service.

Kerr, Charles. "Dog-Team Express Days." *Okanogan County Heritage*, Winter 1974-75.

Knott, Greg. US Forest Service Minerals Expert. Interview. Winthrop, Washington, summer 1990.

Methow Valley News. Dec. 2, 1976.

Moean, Wayne. "Mines and Mineral Deposits of Whatcom County, WA." Washington Dept. of Natural Resources Division of Mines and Geology Bulletin #57, 1969.

Okanogan County Heritage. "Robinson." Author unknown. March 1964.

Roe, JoAnn. *The North Cascadians*. Madrona Publishers, Seattle, 1980.

——. North Cascade Institute Class. Sun Mountain Lodge, Winthrop, Washington, fall 1991.

Smith, Richard. "The Winter I Spent at the Old Azurite Mine." *Coyote Tales*, 1974.

Twisp, Winthrop Conconully Cultural Resource Overview. US Forest Service, Winthrop Ranger District, 1979.

Weller, Howard. "From Horses to Helicopters." *Okanogan County Heritage*, Spring 1988.

Whiting, Keith. "The Azurite Mine Story (1915-1942)." February 1975, from ASARCO Records, August 1982.

Chapter 6

PAVING THE WAY TO
SHANGRI-LA

Pioneer Routes Into the Methow

When pioneers began their daredevil forays into the Methow, the valley was like Shangri-La, nearly impossible to penetrate. Even with today's good access, it is easy to imagine what a herculean task it was to get here at one time.

The summits of the North Cascades line up like the Wall of China at the head of the valley. Below the Cascades, the glacier-carved cliffs of Goat Wall hinder travel in or out of the upper valley. At the lowest end of the valley, steep hillsides plunge into the Methow River for 18 miles before the Methow's confluence with the Columbia River. The Sawtooth Range rises sharply along the valley's western border. There is barely a stretch of the Methow not fenced in by mountains and hills and ridges.

Yet in spite of the Methow's formidable boundaries, settlers eventually struck routes into the valley. The paths they forged were fraught with danger, disaster and often with unimaginable discomfort. But the rewards were great once they arrived, so people braved the hardships and kept coming.

Most journeys to the Methow began with safe, dependable sources of transportation, but as immigrants got closer to their destination, travel became rougher, vehicles more rustic, and the trip more hazardous. People coming from the east boarded a train to Ellensburg, Spokane or Sprague—Sprague being the end of the railroad line in the late 19th century. From these bastions of civilization, the pioneers traveled cross-country by horseback and covered wagon.

After taking a train to Sprague in 1891, the Guy Waring family outfitted themselves with a covered wagon and two gray mares for their journey to the new land. Anna Greene Stevens, Waring's stepdaughter, related the daily schedule followed by the family:

> The days were unbelievably long. We were up at
> 3 a.m. to get started on breakfast and chores, so
> we could be ready to be on our way about 5 a.m.
> We covered 30 miles a day. By 4 p.m. we were all
> glad to make camp so we could look out for the
> horses, cook supper and get settled in for the
> night before darkness came.
> —*Okanogan County Heritage*, June 1970.

Before facing the mountain passes surrounding the Methow, the Columbia River had to be crossed. Indians offered their services to the earliest pioneers. On the Warings' first trip to the Okanogan area, the family warily accepted the native transit service. Here is Anna's description of her family's initial river crossing:

Indian dugout used to ferry passengers across the Columbia. Photo from the Okanogan County Historical Society.

> We spent five days alone crossing the Columbia
> River, a perilous and awesome undertaking. The
> river, undammed in those days, boiled downstream
> at an unbelievable speed. Indian dugouts were
> used to make the crossing. They were hollowed-
> out logs with the bark still on them. There was no
> bow or stern. They were treacherous, and only the
> extreme skill of the three Indian paddlers made
> the crossing possible.
> The covered wagons had to be taken completely
> apart and carried across in pieces. Two dugouts
> were tied together to accomplish this feat.
> —*Okanogan County Heritage*, March 1970.

Later, private ferries carried pioneers across the Columbia,
the first being "Wild Goose" Bill Condon's ferry at Goose
Creek, the present site of Wilbur. Samuel Wilbur Condit, the
operator of the famous ferry service, received the name "Wild
Goose" after he encountered a flock of tame geese and mistak-
enly shot one. His business began in 1884 with a fleet of canoes, which a year later he upgraded to a raft made of five
huge logs chained together and propelled by swimming horses.

By the time the Warings made their second Columbia River
crossing, Wild Goose Bill had a cable ferry in use. Anna Stevens
described this comparatively tame traverse of the Columbia:

> This time there was a ferry that the covered
> wagon could drive onto, which crossed the river
> attached to a trolley. The boat, hauled at an angle
> against the swift current and held by the trolley,
> sailed across by water pressure.
> —*Okanogan County Heritage*, June 1970.

If a pioneer family planned on braving the Chiliwhist Trail to
the Methow, the Okanogan River was the next big obstacle on
this route. Alice Rader Burge's family in 1888 forded the
Okanogan River near Malott. To prepare for the passage took
several days according to Alice. During this time, the wagons
soaked in water and were caulked with rags so they'd float
without leaking. A thick, long rope was fastened to each vehicle. A man grabbed the rope, and while his horse swam the
river, he guided his wagon across.

Once pioneers had navigated the Okanogan River, the mountain range between the Okanogan and Methow valleys had to
be negotiated. To do this, the Chiliwhist Trail was virtually

The driver of the stagecoach, Frank Fulton, operated the Brewster-Twisp Stage Line. Sitting next to Frank in this 1908 photo are Bertie and Maud Prewitt. Photo from the Dick Webb collection.

the only choice for early comers. Originally an Indian path, the Chiliwhist was a safe route on foot, rough but reasonable on horseback, and a two-and-a-half-day ordeal by wagon wheels. Pioneers were no strangers to ordeals though (they had gotten this far, after all), so most lumbered over the grueling 50 percent pitches to the summit, feeling victorious once they reached the road down Benson Creek, fashioned by three Methow forefathers—Mason Thurlow, Harvey Nickell and Napoleon Stone.

The circuitous Okanogan Valley/Chiliwhist Trail itinerary lost favor fast and settlers soon began to scout out more direct routes through canyons running northwest from Pateros and Brewster. One might ask why a route as the crow flies wasn't attempted sooner. The answer: too steep, too dangerous. While the Chiliwhist Trail was no cakewalk, a direct route up the Methow River through the steep-walled Black Canyon was in a hazard class all its own.

Nevertheless, the call of "Wagons ho" was soon heard on ridge lines paralleling the Methow Valley. Gold miner Frank Heath described one of these early routes:

> To get into the valley on wheels the only feasible route was to climb over the Bald Knob Route. This was a mountain road blazed out from Central Ferry on the Columbia River and going

over Bald Knob Mountain. They had no way of grading at this time so they would follow up a ridge or a draw or any way that was level enough that a wagon would not turn over. On the west side they struck the head of Texas Creek, followed along some level-like benches ... then dropped into the Methow Valley.

—*Okanogan County Heritage*, Summer 1972.

Settlers from Winthrop, Twisp and Carlton contributed money and donated labor to improve the Bald Knob Route which they "completed" in 1891. Using plows, scrapers, dynamite and whatever other equipment was available to them, the amateur highway builders carved out a steep, difficult road following hillsides and dipping through passes, avoiding at all costs the cliffs bordering the Methow River which would have necessitated rock drilling.

The tortuous twisting road was a challenge to freighters, related Jessie Schmidt. According to Jessie, one early issue of the *Methow Valley News* told of a freighter who saw a Stetson hat in the road. Climbing down to pick it up, he discovered Tom Barker and his six-horse team virtually buried in mud beneath the hat!

Traffic began to get heavy on the Bald Knob Route so pioneers fashioned another route connecting the upper Methow Valley with the ferry dock at Brewster. Built in 1891, the Brewster Mountain Road traversed Paradise Hill, followed Benson Creek and landed in Silver, south of Twisp. Not quite as scary as the Bald Knob Route, this arterial still presented steep climbs at either end.

Virgil Webb drove a stagecoach from Brewster to Winthrop over the Brewster Mountain Road, with intermediate stops at Paradise, Filer and Silver. Halfway to Benson Creek, the stage would tarry at the little settlement of Filer, where there was a huge building with sleeping units on the top floor, and a restaurant and saloon on the ground floor. The Filer livery stable provided fresh horses for the stagecoach.

During the flood of 1948, the Brewster Mountain Road proved a lifesaver. When a raging Methow River knocked out half the highway bridges, this pioneer pathway provided a connection to the outside world.

The narrow, winding Methow River road. Photo from the Dick Webb collection.

Convicts and a Congressman Build a River Road

Building a convenient river-level road connecting the Methow's towns had been an ultimate goal, but an insurmountable task for the early settlers. It took an aggressive legislator and 100 convicts to accomplish the feat.

W.A. Bolinger, a famous figure from the Squaw Creek mining boom, became a hero after he convinced the state to build a road up the Methow River. Only the state had the resources to build a decent highway on such a crooked, narrow route, claimed Bolinger, and with this as his platform, he was elected to the state House of Representatives in 1904.

Bolinger was a large, good-looking man according to miner/ admirer Frank Heath. Well-educated, he was a good talker.

When the 1905 legislative session opened, Bolinger immediately introduced a bill creating a state highway from the town of Methow to Barron (a mining town west of the Hart's Pass summit) and appropriating $10,000 to pay for it. Bolinger's persuasive powers got the bill passed.

The Washington State Highway Department came into existence the same year that Bolinger's bill passed. The Methow Valley's river-level road won the distinction of being the first highway to be built under the jurisdiction of the state of Washington, and was the means of bringing the state Highway Department into being.

When $18,700 in state and county funds became available in 1906, intense work began immediately on the road. The first 30 miles were roughly graded and soon the new river-view route was proudly opened to the public. "There was little danger of anyone having to turn back once they'd started," the contractor promised. It was a rough road and needed a lot more work, but it received heavy use right away.

At the next legislative session, Bolinger managed to secure state-funded convict labor to work on his road project. Twenty-nine convicts from the state penitentiary at Walla Walla were assigned to work on the Methow highway as hired laborers. Their pay was to be 60 cents a day. Barracks with iron-barred doors, a stockade, and a high fence with four watchtowers were constructed four and a half miles up the Methow River from Pateros.

The felons slaved eight hours a day for nearly four months.

Convicts built this part of the Methow River road. Photo from the Shafer Museum collection.

They blasted out solid rock in a perpendicular bluff; each man moved about a cubic yard of rock a day. When the convicts finished in December, they were healthier than when they arrived, most took pride in the work they'd done and three were paroled for good conduct. The difficult section of road they dynamited came to be called "convict grade," and the name stands to this day.

Convict labor worked so well, Bolinger asked for 45 more inmates in 1909 and the 70-mile river-grade road from Pateros to Robinson Creek was completed by the end of that year. The new highway became the Methow Valley's primary arterial. Bolinger served several more terms in the House of Representatives and one in the state Senate. Later he was widely praised as "the father of good roads in the Methow."

The Short, Sweet Steamboat Era

For a short time (early 1890s to 1914) steamboats chugged up and down the Columbia River, from Wenatchee to the landing at the mouth of the Methow. Despite their somewhat brief tenure, the appealing riverboats were instrumental in opening up the Methow to settlement and development. Arriving from the East Coast, the Midwest, West Coast, or the South, early settlers got off the train at Wenatchee and got on a stern-wheeler. The steamboats hauled settlers and their worldly goods to the mouth of the Methow River. They transported Methow apples and ore to outside markets.

At various times, 20 stern-wheeled riverboats operated on the Columbia north of Wenatchee. The *City of Ellensburg* and the *Thomas L. Nixon* were the first to provide service to the Okanogan country. During the 1890s these two steamers had a monopoly on river shipping in the area.

Barreling through the rough waters of Priest Rapids and Rock Island Rapids, Captain Gray victoriously delivered the Pasco-built *City of Ellensburg* to its Wenatchee dock, a feat others had attempted, but unsuccessfully.

Ellensburg interests had built the boat in order to trade with northern mining areas, including the Methow's Squaw Creek and Slate Creek mining districts. It was an attractive boat boasting the luxuries of a passenger lounge, dining room, windowed salons and a wide-railed promenade all around the upper captain's deck.

Steamboats transported Methow-bound pioneers up the Columbia and Okanogan rivers. Photo by Frank Matsura; courtesy Methow Valley News.

The *Thomas L. Nixon* steamboat, built in Pasco and piloted by the Gray brothers, was named after a wealthy Tacoma man who provided capital to build the vessel. Ore from Okanogan County mines inspired Mr. Nixon's investment.

Although considered a safe means of conveyance, the stern-wheelers still ran into problems, a major one being rapids. Anna Greene Stevens described how steamboats tackled white water:

> The Columbia was very shallow in spots and where other rivers joined there were rapids ... The method used to work up through fast water was called "Lining Up," a hazardous operation. Arriving at the foot of the rapids ... a crewman jumped ashore with the "Lining Up" cable with its big hook. He made his way along the side of the river to the top of the rapids and hooked the hook into a huge iron ring bolted into a rock. The forward winch on the steamer would then take in the line, the engine groaning and steam pressure almost bursting the boiler.
> —*Okanogan County Heritage*, September 1970.

When the rapids proved too powerful, the steamer literally ran out of steam and was dashed back downstream. Guy Waring was aboard during one "Line Up" when the cable broke, snapped back and killed the captain. The steamer swung out, hit a submerged ledge and sank, according to Waring's stepdaughter.

When bridges were built and the railroad completed from Wenatchee to Oroville, the era of the scenic riverboats ended. During their short two-decade life span, the steamers delivered the lion's share of pioneer families and their freight to the doorsteps of the Methow Valley.

Hauling Freight and Passengers Up the Methow Valley

After Methow-bound passengers left the boat at the Columbia River, many boarded custom-made freight wagons which hauled them and their household goods to a new home.

The early freighters provided an invaluable service to remote areas of the Methow 85 years ago. One freight load might total 4,000 pounds of goods, according to Winthrop researcher Frank Kenney. If heading south, Frank said, the wagons carried kegs of butter, apples or possibly a bar of gold bullion. A rear wagon might be piled high with raw beaver pelts, bales of cow and sheep hides and furniture. On the return trip, the cargo might consist of kerosene, axle grease, flour barrels,

Freighters transported pioneer belongings. Photo from the Dick Webb collection.

The first Methow Valley truck transport. Photo from the Okanogan County Historical Society, negative 2621.

whiskey, a keg of blasting powder and the furniture of new settlers. Freighting companies charged $20 to $40 per ton and the driver earned $6.00 per day.

Since early Methow freighters drove on deeply rutted routes, freight wagons by necessity were heavy road warriors with high suspension. A typical freighter drove six to eight horses pulling two wagons. A string of bells hanging from the harnesses of the two lead horses jingled advance warning to other vehicles on the road.

Warning bells were obligatory since the Methow's narrow, precipitous roads prevented turning around and if two teams met head on, one might be forced to back up a quarter mile to a wide spot. This maneuver was even harder than it sounds for freighting teams were noted for their high spirit. It often took several men to harness and hold them until the rig was ready to leave.

Especially fearsome were the times when teams encountered an automobile. The early vehicles were a noisy, alien menace to the horses and nearly scared the beasts to death.

Twisp brothers Leonard and Paul Therriault launched the Therriault Brothers Freight and Transfer Company in 1915. Each started at one end of the Pateros to Winthrop run and took four days for the round trip. One team of horses pulling two wagons left Pateros at 6 a.m. while the other left Winthrop at the same time. The brothers picked up mail and parcel post at each town along the way. The teams rendezvoused at the

"Noon Station" up Gold Creek, halfway between the two desti-
nations. Passengers enjoyed lunch at the inn while the freighters hitched fresh horses to the rig. Sometimes the wagon stayed
overnight at the halfway house.

With his four-horse freight wagon, G. E. Nickell hauled
merchandise, lumber and ore the length of the Methow Valley.
One morning when G. E. was returning from Mazama with a
particularly weighty load of ore, his team started across a
bridge at Winthrop when suddenly the structure collapsed.
Horses and bullion plunged into the Methow River. Legal suits
for accidents were unheard of in those days, but Nickell was
so low in cash he went to the Okanogan County commissioners
and asked for $20 to help pay for wagon repairs. They paid
him right away—in gold!

In the mid-1910s Nickell's sons Ben, Newt, Frank, Carl
and Walt took a technological leap in the freighting business.
Walter Nickell described the advances:

> We were the first to haul freight in 1915 via
> trucks to Winthrop instead of horse-drawn wag-
> ons. Our first truck was no more than a Model T
> with a truck bed made out of lumber. In 1916 we
> bought a Mack truck—a dandy with rubber tires.
> The top speed was 15 miles an hour.
> —*The Way It Was,* June 1990.

The Nickells' first truck was a homemade beauty with chain
drive and sprocket wheels. With this prototype they hauled
merchandise from Pateros trains to their store in Winthrop.

Therriault Brothers Freight Company jumped right on the
automotive bandwagon, producing their own Model T truck
with chain drive and hard rubber tires in 1916. As their
business grew, the Therriaults added first a Reo speed wagon
which could handle 11 passengers, then a Studebaker and
Packard car for summer passenger service and a White truck
for freight. Cars and trucks sometimes couldn't barrel through
the snow in winter so the company kept their dependable
horses and antique equipment for the most challenging weather
conditions.

During World War II, Joe Lockhart saw the need for a bus
service in the Methow, since at the time it was both hard to get
a car and hard to get parts to repair one. Joe started his business around 1944, operating out of a garage in Winthrop. His

26-passenger bus service between Winthrop and Wenatchee became an instant success and Joe soon had all the business he could handle.

The availability of cars after the war killed the Methow's convenient transit system. Joe Lockhart sold the bus and mail contract in 1966.

Of Cars and Trains

The first taxi, a Model T Ford driven by Wendall Stevens, rattled about the town of Twisp around 1908. Several pioneers claimed the same Wendall Stevens drove the very first car ever seen in the valley.

During the early 1910s there were 38 licensed cars in Okanogan County. Several of these "horseless carriages" were registered to Methow Valley citizens. The semi-rich and famous Lord Thomas Blythe of Twisp chugged about in his Brush car and the Methow Canal Company (Blythe's irrigation association) owned a Ford, as did J. A. Risley of Twisp.

Dr. James B. Couche owned one of the first cars in Twisp. Unfortunately, the time of his arrival to patients' homes was less predictable by automobile than by horse.

Once cars arrived, roads became very dusty and full of washboard, recollected Nedra Horn. If you went anywhere, you could count on one or two flat tires. Everyone carried a kit with a pump as a matter of survival and old tubes often looked like patchwork quilts.

In the early days, trains linked markets and were a springboard for growth in Eastern Washington communities. Methow businessmen believed railroad service to the valley would boost the economy and spur development. Miners could export ore, farmers could send produce, and ranchers could transport cattle by rail.

A representative from the Great Northern Railroad examined the Methow for train service potential and concluded the valley's apple orcharding and gold mining warranted a line from Pateros to Early Winters. Armed with the Great Northern report, local sponsors lobbied for a feeder line from Pateros through Twisp to Winthrop around 1916. The project gathered momentum. A contract to build the line was announced! Then ... nothing. Not a track was ever laid.

There is one story that appears to solve the Methow's lack-

A footbridge across the Methow River. Photo from the Okanogan County Historical Society, negative 2620.

of-a-rail-line mystery. It concerns Jim Hill, a railroad tycoon. Hill owned all the land around Pearrygin Lake except for parcels claimed by Washington state and homesteader Benjamin Pearrygin. Hill dreamed of building an attractive resort on the lake which would lure tourists to travel by rail to his getaway. When Hill approached Mr. Pearrygin the latter asked such an exorbitant price for his land, Hill couldn't afford it. Since he couldn't claim title to all the land, Hill abandoned the project. Many old-timers feel this is the reason the Methow Valley never got a rail line.

Fords and Bridges

Before settlers built bridges, they crossed Methow rivers and creeks at established fords. "The same trails worn deep by the hooves of Indian ponies led pioneers to the best places to cross the Methow River and its tributaries," wrote Jesse Schmidt in an *Okanogan County Heritage* article. "But only a fool would try it during high water in May or June." Spring runoff, fast currents, undertow, river holes, rocks and logjams all made fording a dangerous business.

Fords bore the names of homesteaders who owned adjacent property such as the Fulton-Dibble Ford on lower Bear Creek. There were fords near every town, usually named after that town. Settlers named Rocky Ford between Twisp and Carlton for the numerous rocks encountered plus the rough crossing they created.

Despite the precarious nature of fords, pioneers constantly traveled across them. Kids crossed fords to attend Fairview School between Twisp and Winthrop and Lakeview School near Twin Lakes. Families forded rivers to attend the Fourth of July picnic and other social events. A skittish horse, the need to cross a stream during high water—or both—sometimes led to disaster, and there are many tales of lost lives due to fording accidents.

Eventually a man named Bill Burger built and operated a ferry which crossed the river at Twisp. His ferry was attached to a cable anchored on each side of the river. When Bill angled the craft into the current the force of the water propelled it to the other side. Burger's ferry ran on a straight line with the road passing by the Methow Valley Inn in Twisp.

Because the river often froze solid in winter, people built cage contraptions that crossed by pulley and cable like a skier's gondola. Several people could traverse together. To get to church meetings in Winthrop during the winter, many families arrived at the river by sled then crossed by way of a cage at Walter Frisbee's place. This cage was heavily used during the 1894 flood after a low-water bridge and later a ferry built to replace it washed down the river.

At first valleyites constructed bridges for pedestrians only. They were either narrow plank suspension bridges, the type that bounced as you walked and wavered in the wind, or a simple footbridge made by felling a log across a narrow spot in the river.

To accommodate teams and wagons, pioneers split logs, then nailed them together across a water course. These so-called low-water bridges were temporary sorts; barely a gap existed between water course and bridge bottom; consequently each year they washed out and had to be replaced. An unexpected flood might whoosh one away as soon as carpenters laid the final plank.

As a result, people built higher, steel-supported bridges in the Methow. At first these proved not much more sustainable than the low-water-washouts. Poor mixtures were often used for supporting concrete piers and they'd occasionally collapse under an unsuspecting customer. Signs warned travelers never to cross at faster than a walk. A violator could be slapped with a $20 fine! A dropped "stogie" could set a steel-supported bridge on fire, and the dirt-filled bridge approaches sometimes washed out.

Ignoring these drawbacks, workers built six steel-supported bridges in the Methow Valley—one at each town, except Winthrop, which received two. One was erected at McFarland Creek and another below Gold Creek.

Concrete bridges slowly supplanted steel-supported bridges. The 1948 flood accelerated the change by clearing out many remaining steel-support types. One at Squaw Creek blew out in a matter of minutes. Today, if you travel the length of the Methow Valley, you will cross 11 concrete bridges.

The North Cascades Highway

What motivated men to carve a road through the solid rock heart of the North Cascade Mountains was simple enough—gold! In support of the herculean highway project, the Washington State Road Commissioners' 1896 report claimed:

> At the summit of the Cascades, where the (future) road crosses, there are vast deposits of gold, silver and lead ores which must have good roads before any amount of development can be made. The opening up of these great mineral fields is one of the greatest works the state could aid, for from no other one source can a greater degree of prosperity be dispensed among people of the state.
> —*Washington Highways*, September 1972.

The state Legislature had used the same overly optimistic assessment of the North Cascades' mineral deposits as did the road commissioners when the government had appropriated $20,000 in 1893 to build a wagon road from Bellingham to Spokane. The expert opinion of the commissioners convinced legislators that the Cascade road could soon be paved in gold.

Along with the $20,000 allotment, state officials submitted a sketchy map of the wagon route which ignored the 260 miles of imposing real estate through which the road would pass. Lawmakers apparently failed to comprehend that their proposed road sliced through some of the tallest, steepest, most remote and barely explored mountains in the United States!

Dutifully, the state road commission sallied forth into un-

Giant machinery carves a road through the solid heart of the North Cascades. Photo from the Shafer Museum collection.

charted realms of 8,000-foot North Cascade peaks. Several possible and impossible routes were explored by some state workers who turned out to be incredibly capable climbers. The Skagit Pass route won favor over the others. According to a commission report, "The board found the route up the Twisp River over Twisp Pass, down Bridge Creek, up the Stehekin River, over Cascade (or Skagit) Pass, and down the Cascade River (to Marblemount) the shortest, most feasible and practical." (*Ibid.*)

Miraculously, the so-called Cascade Mountain Road opened soon after the plan was laid, according to an 1897 newspaper account. The author insisted freight wagons could pass through the route except perhaps in steep places. "Sheer falsehood," is how historian JoAnn Roe summed up this journalistic effort. Newspapers at the time were "fast and loose with the truth," she warned. "Anything might be said based on hearsay."

Sure enough, a government surveyor checked out the trail in 1905 and concluded that all the money invested in the Cascade

Road so far had been wasted. The road wound up the Twisp River a ways, but beyond that it was just a pack trail and even much of that had washed away.

After this inauspicious start, the highway plan simmered on a back burner for years. Then in the early 1930s promoters resurrected the North Cascades Highway project. Once again, gold motivated road building. The Slate Creek District, one of the mining meccas to originally inspire the highway idea, revived in the '30s when the Azurite Mine began shipping ore once more from this remote area of the Methow.

Building a road to the coast became the personal goal of Congressman E. F. Banker of Winthrop. In 1932, Banker obtained $15,000 for a new survey of the highway. Wenatchee highway engineer Ivan Munson took the assignment, and with his crew of 30 men set up camp at Early Winters Creek in Mazama. They scouted an alternative route up Early Winters Creek to Washington Pass, down Slate Creek and Bridge Creek, up the Stehekin River, across Cascade Pass and down to Marblemount.

Ivan and his surveyors were the first to recognize that a route over Washington Pass might work. Plus Munson explored a potential new portion of the route along Granite Creek which he reported would be less costly and easier to build.

After his first road-surveying adventure in the North Cascades, Munson began singing the praises of the transmountain highway. His casual suggestion of the Washington Pass, Rainy Pass, Granite Creek alternative became the eventual route the highway would take.

No work was done on the road during World War II. Ivan Munson, promoted to district engineer, got the ball rolling again in 1956, when he invited the highway commissioners on a horseback reconnaissance through the area slated for highway development. Also invited on the expedition was Methow orchardist George Zahn who was smitten by the terrain and became a leading proponent of the highway. When Zahn later was appointed chairman of the highway commission, he proved to be a talented fund-raiser for the road development.

Zahn hired contractors to make the difficult 5.3-mile link between Diablo Dam and Thunder Lake for $870,069. From then on, contracts were steadily awarded. The state negotiated 35 separate contracts for the 63.5 miles connecting Diablo Dam and Mazama.

From the Methow Valley, the completed road ascended to 5,475-foot Washington Pass, then Rainy Pass at 4,860 feet before following Granite and Ruby creeks to Ross Lake and the Skagit River country. An estimate for the total cost of the highway was $33 million, a bargain compared to price tags on today's roads.

Originally the road had been intended for commercial use —a link between North Cascadian gold fields and coastal coffers. Over the years, however, the economic situation changed. By the time contractors were hired, the potential tourist trade abetted by road construction became a more lucrative prospect than prospectors' gold. With this in mind, contractors set out to make the highway a scenic drive. Trees were cut to allow for better views. Road crews created a spectacular overlook at Washington Pass, where travelers could enjoy a mountain panorama of Silver Star, the Liberty Bell Range, Kangaroo Ridge and the Wine Spires. Scenic turnouts, interpretive signs and hiking trails enhanced the new route.

When the governor cut the ribbon in September 1972, the North Cascades Highway officially opened its portal gates. Winthrop had begun its western-style face-lift that year, new businesses in town began to attract tourists, and the town's economy boomed. The link had been completed between North Central Washington and Puget Sound on one of the most scenic arterials in the world.

Bibliography

Borg, Ted. "The Last Riverboat." *Okanogan County Heritage*, Summer 1984.

Duffy, Barbara. Notes from Wenatchee Valley College Class on Methow Valley History.

———. "Pioneer Girl." *Okanogan County Heritage*, Winter 1975-76.

Heath, Frank. "Gold." *Okanogan County Heritage*, Summer 1972.

Hottell, Diana. "Nickell Recalls Family History." *Methow Valley News*, Oct. 12, 1978.

———. "Virgil Webb." *Methow Valley News*, Oct. 13, 1977.

———. "Marie Risley ... She is One of the Few Who Remembers." *Methow Valley News*, June 11, 1981.

Kenney, Frank. Untitled article on freighters. *Methow Valley News*, February 18, 1988.

Lockhart, Lola. Phone Interview. Winthrop, Washington, summer 1990.

Martin, Arthur, editor. "Building the North Cascades Highway." *Washing-

122

ton Highways, September 1972.

———. "Final Report of the Board of State Commissioners of the State of Washington, 1896." *Washington Highways*, September 1972.

Nickell, Walter. *The Way It Was*. Naples, Florida, June 1990.

Pidcock, Emma Rader. "Pioneer Life In the Methow Valley." *Okanogan County Heritage*, March 1969.

Roe, JoAnn. *The North Cascadians*. Madrona Publishers, Seattle, 1980.

———. North Cascade Institute Class. Sun Mountain Lodge, Winthrop, Washington, fall 1991.

Ross, Orrin C. "O'er Mountain Trails." *Okanogan County Heritage*, Spring 1985.

Schmidt, Jesse. "Evolution of Roads in the Lower Okanogan County," *Okanogan County Heritage*, Fall 1972.

———. "Methow Valley Fords and Bridges." *Okanogan County Heritage*, December 1968.

Stevens, Anna Greene. "Life in the Okanogan." *Okanogan County Heritage*, June 1970; March 1970; and September 1970.

Stout, Eula. "Chilliwhist Trail-Tough." *Okanogan County Heritage*, December 1969.

Therriault, Leonard. "Leonard Therriault Pioneer." *Okanogan County Heritage*, March 1971.

Victor, Guy (Kewpie). "I Ran Wild Goose Bill's Ferry." *Okanogan County Heritage*, March 1966.

Wilson, Bruce. *The Late Frontier*. Okanogan County Historical Society, 1990.

The Methow was a land of plenty where "bunch grass grew belly deep to a horse." Photo from the Shafer Museum collection.

Chapter 7

THE PIONEERS FIND A PARADISE

Bunch Grass Belly Deep to a Horse

Because of its remoteness, the Methow Valley remained unsettled after most of the nation had already been homesteaded. Inhabited only by small bands of Indians and a handful of trappers and miners for decades, the Methow lay undisturbed like a secret garden, awaiting discovery. The first pioneers to find the mountain-guarded valley came after the Indian reservation that included the Methow was opened to white settlement. It was a rumor that lured them here.

A trapper, passing through Ellensburg in the late 1880s, spread stories about a land of plenty where "bunch grass was belly deep to a horse," where an abundance of clear water flowed and game animals were plentiful. Natives called this land of promise the Methow Valley, said the trapper. Mason Thurlow, Harvey Nickell and Napoleon Stone, all Texans who had migrated to Ellensburg, heard the trapper's tales and decided to seek their fortunes in this little-known territory in Okanogan County.

To take up untrammeled land, to own their own kingdoms on 160 acres—this was their goal in 1887 when the three friends headed to the Methow Valley. En route to the Methow, the adventurers probably started wondering if their romantic quest was worth the tortuous journey. They followed the traditional route called the Chiliwhist Trail, which had linked the Okanogan and Methow River valleys for over 3,500 years. Ancient Indians had used the route, followed later by Methow Indians, Hudson's Bay Company fur traders and military expeditions. After this vanguard of Texans, many future homesteaders labored over the same hazardous path.

Beginning as a horse track up from Malott by way of Chiliwhist Creek Canyon, the Chiliwhist Trail leapt up a steep hogback, lurched along mountainsides known as the Three Devils and Seven Devils, then finally crossed a summit. With ascent pitches of 30 percent to 50 percent, this route seemed to serve as a rite of passage for Methow pioneers. If you survived the Chiliwhist, you could survive in the Methow Valley! Thurlow, Stone and Nickell made the grade, so to speak, descended Benson Creek and landed on the banks of the Methow River near the future location of the town of Silver.

The Homestead Act of 1862 offered 160 acres of land to any citizen 21 or older who wanted to settle the land. The law required that a settler live on the site for five years, make improvements on it and pay a $15 filing fee. This was an unbeatable deal. The one catch was that to be claimed as a homestead the land had to have been surveyed by the government. Since most of Okanogan County had been Indian reservation until 1886, the federal surveyors had ignored the area. In the Methow, government surveyors finally arrived in the late 1890s. Before that, many settlers took land under squatters' rights, which were not legal claims but boundaries to respect if the squatter was serious about the land, protective and tough.

When Mason Thurlow arrived in the Methow, he met one of the first known squatters here, Joe White, who had settled in the midvalley Beaver Creek area. Setting the pattern for later pioneers, Joe ingeniously dug the first irrigation ditch by pulling logs behind his horse from Beaver Creek to his fields, thereby creating nice grooves to channel life-giving water.

Joe White sold his 160-acre squatter's-right claim to Thurlow along with a rough dirt-floored cabin—all for $22.50. Across the creek, the Nickells settled on a fine piece of real estate, while Napoleon Stone continued upvalley to homestead near Bear Creek, closer to the future town of Winthrop.

At first Thurlow regretted his extravagance and haste, but soon he realized he'd made a fair trade for his money. Water was plentiful, the place needed little clearing and the grass grew tall and thick.

Before leaving Ellensburg, tragedy had befallen the Thurlow family. Mason's wife Mary Ellen had died of pneumonia after a bout of measles. Mason was probably glad to exchange a place he associated with loss and grief for a place that offered hope and a fresh start in life. After his initial scouting trip and purchase of a squatter's right, he brought his family to the Methow in 1888 and in 1891 married Lois Nickell, widow of Harvey Nickell's brother. Thurlow already had four children, Lois brought two to the marriage, and together they produced seven more children for a total of 13 offspring.

Mason Thurlow told his children he had only one year of formal schooling and could not sign his name when he married at the age of 18. Yet he taught himself to read and became an ardent reader. Mason's self-education included mathematics as far as calculus and he was a whiz at doing calculations in his head.

Mason took his civic duties seriously. He sat on the first election board, provided the first polling place and cast one-twenty-fourth of the ballots in the first presidential election held in the Methow in 1888. To welcome the other 23 voters who came from as far downriver as the town of Methow and as far upriver as Mazama, Thurlow got down his trusty Winchester rifle, killed a deer and treated the electorate to a venison supper. When Beaver Creek School District formed in November 1890, Thurlow sat on the original school board.

Like so many Methow pioneers, the Thurlows were industrious and blessed with hardy constitutions. Together they built up a fine cattle and hay ranch in the pastures and hills above Beaver Creek. It was the earliest ranch in the Methow plus one of the most productive and enduring. The Thurlows worked it for nearly a hundred years. (See chapter on cattle ranching for details of the Thurlow Ranch.)

Meanwhile, the Thurlows' neighbors, the Harvey Nickells, were settling in with their four children. In May 1889, Alcena Nickell, Harvey's wife, gave birth to daughter Ellen, the first white baby born in the valley.

Lee and Rena Ives had staked a claim where the town of Pateros now stands even before the Texans arrived in the Methow. In 1885 the pair reached the banks of the Columbia River where they camped near some friendly Indians and crossed the river in Indian canoes. On the north bank of the Columbia at the southernmost point of the Methow Valley, the Ives built a home. Being sociable, they fed and lodged the many travelers who landed at this big intersection of the Methow and Columbia rivers, and their home eventually became a community center. Later, the couple built a hotel, known as Ives Landing, where many homesteaders spent their first night before traveling up the Methow. They also operated the Central Ferry which crossed the Columbia River above Pateros.

A well-remembered settler was Sarah Metca'f, wife of S. M. Metcalf, who farmed near the town of Silver in the 1890s. Sarah owned the first, and for a long time the only, pump organ in the valley, and it was in great demand for social events. By wagon or sled, pioneers hauled the hefty instrument to weddings, funerals, and festive functions.

Almost singlehandedly, Sarah shouldered the social welfare of the valley. She taught school and Sunday school. She delivered babies even when it entailed riding horseback in blizzards. She nursed the sick and sat with the deceased. If kids lived too far from school, she boarded them at her home, offering meals for 12 cents.

Farther up the valley, George L. Thompson took up a squatter's right on Moccasin Lake which in the 1890s was called Thompson Lake after this original homesteader. Being a

Pioneer architecture at the Ventzke homestead. Photo from the Shafer Museum collection.

leader and a teller of tall tales to boot, Thompson became rather a legend in his own time. Local citizens often asked George to be master of ceremonies for programs, especially the Fourth of July celebration. His orations included so much kidding and so many tall tales that Thompson Creek, which flowed through his land, was changed to Liar's Creek!

George Thompson was not all talk though. He proved to be a Good Samaritan to his new neighbors, Laura and Fred Thompson (no relation to him). The Thompsons arrived in the valley in September 1889, to face one of the Methow's most cruel winters. It snowed and snowed; when it got so bad the horses couldn't paw down for feed, George walked several miles to Fred Thompson's through head-high snow to share his feed with his neighbor's horses. Without his generosity the horses would have starved.

George also supplied food to the Thompson family and when Laura ran out of grease, he shared some big cakes of tallow. He was the last person Laura and Fred saw until mid-February, when another neighbor, Walter Frisbee, skied in to check on their health. He found them well, well fed, and fairly unscathed by cabin fever, since they'd brought books from their old home in Kansas and read each tome six times apiece that winter.

Early settler Walter Frisbee chose one of the most well-watered spreads in the entire valley. Arriving in the Methow in 1888, Walter established his 160-acre homestead in the area where the original federal fish hatchery is now, near Winthrop. Sloughs, creeks, and beaver dams threading through his land made it easy to irrigate. The clever Frisbee designed an irrigation system that watered his fields and ran through his spawning pools, well stocked with trout. Walter took first water rights out of the Methow River in 1888. His water system became known as the Frisbee Irrigation Ditch and Right-of-Way.

The Fruits of Their Labor

During the growing season and preserving season, the pioneers must have been constantly at work. They produced and preserved their own food. Then they earned a little money to buy what they could not produce themselves. Enid Milner, Twisp resident in the early 1910s, described the pioneer labor load:

> Life was a round of seasonal work, a constant and necessary cycle that everyone shared, since it

128

was shared, often enjoyed; hunting in the fall, cutting ice in the winter, storing wood, planting and reaping, haying and cooking for the crews.
—*Methow Valley News*, July 5, 1979.

Fortunately, their labor produced bountiful amounts of food and also, for many, a satisfying and even exhilarating lifestyle.

Harvey Nickell's daughter Ellen recalled her family's pioneer lifestyle. The Nickells lived in a one-room cabin where they slept, cooked, ate, washed, ironed and relaxed.

> There was an ice house in back where we kept milk, cream, butter, etc. We could always make ice cream. We even had cantaloupes and watermelons buried in sawdust covering the ice. When we needed meat, father would hunt grouse, prairie chicken, bear and deer. Venison was jerked for winter but the men could kill deer anytime they wished. But they only did when food was needed.
>
> Father raised cattle and always had two to three hogs to kill. Spareribs were cooked fresh, ham and shoulders were smoked, the fat sides rendered into lard and stored for shortening. With dried apples and strawberries it made a yummy pie.
>
> —*Okanogan County Heritage*, March 1965.

Three factors favored the early pioneers in their pursuits of survival. They tilled untapped earth, enough moisture blessed the Methow in the early years, and a preponderance of pioneers had green thumbs and the knowledge of how to grow food even in the Methow's gravelly, glacial soil.

Pioneer child Emma Rader listed her family's mouth-watering produce department: onions, cabbages, carrots, rutabagas, parsnips, squashes, pumpkins, quantities of sweet strawberries, luscious raspberries, fat blackberries, gooseberries, and currants. How many Methowians today can grow the following delectables raised so proudly by Emma's clan?

> Watermelons and cantaloupes grown on our farm were among the best produced anywhere. People from Twisp gathered at our house on summer evenings for "melon feeds." In this day and age folks won't believe that good melons will grow and mature here, but I know they will!
>
> —*Okanogan County Heritage*, June 1969.

Methow pioneer women in the late 1800s and early 1900s didn't use electric stoves, temperature controls or timers, but

IN THE UPPER METHOW VALLEY.
NEAR WINTHROP, WASHINGTON.

Pioneers produced bountiful amounts of food. Photo from the Shafer Museum collection.

no matter. They turned out feather-light biscuits, world-class pies and all manner of homemade treats from scratch. "Saturday was bake day," said Ruth McLean. "Mother baked pies, cakes, cookies, lots of homemade breads too. There was no temperature gauge on the oven so you had to know by thrusting your hand in, then testing the heat." (*Okanogan County Heritage*, Fall 1974.)

Junk, trash, throwaways and garbage were seldom heard words in pioneer times, because most everything had a use! After the McAllister family dried applies, pears and peaches on their sunny rooftops, the skins and cores of the apples became ingredients for jelly, the skins of pears and peaches for syrup. Jelly glasses weren't available to Mrs. Dan McAllister, so she fashioned her own from old bottles she saved. Her recipe was to soak yarn in kerosene, then wrap it around the wide part of a bottle. Next, ignite. Once it's burning all around, plunge the glass in cold water and the top will snap off. Use a handy small stone to smooth the edge.

The resourceful Mrs. McAllister used her cool well to refrigerate milk and butter and, as with all the early settlers, a root storage area was essential. Mrs. McAllister advocated an outdoor storage cellar made of logs framing a hole dug two to three feet down or into a bank. After being covered with soil, the top became firm with vegetation growing on it. Canned fruit and hardy veggies kept well there all winter.

Other pioneers employed equally successful preservation methods. An open milk house built over a creek among willow trees kept the butter and cream fresh for Emma Rader. Her family stored dairy products in large stone jars with lids, then placed them in a box-like trough set in the cool, flowing water.

Without Whirlpools and Maytags, could laundry have been anything but pure drudgery in pioneer days? Still, women didn't gripe about the tedious task, at least not in the pioneer literature. Ruth Davis' family rubbed their dirty clothes clean on a washboard. But even before the elbow grease application had begun, water had to be carried from a stream or well, then heated in a huge boiler on top of the wood range. A second tub held the clothes being washed. After each load, the laundress carried out, emptied and refilled the heavy tubs.

Ruth Davis remembered her mother making lamps to light their cabin at night. Melted tallow served as fuel and a tightly braided piece of flannel became a wick. A recycled tin can made a choice lamp. "It had an awful smell and a flickering light," said Ruth. Later, kerosene lamps came into use, then the high-tech gasoline lamps with mantles which were a great improvement, Ruth recalled.

Ruth slept on an "old straw tick" which consisted of a mattress-sized bag filled with straw. Perhaps it started springy enough, but Ruth remembered the hay had to be changed often because it got quite powdery and uncomfortable.

When it came to clothing, women handmade their own fashions. They designed and sewed dresses and skirts which they wore every day for every activity. Pants were not female pioneer apparel, though a long culotte-styled skirt was acceptable for horseback riding.

When girls wanted to look beautiful, they curled their long tresses with a curling iron or rolled them around a large spike to create lively effects. Cornstarch powder softened a ruddy complexion, and red-powdered sugar made lips look alluring.

Despite their resourcefulness, the pioneers were often forced to travel to obtain necessary supplies. A five-day trip by horse and wagon landed Emma Rader's family in Ellensburg, one of the Methow's main supply depots, where they bought flour in

Cream day. Photo from the Dick Webb collection.

50-pound bags and other staples in quantities to last up to a year. The men chose shoes, shirts, overalls and underwear. The women shopped for shoes, underwear and fabric—calico, flannel and denim—to sew their clothes by hand.

Flour, sugar, coffee, rice and possibly some fun treats like raisins were the only food items most pioneers purchased. But to buy these staples, plus material for clothes and maybe a special bonnet for Mom, meant cash, which was a scarce commodity within the Methow barter system.

To make money, enterprising pioneers produced goods or sold produce. Once a year, Emma Rader's family took tanned hides and smoked shoulders from deer to trade for supplies in Ellensburg. Some people sold berries and vegetables to miners. Emma sold berries in gallon pails for 25 cents, or five gallons for $1.00, which seems a pitiful earning until you find out Emma's mother saved enough from the berry fund to carpet their parlor!

Freighting furnished another means of support for Emma's family. Her father, Pleas Rader, hauled groceries, dry goods and hardware from the Brewster landing on the Columbia River up the Methow Valley to supply the Burke Brothers, Methow Trading Company and other businesses.

To make ends meet, many pioneers, like modern-day Methow immigrants, had to be jacks-of-all-trades. Clarence Heckendorn stands out as a good example of the versatile valley man. He moved to the Methow in 1899 and never left. He ranched, farmed, herded cattle, cut and split 75 to 100 cords of wood annually for five years, horse logged, packed for sheepherders, packed crews into mountain fires, dug wells, shoed horses, did carpentry, drove a hearse, dug graves, hauled fuel to the Azurite Mine and helped build the mill there. "A little bit of everything," is how Clarence described his career.

At harvest time, a regular exodus occurred from the Methow to the Big Bend country where men worked in wheat fields for $1.00 a day.

Most Methow farmers raised a small dairy herd, and the only cash they ever received was the modest but dependable cream check. This provided enough money to buy most necessary supplies. In 1905, the first creamery in North Central Washington, the Methow Valley Creamery, began churning butter in Twisp. Cream separators were unknown here before Jim Holcomb opened his new business and became the first Methow butter-maker. Following his example, the Star Creamery, owned and operated by Englishman Evelyn Aldritch,

Newt Nickell molding butter at the Winthrop creamery. Photo from the Okanogan County Historical Society, negative 3048.

opened in Winthrop in 1906.

People all over the valley milked their cows for the creamery, giving their old-fashioned churns a rest. Cream day became the most eventful day of the week and the pioneers looked forward to it as a time for social diversion. Besides picking up the welcome cream check, they caught up on news and gossip, bought some extra groceries, and for a super treat, maybe enjoyed dinner out at the hotel or cafe.

Work at the creamery itself was less fun. "A mankiller" is what Marie Risley of Twisp called it. Workers had to lift 10-gallon cans of cream and dump them into a huge pasteurizer. While they syphoned the cream into churns they had to constantly keep the boilers going for pasteurization as well as make ice in huge vats. Workers churned about 1,000 pounds of butter every morning.

Dairying became more and more important in the Methow Valley in the early 1900s. Despite the limited market due to a lack of rail transportation up the Methow Valley, shipments of Methow Valley butter still traveled to the coast in 1902 and 1903 netting producers 28 cents per pound. A Great Northern Railway Company report stated that Twisp creameries shipped $20,000 worth of butter in 1908, and $25,000 worth the next year.

Strict sanitary standards finally caused the demise of the popular creameries. "I don't blame them," said Mary Risley. "We found mice and rags and so many different things in the cream—you couldn't imagine."

As dairying declined, raising beef cattle began to flourish. Drought in the '20s and '30s had made raising dairy cows on irrigated pastures economical but the return of moisture to the Methow in the 1940s through the 1960s produced good feed on rangeland, so farmers began to stock large ranches with beef cattle.

Few people raise dairy cows in the Methow anymore, but many people remember wistfully the days of the creameries, and that all-important cream check which helped keep many farms running.

Bibliography
Coyote Tales: Stories of the Methow Valley. Liberty Bell High School
  Class, Toni Hughes Faculty Advisor, 1974.

134

Davis, Ruth. "Mining Lured McLean to the Methow." *Okanogan County Heritage*, Fall 1974.

Duffy, Barbara. "Pioneer Girl (Alice Rader Burge)." *Okanogan County Heritage*, Winter 1975-76.

——. Notes from Wenatchee Valley College Class on Methow Valley History. Winthrop, Washington.

Hottell, Diana. "Clarence Heckendorn: He's Done a Little Bit of Everything." *Methow Valley News*, August 20, 1981.

——. "Enid Milner." *Methow Valley News*, June 11, 1989.

——. "Enid Milner: Memories Strong and Sustaining." *Methow Valley News*, July 5, 1979.

——. "Frank Thurlow: Four Generations in the Methow." *Methow Valley News*, April 21, 1977.

Johnson, Abbie Williams. "Life in the Upper Methow." *Okanogan County Heritage*, March 1968.

McAllister, Mrs. Dan. "When the Methow Was Young." *Okanogan County Heritage*, December 1964.

Moore, Ellen Nickell. "First White Child in the Methow Valley." *Okanogan County Heritage*, March 1965.

Pidcock, Emma Rader. "Pioneer Life in the Methow Valley." *Okanogan County Heritage*, Part 1, March 1969, and Part 2, June 1969.

Schmidt, Jesse. "Walter Frisbee: Versatile Winthrop Pioneer." *Okanogan County Heritage*, June 1971.

Thompson, Laura. "Laura Thompson Came to Stay." *Okanogan County Heritage*, March 1967.

Wilson, Bruce. *The Late Frontier*. Okanogan County Historical Society, 1990.

Neighbors came from miles around to share in community picnics like this one held in 1907 at the Culbertson Ranger Station in the Poorman Creek area. The pioneers fashioned a table from wooden crates and planks. Photo from The Wenatchee World.

Chapter 8

THE PIONEER SOCIAL CALENDAR

Being Neighborly

Methow pioneers toiled incessantly it seems, yet most relished a rich and rewarding social life. To meet people and make friends in the early days, all one had to do was be neighborly. With old friends and newcomers, people shared their homes, their food, their tools, their talents and their time. House construction parties, barn raisings, quilting bees, storytelling sessions and plain old shooting the breeze with your neighbor were all part of the Methow social scene. According to founding father Mason Thurlow, some neighbors practically wore out his welcome mat:

> I guess the thing I liked best about this country
> ever since I came here was the neighborliness of
> all the folks here. When we got this big house
> built, there never was a night but what there
> would be one to a dozen folks here. They just
> came and stayed and there was nothing we could
> do about it. It weren't any hotel but in a way it
> was. Everybody knew everybody else and what was
> your neighbor's you could always use.
>
> —*Nedra Horn's scrapbook.*

When Guy Waring, intellectual from the East, arrived in the Methow in 1891, he was welcomed with helping hands. "Neighbors came to help build our home, which was the custom in the West," said Anna Greene Stevens, Waring's step-daughter. "Nobody wants pay, they just always help newcomers get established." (*Okanogan County Heritage*, June 1970.)

Pioneers found pleasure in giving when a neighbor was in need. By the time the nasty winter of 1889 flung a final storm at the Methow on March 29, many settlers had empty flour bins and either no money or no means to get to a supply store. Though they, too, were running out of supplies, Laura Thompson's family shared all they had left with neighbors.

Even when they were away, local pioneers left their homes open for others to use. It was the custom to leave houses and cabins unlocked, remembered local Pat Murphy: "The law of the land was that those needing shelter, warmth or sustenance could enter and use what they needed." (*Methow Valley News*, November 13, 1980.) When they were through, visitors either left a little cash, split a little wood or did some favor to show their gratitude.

Fourth of July

All the pioneers talk about the Fourth of July celebration—the biggest shindig of the year in the Methow Valley. Held for the first time in 1891 near the town of Silver south of Twisp, it later moved to a central location halfway between

The Winthrop Brass Band entertains in Twisp. Photo from the Okanogan County Historical Society, negative 3044.

Twisp and Winthrop, near where Bear Creek flows into the Methow River.

The Fourth of July was a time for pioneers to party with friends as well as a time for these patriotic people to honor the nation's independence. The event began with the Declaration of Independence traditionally read by favorite orator George L. Thompson of Liar's Creek fame. A quarrel started once when someone brought up that George was born in Canada. George's supporters speedily overruled the zealous objector and George gave his usual outstanding oration.

Every family brought a picnic basket brimming with hearty, homemade entrees and delectable desserts. Flora Filer Jones remembered best the divine lemonade made from freshly squeezed lemons, served on this occasion and kept refreshingly cold by ice blocks cut the previous winter and preserved in an ice house.

Faithful Mrs. S. M. Metcalf always emerged with her organ in tow to lead the throngs in patriotic songs. Participants entered horse races and foot races and danced all night at the Winthrop log hall. Prizes went to the best-looking lady and the homeliest gent.

Deke Smith remembered during early Fourth of July celebrations a great campground teeming with Indians who brought their race horses, played their stick games and gambled—chanting and hollering all the while.

In Winthrop, a brass band entertained, and participants entered contests of all kinds, like nail driving for women, pie eating for men, and sock races for kids. Of course everyone visited with their valley neighbors. "All talked about the future," said Abbie Williams Johnson, "and how they'd improve the valley."

How to Have a Good Time

One thing seems certain about the early days. Pioneers worked hard, but they knew when work should stop and play begin. "Everybody had the knack of knowing how to have a good time," said Deke Smith, recalling the old days. Methow pioneers were not sit-at-homes; isolation often made people more sociable. Deke recalled: "Anyone would have a dance if their house had a few square feet of space. They'd just kick all the furniture out. We'd dance all night. Once I rode from

Libby Creek to Twin Lakes to go to a dance." (*Methow Valley News*, Summer 1977.) Deke rode a distance of about 17 miles by horseback that one evening!

With the same resourcefulness they applied to building homes and producing food, the pioneers created their own entertainment. Stanley Darwood remembered the great get-togethers of past times with contagious enthusiasm:

> Oh we had parties in those days. The house party was the most entertainment there was. You give it this week, I'll give it next week and so on up and down the valley. Everybody that could play an instrument at all would play, and everybody would dance and sing and have a great time.
> —*River Pigs and Cayuses.*

Pearl Rader and neighbors gathered at a one-room schoolhouse near Twin Lakes for social occasions. Come Saturday night, people congregated at the school to share a potluck supper followed by all-night dancing to the twangs of a mandolin and strumming of a guitar. Pearl remembered performing once at one of the many "literaries" held at the schoolhouse. She and her sister, Arulu, sang "When the Harvest Moon is Shining, Molly Dear," while Pearl pounded away on the organ.

A shortage of women often hampered pioneer social functions, for in the early years lots of bachelors lived in the foothills, but few women. A local lonely hearts club magazine was chock-full of advertisements from single men pining for partners. A few women traveled from the East to marry local bachelors.

The settlers overcame that common winter malady, cabin fever, with zest and resilience. In his inimitable way, Deke Smith described recreation in the cold season.

> Hoedowns! ... In the early days that was our recreation. Wintertime we were more or less snowbound but that didn't make no difference. People gotta have company or they'll climb the walls. Families was all scattered out. So every Saturday night they'd hitch up the old sleighs. People thought nothing of going out at 10 below zero, maybe in a snowstorm, eight to ten miles to some house.
>
> The whole tribe would go and wedge in there— Grandpa, Grandma, babies. At midnight they'd

Folks would hitch up the old sleigh and drive to a hoedown. Photo from the Methow Valley News.

call a halt for a great feed. And if anybody had
any booze, they'd drink. Hard cider used to be
quite a thing.

—Ibid.

These hardy folks would dance all night and rise the next
morning to go home and do the chores!

If there didn't happen to be a hoedown scheduled some
winter eve, but people were still ripe for a good time, they'd
hitch up the team and risk frostbite for a sleigh ride. Stanley
Darwood told about those romantic night escapades:

Everybody had their teams and sleds, hansom
cutters. And we used sleigh bells on the horses so
that when they was running along well—tingle,
dingle, dingle, ding-a-ling. It was lots of fun. The
highway wasn't maintained but people used to get
out in the wintertime and just go sleigh riding.
Bundle up with a few blankets around you and set
in that old sleigh and ride up and down the river
just for the enjoyment of it.

—Ibid.

Winter sleigh riding was a wholesome and exhilarating adventure for kids as well, one that matched their exuberance and
filled them with joy. In her recollection, Emma Rader Pidcock
makes the sleigh rides of her youth come to life again:

Harvesting ice on the Methow River. Photo from the Methow Valley News.

Sometimes my brother and I hitched a team to
the bobsled, put in some straw and blankets, gathered a crowd of boys and girls and went riding
over the countryside. It was usually a moonlit
night. The jingling of sleigh bells seemed to keep
pace with the crunchy tread of horses' feet and the
chilly squeak of the sleds as they slipped over the
frozen snow. We were a happy group and expressed our feelings in laughter and song.
—*Okanogan County Heritage*, June 1969.

All locals looked forward to the ice harvest which was as
much a social event as a winter chore. If there'd been a long
freeze, the ice would get to be about 18 inches thick. A heavy
steel saw sliced the ice into blocks about two feet square.
They'd be fished out with tongs, dragged to a sled and loaded
up. Once home, the giant cubes would be stacked in the center
of a refrigerator-type building. A foot or more of sawdust
stuffed between the wall and the ice insulated the ice house. As
needed, people put the frozen chunks into ice boxes to preserve
food. Darwood described the social nature of the affair:

It was fun. There'd be as many as six or eight
people down there all cutting at the same time,
more or less helping each other. Naturally, we'd

plan on a little party afterwards if there was a way
of doing it at all. You betcha! Mostly a kind of
get-together with a jug of some kind. It had to be
moonshine then.

—Ibid.

King Kennedy

There was one professional entertainer everyone remembered:
King Kennedy, the magician and ventriloquist from Chelan who
took his magic acts and wooden doll dummies to remote areas
of Eastern Washington in the late 1890s and early 1900s.

King traveled rough, rocky, potholed roads in the dead of
winter in order not to disappoint his fans. He always scheduled
a one-day stop at the town of Silver in the Methow Valley.
Like a gypsy, King carried all his props in his wagon and slept
there as well.

For just a few cents' admission, people got a bellyfull of
laughs and a raft of surprises. Wherever he went King packed
the place. He had one crippled arm, but put on a Punch and
Judy show that always caused the kids to giggle and squeal,
remembered Walter Nickell. Punch relentlessly pestered and
sassed Kennedy, who'd finally retaliate by smacking Punch in
the snoot.

He was adept at classic magic too. After requesting a hat
from the crowd and receiving a brand new Stetson (high of
crown, wide of brim), King broke a half-dozen eggs into the
hat and whisked up an omelet. The fellow who owned the hat
looked livid until King handed back the headpiece without a
trace of egg in it!

King introduced the first hand-wound phonograph and silent
moving pictures to the Methow Valley, too. "Gosh, did we
look forward to his yearly visit," said Walter Nickell. Undoubtedly that could be said for nearly every other pioneer child
back then.

Fun Just Livin' Here

The natural environment of the Methow Valley is so beautiful that for newcomers, the greatest pleasure often comes from
simply a view of the mountains from a window, a hike over
velvet-green hills, discovering the first spring sunflower, or dipping toes into an icy, clear creek. The early pioneers were no

142

different. Even though they spent many hours outside, most of the time working hard, the first settlers were no more immune than present residents to the glorious Methow landscape. Just living in this place sometimes seemed like heaven. "It was a kid's paradise," remembered Ruby La Fordge.

> The Methow Valley was a beautiful country with many springs, streams and lakes. Bunch grass grew knee high to a man. Wild roses and other flowering plants covered the hillsides. We children lived carefree lives.
> —*Okanogan County Heritage*, December 1965.

Bibliography

Cooper, Mrs W. Z. "Glimpses From the Past." *Okanogan County Heritage*, June 1968.

Horn, Nedra. Notes on her family history. Winthrop, Washington.

Hottell, Diana. "Pearl Rader Risley: Homestead Life on Patterson Lake." *Methow Valley News*, July 14, 1977.

———. "Pat and Mike Murphy: Living Through the Hard Times Together." *Methow Valley News*, November 13, 1980.

———. "Deke Smith." *Methow Valley News*, Souvenir Issue, Summer 1977.

Johnson, Abbie Williams. "Life in the Upper Methow." *Okanogan County Heritage*, March 1968.

Jones, Flora Filer. "Methow Independence Day." *Okanogan County Heritage*, December 1971.

Nickell, Walter. *The Way It Was*. Naples, Florida, June 1990.

Pidcock, Emma Rader. "Pioneer Life in the Methow Valley." *Okanogan County Heritage*, June 1969.

Schmidt, Jesse. "Ruby La Fordge, Methow Valley." *Okanogan County Heritage*, December 1965.

Stevens, Anna Greene. "Life in the Okanogan." *Okanogan County Heritage*, June 1970.

Strickland, Ron. *River Pigs and Cayuses: Oral Histories From the Pacific Northwest*. Lexikos, San Francisco, 1984.

The Wenatchee World. November 10, 1972.

Wilson, Bruce. *Late Frontier*. Okanogan County Historical Society, 1990.

Chapter 9

HOMESTEADS NEAR SUN MOUNTAIN

Author's Note:

I've chosen to write a special chapter on homesteads near Sun Mountain not because they differed from other homesteads in the valley (I believe they were very similar), but because I personally know the area so well.

The Sun Mountain environs are representative of many other localities in the valley during pioneer times. There were homesteads all over the hills in this remote area. A large sawmill once stood where there's now an open meadow. By focusing on this smaller area, I hope readers can imagine how the rest of the valley was populated back in pioneer days.

The Hough Homestead

The Hough homestead is one historic site all Sun Mountain visitors should try to see. An easy one- to two-mile hike on Beaver Pond Trail or Sunnyside Trail leads to this scenic pioneer farm. At the Hough place there are two antique structures—an old semipreserved cabin made of cut lumber and a picturesque broken-down log barn, both standing in a meadow on the banks of a creek. A few hardy lilacs and brilliant red poppies planted by the last homesteaders still thrive.

Joe and Blanche Hough weren't the first folks to live at this lovely junction of meadow, forest and stream, though the

144

*Ken White snowshoes in to the log barn at the Hough homestead. Photo
courtesy Marjory White.*

homestead was named after them. Clyde Dibble owned it before the Houghs; he'd moved there with his wife Selma after
World War I. Early trapper Tracy Heath had settled nearby
in a log cabin located at the lower end of the irrigation syphon
on Little Wolf Creek. Pioneers picnicked and played horseshoes
and baseball in the area where Tracy's cabin stood, testifying
way back then to the recreation potential of the area.

According to local resident Hazel Kikendall, her folks, Joe
and Blanche Hough, bought the 160-acre homestead in the late
1920s. At one time a big house existed near where the present
cabin stands, but it burned long ago. Joe built the little house
that still remains, and the big log barn. The Hough family ran
the place as a cattle ranch until around 1941. In this remote
area, ranching in the '30s was like ranching in the early 1900s
elsewhere. There was no electricity, and all the ranch work was

done by horsepower.

Hazel remembered her folks raised cows and farmed the entire area. It was all pastureland around where Sun Mountain Lodge is now. To earn money to pay for supplies, the Houghs sold berries and wood, and packed for hunters. Walter Nickell said, "It was impossible to make a living on it (the Hough place) as evidenced by all who tried, including Joe Hough." This may have been the reason Joe and Blanche left to work in the Seattle shipyards in the early '40s.

Their son, Bud Hough, and his wife, Mardi, took over the ranch from 1939 to 1941, living in the idyllic setting all year round, hot summer and frigid winter.

Bud and Mardi never faced the chore of changing irrigation pipes in their alfalfa fields, since rain alone watered their farm. But they harrowed the field with work horses, stacked the hay in the barn, milked their 20 cows by hand, and raised their own chickens. In addition to all the domestic chores, woodswoman Mardi trapped coyotes for their pelts. Whatever the weather she'd ride the trapline every day.

West of the old log barn the Houghs grew a copious garden. Between the poultry, milk cows, cattle and garden they always had plenty to eat.

Every Monday, the couple went to the creamery in Winthrop located where Sam's Place is now. To get to town they lumbered along dirt trails until they got to the luxury of a gravel road which began at Patterson Lake Resort, at the north end of Patterson Lake. In the winter, they drove a dog team to town. The dogs also helped haul water. A good spring running through their property provided the Houghs with drinking water all year.

The Rader Homestead

Open meadows on the shores of a long, clear lake surrounded by rounded hills and distant snow-capped peaks—does this define the perfect homestead site? Three pioneer families who found such a place were the Pattersons, the George Raders and the Leonard Raders.

Patterson was the first settler to light upon this ideal spot. Born in 1864 in Walla Walla, Sam Patterson took a squatter's right on the land at the south end of Patterson Lake before the government surveyed it. Sam and his family built a house at the head of the lake and cultivated the land there in the 1890s. The *History of North Washington*, published in 1904, offered the following description of Sam and his enterprises: "He owns a valuable estate all under ditch and especially adapted for alfalfa raising. He feeds about 50 head of cattle each winter, has a nice orchard and is a prosperous citizen." Historians report the biographies in this book were written and paid for by each settler listed, so Sam likely penned the complimentary entry himself.

Neighbor George Rader thought Sam was a rather difficult man. Nevertheless, the two worked out a lengthy legal agreement in 1896 whereby George bought Patterson's property for $350. George paid $100 down and worked the rest off at $3.00 wages paid per day for 10 hours of work which included the use of George's team of horses. Sam moved to the east side of the Methow River between Twisp and Winthrop.

Soon George secured a patent for the Patterson acreage, then got another homestead patent for 160 acres adjoining the first purchase. Son Leonard Rader obtained a homestead adjacent to his father's which extended into an area now called

George Rader and family in front of their log house at Patterson Lake. Photo from the Robert Rader collection.

The George Rader homestead about 1920. Photo from the Robert Rader collection.

Pine Forest.

Pearl Rader Risley, born in a big log cabin in 1901, enjoyed memories of a delightful family life on the George Rader homestead. The Raders had 15 children; Pearl was the third youngest. Pearl said when she was born there were "only 10 of us in the house," since many siblings had married and moved away. All 10 family members crowded into their cabin until 1910 when the Raders built a big new house with six bedrooms.

Working or playing the family kept constantly active. For the most part, they were self-sufficient. Their land offered the natural resources and they had the basic skills to produce nearly all they needed to survive. Pearl relished every minute of her busy and productive family life on Patterson Lake.

> It was heaven. My dad was a real farmer. He
> kept milk cows and raised a few beef cattle.
> Everything was all neat and clean and fenced, just
> like a backyard. We had five acres of orchard and
> all kinds of fruits and berries. We produced all

148

our food so that was no problem.
    —*Methow Valley News*, July 14, 1977.
    For all farmers fall meant harvest time. Pearl picked apples, dug spuds and gathered cabbages. The family canned and put up jam and spiced prunes in five-gallon crocks.

> For the apples and potatoes we'd dig a pit in the earth, layer it with hay, put in some apples then some spuds, and more hay and so on. Then we'd cover it over with dirt and in the winter dig a small hole down through the snow and earth and bring out as much as we needed. We'd have fresh stuff til heaven knows when.
    —*Methow Valley News*, July 14, 1977.

Late fall heralded hog-killing time. George cured the meat and smoked hams and bacon. "I can still taste the head cheese and pans of homemade sausage," said Pearl.

To get supplies they couldn't produce themselves, the Raders traded jerky and tanned deer hides. When hunting was good they'd take four fully loaded pack horses to Ellensburg for barter. They sold gooseberries, currants, dewberries and other delectable fruits to purchase school clothes. One day the Raders picked 22 gallons of berries which must have bought a lot of calico at 10 cents a yard. Once a week they rode to town to sell their cream, kept refrigerated and fresh by the flume of cold spring water running through their milk house.

Hily Rader, Pearl's mother, sewed all their clothes. "My mother used everything and wasted nothing," said Pearl. "She used to make up bloomers from flour sacks. She'd fix them up real pretty and put lace on them."

The family washed laundry the old-fashioned way in big wash basins by the edge of Patterson Lake. Each Saturday night, the Raders filled one of those tubs with steaming water so every member of the huge family could take a weekly bath. Girls went first, then boys, only changing the water when it got "too thick" remembered Pearl's brother, Jack.

During the winter the workload lightened. Everyone helped cut ice blocks from the frozen lake, "but that was more fun than work," said Pearl. Plenty of wood had already been stacked to heat the stove and there was plenty of stored food. In winter, George took time to sit and read the kids stories of the far north in Alaska. "My dad was a good storyteller, too; he knew how to embroider a tale around the edges and to make it more exciting," said Pearl.

The Rader family celebrated a classic old-fashioned Christmas, with family feasting, homemade gifts and overflowing cheer. All the older brothers and sisters returned to the nest for the occasion. The family decorated the tall, freshly cut Christmas tree with homemade ornaments and long strings of popcorn. Red and green paper ribbons hung in the living room with a red paper bell adorning the center. Cedar boughs filled the rooms with their fragrance. Fancy presents were unaffordable, but Hily bought doll heads, then sewed bodies and clothes for them. The troupe would sing songs accompanied by an old organ and listen to an old phonograph play favorite tunes. The celebration lasted for two glorious days.

The Christmas gathering came at the beginning of a possibly long period of winter isolation for the family. Jack Rader recalled years when up to six feet of settled snow enshrouded their front yard. Sometimes they had to tunnel their way out of the house in the morning after a big snowfall. Jack remembered frigid 40-below-zero weather that lasted for days. When snowbound, the Raders' only contact with the outside world was their father's infrequent snowshoe trips for mail and supplies. The trip could take him three days.

The Burton-Fender Sawmill
and the Leonard Rader Homestead

Just around the corner from the George Rader homestead, the Burton and Fender Sawmill churned out lumber for pioneer houses. In 1909 Clarence and Anna Burton had purchased the sawmill site from Ida and Benjamin Filer, the original homesteaders. The Burtons paid $4,000 for the 320-acre homestead, located near the present entrance to the Pine Forest development. The couple managed a successful lumberyard and planer mill on the site. Their premier planer was the first in the area to produce finished siding for houses. Wood was obtained from Douglas Canyon (named after the Douglas family that homesteaded the draw directly above the mill).

When there was no wood left to cut, the mill closed down and Leonard Rader bought all 320 acres of the Burton's land. Leonard wisely built a dam, creating a reservoir which collected water from Rader and Thompson creeks. The reservoir still exists and is now called Bristlecone Pond. With this stor-

The Burton-Fender Sawmill in the Patterson Lake area. Photo from the Shafer Museum collection.

age system, Leonard irrigated his hay fields and orchards of plums, apricots and cherries. Some of these trees survive today on the site. When his father, George, retired, Leonard took over the original Rader homestead as well. His ranch property then totaled 800 acres.

During the good moisture years in the Methow, the Raders had lots of neighbors in what is now called the Pine Forest area. Drought years came and the homesteaders up above in the drier hillsides had to leave. The Raders held on because their land was very productive and some of their crops were irrigated. Later, even Leonard gave up farming the area.

Nothing remains of Leonard Rader's Pine Forest house. Remnants of an old water diversion from Thompson Creek remain as well as old stumps left from the sawmill days.

Over by George Rader's old estate, nearer to Patterson Lake, the house, barns and big log corrals are all gone, but a foundation still marks the site. The original stonework in the cellar peeks out from the cement that was added later. A sprinkling of poppies and several bushy lilacs growing there have fared the best over time. Walk from Patterson Lake Resort along the scenic lakeshore hiking trail to the south end

of the lake, relax in the meadows there for awhile, and imagine
what life was like for the Raders living in this lovely place so
long ago.

The Houghs and Raders Have Neighbors

In addition to the Houghs and Raders, several other settlers
homesteaded the meadows and woodlands of the Sun Mountain
area.

A pioneer bachelor, known to everyone as simply Mr.
Barnsley, cleared several acres of land for farming along the
old road descending from the north end of Patterson Lake to
Twin Lakes Road.

Mr. Barnsley, a renowned hermit, occasionally enjoyed a social spree in town according to local Ken White. In the early
days, when few owned cars in the Methow, Barnsley would
drive his horses and sled into town on a cold winter afternoon
to tip a few and visit friends at the Winthrop Pool Hall, now
Three Fingered Jacks restaurant. At closing time, he'd unhitch
his team from the post out front, head them toward home,
wrap himself up in a blanket and fall asleep on the floor of his
rig. His horses faithfully plodded home to the hay that awaited
them. Folks on the road recognized the driverless sled and all
politely pulled over so Barnsley's horses could pass.

"Barnsley was a questionable guy," claimed Gilbert Dibble.
"Lots of people were afraid of him, but I loved him when I
was a kid," he said. Young Gilbert befriended Barnsley while
both worked cutting and baling hay in the area. Periodically,
Dibble visited his eccentric pal who would entertain the boy by
playing the guitar, banjo, fiddle or mouth organ. In addition to
being a multitalented musician, Barnsley brewed tasty homemade elderberry wine, and he'd often share a glass with his 16-
year-old companion.

Barnsley taught Gilbert how to drive his Model T and as it
turned out, this was a good idea. One time on a surprise visit,
Gilbert found Barnsley deathly ill with pneumonia. The recluse
had lain sick alone for 10 days. Nearly panicky, Gilbert frantically started up the Model T to make a mad dash to the doctor. His foot never left the gas pedal on that particular trip,
and he wiped out seven gates driving from Barnsley's place
to the highway. (His driver's ed class hadn't included braking.)
He survived the ride, found the doctor and saved his old

152

friend's life.

Thomas Morley, another bachelor homesteader in the area, like Barnsley, had an eccentric side. Sun Mountain Lodge is set on the northwest corner of Morley's land.

Morley raised hay on the level benches near the lodge and grazed cattle on land right where the lodge stands. Instead of building a home, Morley just burrowed into the banks of a creek. Officials insisted Morley build a real house on his land if he wanted to claim title to his homestead. To satisfy the bureaucracy, Morley constructed a house one-quarter mile down Patterson Creek from the present dam at the north end of Patterson Lake. However, he refused to live in the above-ground abode, preferring the security of his dugout shelter.

The nearby hand-hewn Powers' homestead vintage early 1900s is fairly well preserved, partly due to renovations made by the local Athletic Club when they used the cabin as a warming hut for skiers. It is a small house and one wonders how the Powers and their seven children all fit into it. Remnants of an old root cellar still exist by the log cabin. Frail-looking fruit trees grow near the house alongside several healthy lilac bushes. A good creek runs through the property.

Henry Harrison Williams homesteaded 160 acres south of Patterson Lake and four rough road miles from the Methow River. In the summer of 1889, he constructed a 14- by 20-foot one-room cabin near the lake. Williams built a roof of hand-split shakes, and he shaved cottonwood logs for the cabin floor, both luxuries at a time when many homes had dirt floors and roofs. Across the lake from Henry Williams, his son, Newton Williams, from Helena, Montana, settled on a homestead where Patterson Lake Resort is located now.

Bibliography

Dibble, Gilbert. Phone Interview. Pleasanton, California, spring 1991.

Hawkins, Mike. "Jack Rader." Souvenir Program, Winthrop 49ers, May 25, 1968.

Hottell, Diana. "Pearl Rader Risley: Homestead Life on Patterson Lake." *Methow Valley News*, July 14, 1977.

Hough, Mardi. Phone Interview. Twisp, Washington, spring 1990.

Johnson, Abbie Williams. "Life in the Upper Methow." *Okanogan County Heritage*, March 1968.

Kikendall, Hazel. Autobiographical Letter about Methow Valley History. Twisp, Washington, summer 1990.

The Powers' homestead. Photo by Don Portman.

Nickell, Walter. *The Way It Was.* Naples, Florida, June 1990.

Rader, Robert. Phone Interview and Letter. Asheville, North Carolina, May 1990.

Schmidt, Jessie. *The Wenatchee World.* May 14, 1968.

Steele, Richard F. *History of North Washington.* Western Historical Publishing Company, Spokane, 1904.

White, Ken. Field Trips. Winthrop, Washington, summer and fall 1990.

154

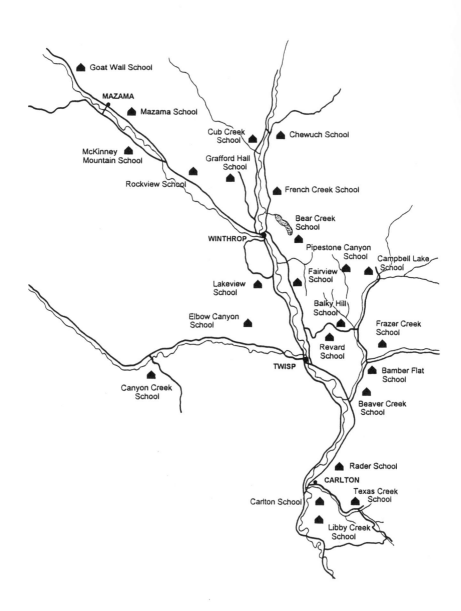

Location of Early Methow Valley Schools

Chapter 10

SCHOOL DAYS
IN THE METHOW VALLEY

A One-Room Schoolhouse for Every Methow Community
Educating their children was a top priority for Methow
Valley pioneers. No sooner had a handful of settlers formed a
small community than some literate person became a teacher,
turning his or her family home into a neighborhood school.
This always sufficed until a real school could be built.

One of the first recorded schools in the valley was held in
Thad Bamber's cabin on Beaver Creek, where the Methow's
first pioneers had settled. In 1890, Ida Malott taught 10 pupils
in the little school.

The first building ever constructed strictly for education was
located five miles south of Winthrop above today's Methow
Valley State Airport. Pioneers called it the Fairview School
because of its placement on the brow of a hill where students
beheld a "fair view" of the valley and river below. Like many
early pioneer schools, it was made of hand-hewn logs and built
by parents of the pupils.

Fairview School had its origin in 1891, when the Filer,
Stone, Prewitt and Davis families all wanted to establish a
school district and maintain a school building for children
living north of Twisp. A school district in those days consisted
of at least seven children, and once approved, school had to be
conducted for at least a three-month term. The four pioneer

families felt these requirements could be fulfilled, so they set to work on a one-room, squared-log schoolhouse with the luxury of three full windows on each side.

The Robert Prewitt family donated lumber for desks and tables—building material that had been destined to finish their house. By the second month of school, the men had whipsawed and planed the donated lumber and fashioned furniture for the students. Because of the Prewitts' generosity, the family suffered chilly feet all winter, padding around on a dirt floor instead of floor boards.

Even with a wood floor, temperatures in the school stayed pretty cool. A box stove provided heat but never quite warmed the whole room. Kids didn't suffer the cold much, however, since the Fairview School closed in the dead of winter due to its remote location and the great depth of snow in those days.

No day-care existed in early times, so the first Fairview teacher, Mrs. Mott Bryan, greeted her students with 18-month-old son Morris in her arms. Some of the early teachers boarded with a family in the neighborhood, while many, like Mrs. Bryan, lived right at the school. A stage or cloakroom doubled as the teacher's living quarters—a bit cramped but the commute to work was nil. Fourteen children attended the Fairview School the first month it opened.

Fairview students enjoyed a special treat the summer of 1898, when the Owen Wisters visited the school. Wister, already a well-known author at the time, thrilled the kids with his visit. Lively Mrs. Wister organized games and contests for the kids and awarded the winners prizes. It was an event the children forever remembered, and when Wister published his famous western novel, *The Virginian*, they couldn't wait to get a copy.

Way up the Twisp River the living room of Fay Bolin's house served as the first school in the area. When the student body exceeded eight, the community agreed a new schoolhouse had to be built. This was in 1922, long after the opening of the Fairview School. Nevertheless, the Canyon Creek School, as it was named, was planned and built the same old-fashioned way. Mr. Bolin deeded his own property at the junction of the Twisp River Road and Buttermilk Road for the school. It was a pleasant spot, lined with tall pines and fir trees and with abundant space for children to play.

The Fairview School (which appears as a dot on a bench midphoto) had a "fair view of the valley." Photo from the Shafer Museum collection.

The men of the community built the Canyon Creek School with their own hands, using lumber furnished by the local mill. Typical of early-day schools, the carpenters cut space for windows on only one side. Secondhand desks from the Campbell Lake School, located in a part of the valley that was losing students, provided furniture for the schoolroom.

Canyon Creek students never tired of any teacher since a different one appeared every term. Only 19-year-old girls fresh out of normal school applied for the job. In those days, young teachers such as these often moved from one school to another, teaching a term or so at each in order to work most of the year. This may explain why the Canyon Creek School changed teachers so often. Or perhaps lonely, local farmers enticed the educated, eligible schoolmarms to leave their careers behind.

In the early 1900s one-room schoolhouses dotted the entire Methow Valley. In the lower valley, there was a school at Squaw Creek, the town of Methow, Gold Creek, Carlton, Libby Creek, two schools up Texas Creek and the valley's most famous school, Beaver Creek.

Like the other valley schools, volunteer labor built Beaver Creek. But unlike the others, it had the benefit of a master carpenter, Sam Metcalf. "He was a craftsman when it came to hewing logs on all four sides and notching ends so they all

158

Beaver Creek School, 1992. Photo by Don Portman.

fit perfectly together," remembered Walter Nickell. "He chinked every little gap with clay which became hard as rock when it dried."

At first the Beaver Creek School term lasted a short four months, since children left to help with harvesting and planting the fields. By 1907, students attended the school for six months. The sturdy little place of learning served students from 1891 until the mid-1940s when the district consolidated with the Twisp School District.

The Beaver Creek School still stands—proof of its builder's skill. It is one of the few one-room schools remaining in the Methow Valley. In 1984 it was donated to the Okanogan County Historical Society which has restored the structure and plans to preserve it as an historical site.

North of Beaver Creek, settlers built rural schools at Frazer Creek, Campbell Lake, Pipestone Canyon and Balky Hill. Schooling in this area started in 1908 at the Revard home on Beaver Creek. Two years later parents constructed the Balky Hill School on the first bench above Beaver Creek on the west side. When this school overflowed with students, locals raised another school just over the hill, called the Campbell Lake School. The latter school was short-lived because drought struck and the dryland farm area quickly lost its population.

Settlers erected country schools in the Winthrop area and all the way north to Mazama. Names of some of the early ones were Cub Creek, Chewuch and French Creek (all up the Chewuch Road), Rockview, Lakeview, Upper Bear Creek, Grafford Hall, Mckinney Mountain, Goat Wall and the Mazama School.

Methow pioneers who sent their children to these one-room schoolhouses truly valued education. Their commitment showed in their willingness to hold school in their own homes, then build schools with whatever resources they had. The school was the community's responsibility and its pride.

Why Pioneer Kids Could Read

Pioneer children learned to read because they were motivated to learn and because their instructors were good.

Children cared about school and got there whenever they could, related Glenn Parker, who attended the one-room Lakeview School on Moccasin Lake Ranch. In the early 1920s when Glenn went to Lakeview, many small ranches were scattered in the neighboring hills. Teacher Mrs. Dan Holland had her hands full with 35 students at all levels from first through eighth grade. Like a pro, Mrs. Holland taught the consecutive rows, each row corresponding to an entire grade level.

Glenn enjoyed it immensely. "It was like a big, happy family," he said. He compared small schools versus a big, centralized school to country towns versus a metropolis. "In the one-room schools, teachers had more time to deal with individuals," said Glenn.

Students at other single-room schools in the valley pledged the same allegiance Glenn did to a small-is-better philosophy of education. At the Canyon Creek School, Carol Bolin Hansen said never more than 12 students attended class and often only one child per grade. Younger learners listened to upper classmen recite, thus absorbing extra knowledge. Some good listeners skipped grades as a result.

Nedra Horn experienced the same top quality education at the Beaver Creek School, which she attended for eight years. Faced with the eighth grade test, "to see if country kids knew enough," as Nedra phrased it, the small towners passed with flying colors. Individualized study and lots of personal attention contributed to student success, said Nedra, as well as the inspired instruction the students received. Nedra offered a glowing description of her teachers:

> I often think of those teachers giving us all they
> had in teaching ability and their desire to help
> these isolated children having almost no teaching
> materials at their disposal. There were a few obsolete maps, a large dictionary and a few books that
> had been donated. When Mrs. Brown taught, she
> brought many of her own good books—classics we
> learned to love. We read and memorized much
> poetry.
> —*Yellowjacket*, Volume 1, by Twisp
>   School Alumni Members, 1980.

In addition to their academic studies, students were responsible for certain chores at school. At the Canyon Creek schoolhouse, the boys carried buckets of water from either Canyon Creek or the Twisp River, both quite a distance away. Carrying wood to feed the ever-hungry stove was another task they routinely performed. Work, physical or mental, was a natural part of life for pioneer children.

The Many Faces of a Schoolhouse

Early Methow schoolhouses served multiple purposes. Since one was located in each small Methow community, the schoolhouse became the obvious site for a community center. Sunday morning the local school became a church: it made sense to use the one completed public building for services and Sunday school rather than build a whole new structure. When King Kennedy came to town with his puppets and magician's tricks, the school metamorphosed into an entertainment center.

In the evenings pioneers regularly scheduled "literaries" at schoolhouses. These were local talent shows with every person of every age encouraged to perform on stage for the community's pleasure and pride. Katie Mattison remembered the "Literary Society" held at the Beaver Creek School. Katie's father played the fiddle for various virtuoso singers. Katie herself recited poems to her peers which she'd learned from her mother. Amateur actors performed short plays called "dialogues." Sarah Metcalf's heavy organ, hauled on a sleigh in winter, livened up the tempo at the literaries. A men's quartet sang "Aunt Dinah's Quilting Party" along with other top harmonizing tunes from the era.

Pioneers knew how to make a holiday festive and the schoolhouse was where a lot of the celebrating took place. Every year at the Beaver Creek School, Nedra Horn remembered a Christmas program extravaganza during which the little schoolhouse practically burst its seams with teeming children and adults. On a platform stood an enormous tree which tickled the ceiling with its pointed tip.

The children's eyes sparkled when they saw the end result of their own brilliant decorations handmade for the occasion— paper chains, snowflake cutouts, tinsel and toys. Candles glowed from the conifer's lacy branches. Two students watched vigilantly with wet towels handy to douse any candle that caught fire.

On the last day of school, the whole community celebrated. Everyone brought copious comestibles for a potluck picnic. Children and adults played ball games and ran races. The one-room schoolhouse of old was not only a great place to learn, but a great place to have fun.

Nedra Horn Taught at Beaver Creek

Who organized all these festive social occasions centered at the schoolhouse? Lots of people, including students, helped, but the teacher was the activities director.

Teachers have always had to have multiple talents and skills, and in pioneer times this seemed especially so. When she was the solitary instructor of Beaver Creek School, Nedra Horn organized Christmas programs, directed plays, devised dances, designed literaries, and planned Halloween parties. Extracurricular activities didn't faze Nedra. She loved being activities director just as she loved being the teacher at Beaver Creek.

Growing up in the 1910s and 1920s, Nedra's concerns for the future were surprisingly similar to those of a girl today. Nedra wanted to get a job. Compared to today's job market for women, however, Nedra's choices were far more limited. A girl could go to business school, take nurse's training, or attend normal school and train to be a teacher. Coming from a culture-minded family, it seemed natural for Nedra to teach. She graduated from teachers' school in 1931 and began her career at the Winthrop District's Grafford Hall School up the Rendez-vous Road. She earned $60 a month.

Next, Nedra accepted a teaching job at her alma mater, the Beaver Creek School. She looked around to see the same three pictures that adorned the walls when she was a student—Abe Lincoln, George Washington and "a girl with dogs." For instructional aids, she had a Book of Knowledge set, a dictionary and several obsolete maps. Lack of materials didn't upset Nedra. She knew the kind of education you could get at these mini-schools, and she could give as good as she had received.

Nedra stressed English, penmanship and spelling. Her students studied the three Rs as well as geography. She remembered vividly when the eighth grade test time neared. This test was a student's passport to high school and failure could mean the end of education. These final exams were no cake-walk either; in fact, they were quite difficult. Students had to review, then often do extra research to pass. Nedra drilled and drilled her students on questions. "They were all very nervous," she said, "but they all passed."

Maintaining discipline was no problem for Nedra. She remembered one bright young boy who came from the town school and knew some tricks. One day when he amused himself

When not teaching, Nedra Horn enjoyed the backcountry. Photo from the Dick Webb collection.

by throwing spit wads, Nedra kept him after school for his transgressions. She offered him lots of paper to make all the wads he wanted. "What fun!" his expression said. Later, however, Nedra looked up from her paperwork to see huge tears streaming down his face. "I don't like to make spit wads," he sniffed, and Nedra welcomed him back to the fold.

Teachers needed to have tough constitutions in the old days. "We did our own janitor work," said Nedra. "When the weather got cold, the teacher had to build a fire in the morning." Nedra was an early supporter of the hot school lunch program. On frosty days, she would brew hot soup on the stove for the children to share at noon.

Getting There Was the Hard Part

Even though early schools were located near the homes of children who attended them, commuting could still be difficult, even dangerous. Buses, if they had existed at the time, could never have navigated some of the trails leading to the one-room schoolhouses. Children often rode sleighs when it snowed, and rode horses or walked in fair weather.

Pioneer kids were determined to attend school despite the physical challenges involved. One case of supreme dedication to attendance was Vernon LaMotte, who had to cross the Methow River to get to school. In the summer, he navigated a narrow footbridge with ease. In winter, however, icejams often destroyed the bridge. When that happened, he and some classmates would cut a channel for 20 or 30 feet to get out to the mainstream, then row a boat across. Surviving this, still another mile and a half of cold country had to be crossed before the schoolhouse came in sight. "When snow was deep, that was kind of hard," said Vernon.

Glenn Parker commuted from his family's house to the Lakeview School several miles away. One winter evening returning home from school, Glenn and his companion sleigh riders encountered another sleigh head-on, on a one-lane road. Since the snow measured three feet deep and the road was extremely narrow, skirting around the other vehicle appeared impossible. A shouting match ensued between the two drivers. Glenn sweated during the entire encounter, because the opponent sled driver was over 6 feet tall and a husky bully. A fight looked imminent, then abruptly one driver risked all and pulled by the other. Not a pinky finger could have fit between the two rigs, said Glenn.

Beulah LaMotte recalled a hair-raising trip to school in Twisp by covered wagon. Her uncle Claude Prewitt, possibly distracted by his sweetheart sitting beside him, suddenly dropped the reins. When he tried to retrieve them, he scared the horses. Claude fell under the stampeding hooves of the animals and all seemed lost when heroine Hannah Jones Worthen grabbed a whip, recovered the reins, and regained control of the team. Claude's clothes were shredded and his pride tattered as well, but all survived the crisis.

In 1913 when several country schools consolidated with Twisp, children from outlying areas could ride the first bus to school. Viva Hoogterp remembered riding the original Methow Valley school bus. It was a small horse-drawn wagon and only a limited number of children would fit, so if you lived two miles or less from the school the law stated you had to get there under your own steam.

In winter, students slid to school on a sled hitched to the school's horses. A tarp draped over the top of the wagon provided minimum protection from the cold. An iron-drawer box containing glowing coals warmed the children's feet. Twisp River kids rode this style of horse-drawn wagon/sled "school bus" for many years. By the late 1920s motorized vehicles took over the job.

Schools in the Town of Twisp

Everyone in the town of Gloversville (later named Twisp) agreed they needed a school, and the likely place was the town's first drug store, known as the Doc Barnes Building. In 1896, 10 students, all under 12 years of age, flocked to this temporary school. They sat on small wooden boxes and used large grocery boxes for desks. Townspeople bought lumber from the Red Shirt Mine a year later and built a new one-room school in Twisp equipped with bona fide chairs, desks, benches and a heating stove. The school offered two terms: September, October and November; and April, May and June.

Soon the population outgrew the one-room structure so Twisp residents built a second, larger school. Like the country schools, the new town school doubled as a community center where Saturday night dances, box socials, debates and Sunday school were held. Everyone felt proud of the new school, especially when Governor Mead came to call. Unfortunately, a cow wandered in during the dignitary's visit, signaling Mead with a loud "MOO!" Defending the bovine bugler, teacher Grace Job remarked, "The governor should expect to see cows in cow country."

In 1911, people began laying bricks for the big school building which now serves multiple purposes as Twisp's community

The Frazer Creek School north of Beaver Creek. Photo from the Okanogan County Historical Society, negative 3385.

center. Two years later, school in Twisp ran a full nine months.

In 1913 Robert W. Dow arrived here to change the course of local education. Dow's self-appointed goal was to establish a high school in the Methow Valley. Professor Dow canvassed the territory for students who had completed eighth grade, hoping to find at least one person for each of the four years of high school.

Dow discovered second-year high school students were nearly nonexistent. Local pupil Herald Bolin didn't feel prepared for the second year, but friendly persuasion convinced him to enter that grade for the good of posterity. In 1914, the first graduating class in Twisp, a grand total of five proud and smiling students, donned caps and gowns and received their diplomas.

For many years the big brick building in Twisp housed both grade school and high school. When things got too crowded, the town built Allen Elementary on the hill above, relieving the old school of grades one through six.

The last high school class to graduate from the brick school was in 1973 when the Twisp and Winthrop schools consolidated to form Methow Valley School District 350. Now the antique structure survives and thrives as a senior center, library, information center, a place for theater and music performances and a variety of community functions.

Winthrop Schools

A little house situated on the Methow River between Winthrop and Heckendorn, a community just east of Winthrop, functioned as the first school in the upper valley. A log house standing right in the center of town served as the second Win-

Winthrop's Central School from the bridge crossing the Methow River. Photo from the Bob Ulrich collection.

Making bricks for Winthrop's Central School. Photo from the Shafter Museum.

throp school; Castle Avenue, overlooking the town, was the site of a new school in 1903.

In 1912, Winthrop built the stately, red brick Central School just south of the bridge crossing the Methow River. Citizens felt pride in their new school built entirely by locals with locally hewn rock and locally forged bricks. Master stonemasons, the McLean brothers, dug out huge rocks nearby and split them with mauls for a 4-foot-thick foundation. On the inside, where the walls had been cut flat, one could see all the different colors and minerals in the stones—browns, greys, blues and greens, remembered ex-Central School student Ken White. Ken was furious when a superintendent with no sense of aesthetics ordered the whole rock face whitewashed. "Covered the whole beautiful surface," lamented Ken.

Both grade school and high school students attended Winthrop's Central School. In 1921, Paul Kennedy became the school's first graduate. In 1927, buses began to transport country kids to the Central School, and by 1939 the school had become so crowded, townspeople were forced to build additions.

Disaster struck in the form of a fiery inferno which burned the solid rock and brick structure to the ground on New Year's

Day, 1961. People built a grade school (which later became the Intermediate School) on the same site, and constructed Liberty Bell High School three miles south of Winthrop.

Methow Schools Consolidate

In the mid-1980s, it became clear that Methow Valley schools needed reorganization, remodeling and repair.

The leaking roof at Allen Elementary in Twisp had caused extensive damage to the structure. Bad wiring at the school prevented computers from being hooked up. Insulation was nonexistent and both the heating and plumbing were shot.

Limited space interfered with education at the Intermediate School in Winthrop. The student population could barely squeeze into the 18,000-square-foot structure. Half the students attended class in portables, while the six acres of land surrounding the school left no room for expansion.

In the late 1980s two bond issues failed and the future of the schools looked dim. After Suellen White became school superintendent in August 1991, the idea of new school construction and a single campus for all the local schools began to gain support.

Local voters eventually approved a $6 million bond to construct a new school and refurbish and expand an old school on the Liberty Bell High School campus on Twin Lakes Road. By the fall of 1995, an imposing and attractive new high school opened its doors to students. At 94,248 square feet, the school could accommodate future growth in population.

Elementary school students joined the campus in September, 1996, when workers completed remodeling the original high school to accommodate the lower grades. The school expansion included four additional classrooms and a large new library.

A phenomenal community effort went into developing the recreation area surrounding the two schools. The two-year volunteer effort transformed alfalfa fields into baseball parks, a football field, and tennis courts. Volunteers who owned a bulldozer, a grader, a dump truck or back hoe donated their equipment and labor to move hundreds of tons of dirt, cut away hills, flatten areas for athletic fields, and install an underground sprinkler system. Locals contributed an estimated quarter of a million dollars worth of free labor.

Students have shown great pride in their schools. In the spring of 1998, students and staff painted a beautiful, uplifting mural at

The new Liberty Bell High School, 1999. Photo by Don Portman.

the entrance to the Methow Valley Elementary School. It depicts the scenery of the valley and the activities people who live here enjoy. By putting 4- by 4-inch painted tiles together, Liberty Bell Junior-Senior High School students created two stunning landscape murals to decorate the interior walls of their school.

Bibliography

Bolin, Henry. "Young Schoolmaster." *Okanogan County Heritage*, Autumn 1971.

Burbank, Mary Webb. "School Buses." *Yellowjacket*, Volume I, Twisp Alumni Members, 1980.

Duffy, Barbara. Notes from Wenatchee Valley College Class on Methow Valley History. Winthrop, Washington.

Eiffert, Billie Bond. "Twisp Schools." *Yellowjacket*, Twisp Alumni Members, 1980.

Hansen, Carol Bolin. "Canyon Creek School." *Yellowjacket*, Twisp Alumni Members, 1980.

Horn, Nedra. Interview. Winthrop, Washington, summer 1990.

——. "Beaver Creek School Days." *Yellowjacket*, Twisp Alumni Members, 1980.

Hottell, Bill. "Katie Mattison." *Methow Valley News*, March 31, 1977.

Hottell, Diana. "Viva Hoogterp and the Webb Clan." *Methow Valley News*, February 2, 1978.

——. "The Adventures of Nedra Horn." *Methow Valley News*, November 8, 1979.

——. "Nedra Horn: The Ideal Childhood," *Methow Valley News*, November 1, 1979.

Jones, Flora Filer. "School in the Gay 90s." *Okanogan County Heritage*, Fall 1971.

Lehman, Marrene McNees. "Fairview School (1891-1910)." *Yellowjacket*, Twisp Alumni Members, 1980.

Methow Valley News. Article on Beaver Creek School. September 6, 1984.

Methow Valley News. March 31, 1994.

Methow Valley News. May 5, 1994.

Methow Valley News. September 7, 1995.

Nickell, Walter. *The Way It Was.* Naples, Florida, June 1990.

Parker, Glenn. Phone Interview. Winthrop, Washington, summer 1990.

White, Suellen. Phone interview. Winthrop, Washington, summer, 1998.

Chapter 11

CARLTON TAKES SHAPE

Modern day Carlton, 24 miles upriver from Pateros, is a road-side town with a general store, motel, café, RV park, beauty shop and post office. Compared to Twisp and Winthrop, it seems small and quiet. At one time, however, Carlton bustled with pioneer enterprises and, according to historian Shirley Mantei Schade, just as many homesteaders settled in the Carlton area as did near the upper valley towns.

In one bold stroke, William J. Fleming created the town of Carlton in 1907 when he moved a two-story store, a hotel and two houses from the town of Silver to the mouth of Texas Creek. Freighter Claude Sykes performed the challenging task with a team of six horses and eight logs. Soon afterward the Carl Dillards purchased the Locust Lodge named for the locust trees planted in the new town—trees which survive to this day.

Apparently Carl Dillard was a popular man since women at a Ladies Aid meeting at the Dillard's home suggested the new town be called "Carl's town" in honor of their host. The group agreed to shorten the name to "Carlton" which they felt was easier to remember. The first Carlton was platted August 23, 1907.

Dave Nagle and C. Hoover began planning a hotel for the new town of Carlton in the spring of 1907. Their two-story 24- by 34-foot establishment with office, dining room, bar and 14 guest rooms opened for business that very summer. Since he'd worked as a chef on Columbia River steamboats, Nagle took charge of the kitchen. The hotel became an instant hit. People gathered there for dances, parties and other special events.

The hotel not only accommodated travelers but in the winter months some families from outlying homesteads rented rooms so their children could continue to go to school in town. Often the mother lived with the children at the hotel while the father stayed back at the ranch keeping up the farm work.

When Carlton residents learned in 1927 of plans to build a new highway one-half mile from their town site, they packed up their buildings and relocated them in a handier spot adjacent to the new road. All of which necessitated a new bridge across the river.

The bridge piers were a sturdy concrete construction with a metal framework overhead while the rest of the bridge was made of lumber. Reflecting safety concerns a warning sign read, "$25 fine for anyone riding or driving over this bridge faster than a walk." Despite precautions, when freighter Sykes crossed the bridge with a six-horse team pulling two wagons one span broke through depositing a wagon in the water. The team yanked the second wagon to safety.

Well-known Carlton Pioneers

Many well-known pioneer families lived in the Carlton area before it officially became a town. By 1888, A.C. Libby, Pleas Rader, George Rader, Harvey Nickell, Josh Risley and Ed McConnell had all settled in the vicinity. Joe Liebl, Charles D. Smith and brother William Smith came in 1894. 1897 brought Arthur Countrymans, the Reynolds, Williamses and Heaths. The home of "Link" and Effie Fender on Texas Creek became the stage stop for freight wagons and stage coaches traveling from Ives Landing (Pateros) to Winthrop.

George Rader's experience moving to the Carlton area was typical of many of these pioneers. After visiting the area on an exploratory trip, George decided the country looked good to him. He built a log house near Carlton, then returned to Ellensburg for his family and cattle.

Bringing his wife and three children, it took seven days for George to drive his loaded-down wagon and 50 head of stock to the new homestead. Going over the Chiliwhist route which was "anything but a road," according to George, he had to cut down trees and dig rocks out of the way. "My wife was pretty disgusted," said George.

There was worse to come. The Raders arrived the summer of '89 just in time to weather the hard winter that followed. George described the Raders' rough first winter:

> When the snow melted, I had 17 out of 50 head of stock left. Some of the hay I had figured on feeding had burned up and I had fed (to the stock) all the bed ticks and all the seed grain I had figured on planting the next spring. We paid more attention to saving the horses than the cows because in those days a team was about the most valuable possession a man had. Those bed ticks and that seed grain saved my horses.
>
> —*Wenatchee Daily World*

Schools and a Church

Before Carlton citizens constructed a real school, Mrs. George Williams taught Libby Creek children to read in her home.

A.C. Libby place at Libby Creek. Photo from the Dick Webb collection.

A.C. Libby, Reynolds, Arthur Countryman and all their sons pooled resources to construct a one-room schoolhouse one-half mile north of the Libby homestead. Other area schools included the Texas Creek School conveniently located near the Fender homestead so all of the Fenders' eight children could walk to class, plus the Rader School located on the George Rader homestead.

The town of Carlton got its first school in 1907. A brick school built in the 1920s replaced the old school which then became a place for a teacher and family to live. The new brick school accommodated all grades in two classrooms; one held the lower four grades and the other the upper four. The front entryway became a library.

The Methodist Church organized prior to 1925 held services in the brick school. With $370 and land donated by A. D. Lang, the community began construction of a church building in 1939. Often 30 men, all volunteers, worked on the church at one time.

Besides church services, the building functioned as a community center where many groups such as the Ladies Aid, Boy Scouts and Community Club met. Later locals built bookshelves and contributed books to form a library in the church. Dedicated in 1945, the Carlton Methodist Church stood only three more years before the Methow River swept it away in the flood of 1948.

Time for Fun

While Carlton people built hotels, schools, churches and homes, they still made plenty of time for recreation and fun. They raced, roped and socialized at rodeos held regularly behind the present fire hall. Indians joined in the festivities, playing their stick games and competing in rodeo events.

The popularity of baseball soared in the entire valley from 1912 on. The Carlton team competed with other Methow teams and later teams from CCC encampments. The CCC Carlton team from Foggy Dew Camp was the unbeatable team.

Harold and Osa Kirkham had the brilliant idea of remodeling a Carlton building into a roller skating rink. They put in a beautiful maple floor and soon Harold and son Quentin, who could both dance on skates, were teaching others to do the same. Saturday nights the rink doubled as a dance hall. Like a modern day "open mike" session, any musician could play and pass the hat. George

Burnside, a one-man-band local favorite, often could be heard
playing the fiddle or harmonica while pounding out his own percussion on a bucket or tub with his foot. Weekend gatherings
might also include cards, bingo and a potluck supper—the party
lasting until dawn when everyone headed home to milk cows and
do chores.

Carlton General Store

The hub of the present town of Carlton is the Carlton General
Store where one can buy anything from gas and groceries to local

*The Carlton Stage, 1914. Photo by Curtis, from the photo collection
of the Washington State Historical Society, Tacoma. Negative number
30086.*

176

history books. Early resident Del Lang owned the store twice. In 1935 Del ran the post office in the store. The present owners Diana and Bill McAdow say the store has been in that location for 50 years, but historians think the venerable establishment has likely been there for at least 70 years.

Bibliography
Shade, Shirley Mantei. "In 1907 Carlton Takes Shape at Texas Creek." *Okanogan County Heritage*, Spring 1998.
Stoffel, Karl. "Rader's Horses Saved With Bed Ticks and Seed Grain." *Wenatchee Daily World*. (Barbara Duffy Library).

For a while Twisp (here shown in 1912) was one of the largest towns in the county. Photo from the Dick Webb collection.

Chapter 12

TWISP: A CENTER OF TRADE

People have always been curious about how the town of Twisp got its name. One author claimed "Twisp" was a modification of the Indian word: "T-wapsp", which meant yellowjacket. Another researcher agreed that the name was derived from Chinook jargon, the local Indian language, but countered that the original spelling was "Twistsp" to imitate the sound of a buzzing wasp. Certainly, a combination of the two theories is correct; the word probably means wasp and is an example of Indian onomatopoeia as well. There are definitely enough wasps and wasp buzzing in late summer to support both ideas.

There's an historical reference which sheds additional light on both the origin and meaning of Twisp's unusual name. Before it became a town, Indians and explorers frequently camped at Twisp likely because of its handy water access at the confluence of two rivers. The journals of Alexander Ross indicate the legendary fur trader/explorer camped near the present site of the town. In the late 1850s an Indian village called Chilkotahp was located at the mouth of the Twisp River on the north bank. The Indians named the river that flowed by their settlement and emptied into the Methow River the Twisp River, which pioneers assumed meant the forks of two rivers in Chinook jargon.

Gloversville

At one time, Twisp bore a far more ordinary appellation. When H.C. Glover, original homesteader of the land where Twisp now stands, went to Conconully to register the townsite, he proudly named it Gloversville. That same year, 1897, Glover platted the townsite at the mouth of the Twisp River, probably near the original Chilkotahp encampment.

Next John Risley took over Twisp's center stage, buying Glover out and selling lots to the town's first businessmen. On one parcel of the new subdivision, Jim Sewell built a small store which he later sold to the valley's most ubiquitous merchant, Guy Waring.

A prolific pioneer carpenter, James L. Colwell, arrived in Twisp in 1891. His first construction project was a large blacksmith shop in town. Colwell then built the first Twisp residence, a log cabin, followed by a two-room frame house next door. Later, the master builder built the first post office and became the first postmaster, serving Twisp in this capacity from 1898 to 1908.

Doc Barney's drug store was one of Twisp's earliest establishments. Later it became the first schoolhouse in the town.

Twisp, about 1916. Note freight wagons in foreground and Indian encampment on left. Photo from the Dick Webb collection.

Amanda Burgar, who must have been quite an independent and liberated lady in her time, platted a townsite on the quarter section adjoining Gloversville in 1899, and called it Twisp after the river. This name apparently proved irresistible to everyone, for from that time on "Gloversville" was history, and "Twisp" became the permanent name of the town.

"One of the Leading Towns in the Country"

After the enterprising Amanda opened the Twisp Hotel, the town began to develop exponentially. Twisp became "ranked as one of the leading towns in the country," claimed a writer in the *History of North Washington*, published in 1904. New businesses were generated and buildings sprouted to house them in Twisp as a result of mushrooming development and population growth in the entire Methow Valley, the author declared, adding that in one year, the town doubled in size!

When Mrs. Dan McAllister crossed the bridge over the Methow River in 1901 and paraded into Twisp, she found a town of respectable proportions. There was Mrs. Burgar's hotel, Gibson brothers' store, the Methow Trading Company, a drug store, Dr. Jas. B. Couche's office and the dentistry clinic of Dr. Preston.

Mining had been the main economic prop for the new town in the 1890s and early 1900s. The nearby Red Shirt Mine, the Alder Creek and Twisp River mining districts, and even the upper Methow and Slate Creek districts buttressed businesses in Twisp. The mines enhanced Twisp's economy by providing payrolls and generating traffic through the town. Miners relished the fresh produce available in Twisp: they bought all necessary supplies there, and on days off they'd hit town for a good time.

Where All the Action Is

In the early 1900s all the action was in Twisp, remembered local Deke Smith. The bustling little burg serviced settlers with three general stores, two livery stables, two blacksmith shops, a creamery, the Commercial Bank, a newspaper office, a post office, a total of three saloons where people could party, and at least two wooden churches where souls could pray for redemption after a night of carousing. "The hills were chock-full of homesteaders and prospectors," Deke recalled. On Saturdays they would all come to town for socializing and supplies. "You'd think it was a celebration," said Deke.

At this time, the first issue of the *Methow Valley News*, the valley's oldest paper, appeared on Methow newsstands. Originator of the Twisp paper, Harry Marble, set a record for longevity in the newspaper business: for 43 years, from 1903 to 1946, Marble published the local news. The paper survives to this day and remains the main source of information for local events.

In 1900, Twisp hosted a thriving fish hatchery with a capacity of 3 million fry. Located at the confluence of the Twisp and Methow rivers, the Methow Fish Hatchery released hundreds of thousands of salmon into the rivers. When Walter Nickell was a boy, he witnessed the reared salmon returning from their ocean journey. Looking down into the water from a bridge, Walter found the river so thick with fish that the bottom was completely obscured.

Harry Marble in the Methow Valley News office. Photo from the Methow Valley News.

In the early 1900s locals brought their fastest horses to Twisp, where they'd compete on a one-half-mile race track. The course was located on the Twisp side of the Methow River, where the present bridge is, heading toward Carlton. Enthusiasts organized horse races for the valley-wide Fourth of July celebration or whenever a holiday came up on the calendar. From miles around, whole families would troop to Twisp by buggies, wagons or on horseback.

As mining activity waned near Twisp and in the Methow as a whole, agriculture rose in economic importance. Lord Thomas Blythe launched his ill-fated irrigation scheme for Twisp and Carlton, which metamorphosed into a success story in the early 1920s once the Methow Valley Irrigation District adopted the project. Twisp became the hub of the valley's fertile irrigated bench-land farming. Ranchers dry-farmed higher land near Twisp, while livestock ranged in the hill and mountain country of the area.

Roads and Power

At the start of the century, the road to Twisp became a little more conducive to travel. A steel bridge replaced the Twisp ferry around 1906, and convict crews began grading the treacherous road up the lower Methow that same year. Pioneers in 1904 enjoyed mass transit in the form of a daily stagecoach run between Twisp and Brewster.

Back in 1904, when boosters touted Twisp as a booming little metropolis, the *Methow Valley News* insisted accelerated growth depended on the "railroad question being settled." The question was settled all right, but unfavorably for commerce, convenience and fuel consumption, since rails were never laid in the Methow, and trains never chugged up the valley from the Columbia.

By 1913 one could promenade down Twisp lanes in the darkening night lit by the gentle glow of street lamps. Barney Chisholm was the fellow to thank for this modern convenience. Barney received a franchise in 1910 to run an electric power plant on the lower Twisp River to supply the town of Twisp with electricity. According to one local, town lights would flicker and dim once the movie began at the Fraternal Hall.

At first local donors funded the street lights. Chisholm's successor, the Washington Water Power Company, bargained to supply power to farmers outside city limits if they'd buy electric ranges. Ranchers obediently bought stoves and immediately put them in storage. Only a fool would use expensive electricity for cooking when wood-stove energy was free, the ranchers reasoned. People used the precious kilowatts only for lighting and possibly a pump.

During the same period, Twisp installed a gravity flow water system originating on the Twisp River two and a half miles above town. Townspeople had to hand haul water during several winters when the water froze in the system, but this is not such an unusual occurrence for Methow residents even today. Engineers installed a new, improved system which included a well and electric pump in 1938 at the Twisp City Park. To meet increased demands, the system has been enlarged over the years.

The Twisp Fire

Twisp residents would never forget the year 1924, when the town barely survived a holocaust. Late in the night of July 13, smoke and searing heat awakened Dr. Holmes from sleep. He and Mrs. Holmes leaped from bed and rescued their two children from their burning home. The couple was scorched but survived.

Meanwhile, raging flames gained such headway, no fire department could have controlled the conflagration. The townspeople gave it their best with the old-fashioned water system at their disposal. (Water streamed into town by way of a 4-inch wooden pipeline running from the Twisp River.) The whole town mobilized, but the fire could not be controlled. "It was so hot," said Marie Risley, "that the fire hoses that were dragged out into the middle of the street just burnt up like paper."

In half an hour, 23 buildings burst into flames. Within one and a half hours the structures had crashed to the ground. By 12:30 a.m. Thursday, July 14, the main retail business section of Twisp lay in smoldering ashes. People postulated that an iron left on in Dr. Holmes' drug store residence ignited the fire.

Here's the final tally on buildings incinerated in the Twisp inferno of '24: the Commercial Bank, Twisp Mercantile store and warehouse, the Twisp Hotel, Oasis Confectionery, Hagerman's residence, Twisp Pharmacy, Holman Bakery, Hoffman Shoe Shop, the transfer garage, Mutual Creamery, Risley's Pool Hall, the meat market, Scott's Barber Shop, the Twisp

Flour Mill and warehouse and the home of Mrs. Ella Couche.

The Big Brick Store, a grocery and dry goods establishment, remained upright amid the ruins of the disastrous fire. This sturdy structure, which became the Twisp Evergreen grocery, still rests squarely in the center of town. Though badly scorched, Twisp City Hall also survived the firestorm.

Instead of grieving for their losses, people rebounded and rebuilt Twisp. First they reconstructed the area where the Antler's Tavern and Valley Auto Parts were later located. For obvious reasons, brick and cement were the preferred construction materials for the refurbished Twisp.

Hard Times

Hard times hit Twisp during the nation's Depression. Drought continued to sap the dryland soil. 1930 was the driest year old-timers could recall. Less water made it harder to grow crops plus farm prices sank to an all-time low. But two things saved Twisp and the Methow Valley from the suicidal despair that prevailed in the rest of the US. First, most rural families here were self-sufficient, and what they couldn't produce, they could obtain through barter. Second, everyone felt a responsibility to help a needy neighbor.

Twisp rancher Lucille Thurlow described how her family kept food on the table during the Depression and garnered enough to share with neighbors. Potatoes were one crop that survived during hard times, said Lucille. One Depression year, the Thurlows produced around 30 tons of spuds. Here's Lucille's potato tale:

> They weren't worth money then, neither were cattle for that matter. (In the early '30s, cattle were selling for 2 cents a pound.) But we took our potatoes down to Chelan to a friend who had a store who traded them for flour, sugar and bar soap. We were then able to give away a sack of flour and some sugar and soap to people around here who needed those things.
> —*Methow Valley News.* Souvenir Issue, Summer 1977.

To survive, you had to be willing to work any job available for whatever pay was offered, remembered Hazel Kikendall, a Twisp resident.

> I recall in the 1930s haying wages were 25

cents an hour and dinner. $700 annual income
was normal. Some men, singly or in groups, traveled to the Bend Country to help in the wheat
harvest. We learned to make do or did without.
    —*Hazel Kikendall's personal letter on history.*

It took some ingenuity and possibly a little hustling to stave
off stomach pangs and keep life moderately comfortable, but
locals had already learned the fine art of bartering.

People bartered or traded work with neighbors.
We had gardens. We learned to can and dry our
surplus; people who cut wood traded for groceries.
We traded extra plants or vegetables. One time we
traded some veal for a man's flannel shirt.
    —*Ibid.*

The Depression brought out the best in many people. "That
was truly a neighbors-helping-neighbors time," said Hazel.

No one exemplified the generous spirit of the era more than
Cynthia Bailey, who opened the Blue Bird Cafe in Twisp during the Depression. Cynthia not only served delicious, home-
cooked meals, but she never let a soul go hungry in her restaurant, even when they didn't have a dime. "I gave away many a
meal," admitted Cynthia. She gained fame for her generosity
during a time when people could barely support themselves.
And despite her generosity, maybe because of it, she operated
her business successfully until 1950, even giving away butter
when rationing was on during World War II. "Besides that, I
never charged the ministers for their meals," said Cynthia.

One sparkling accomplishment of the 1930s was the successful joint venture of the American Legion Posts of Twisp and
Winthrop to build the Intercity Airport which became a famous
smokejumper base between the two towns.

The Flood of '48

The infamous flood of 1948 slammed into Twisp, washed out
the main bridge into town, sent four tourist cabins built just
below the bridge sailing downstream and forced many townspeople to evacuate their homes. When their front lawn turned
into a soggy mattress, the Leigh Webbs evacuated their home,
located at the confluence of the Twisp and Methow rivers, and
sought refuge at a friend's residence near the Wagner Mill.
When the rising Methow River threatened their friend's house,

The cowboy town of Twisp, 1909. Photo from the Dick Webb collection.

they moved once more, this time to the Twisp City Airport and hangers, where they shared a shelter with several other local families. Canvas partitions were erected for privacy and furniture and beds were sent in. The Red Cross provided food and supplies for the flood refugees.

Back at the washed-out bridge site, Wagner Mill employees worked in two shifts pulling people across the river in a cage on a cable. Water had swooshed the soil away from the mill office, and the only thing that kept the building in place was its basement, anchored in the ground like a deep tree root. Receding floodwaters left the basement walls exposed.

A Glance At Modern Day Twisp

Until about 1970, most Twisp residents made a living either by production such as farming, orcharding, stock raising and logging, or they worked for the US Forest Service or ran a small business in town. According to Vernon LaMotte, only one real estate agent worked in Twisp before 1970 and he could barely make a living. About the time the North Cascades Highway opened, the valley's economic situation began to change radically. Many cattle ranchers sold their land to newcomers, who had traveled over the highway's easy access to the Methow to find the perfect place to live. Real estate ex-

186

change became an important part of Twisp's economy (the same being true, except more so, for Winthrop and Mazama).

Twisp is now a tidy, viable town. Many newcomers have established themselves locally in respected businesses and services. There's a popular farmer's market, a handsome art gallery displaying local art, an excellent library, a medical center, dentist's office, community center, a Neighbors Helping Neighbors organization, many active civic groups and many services. In Twisp today, a healthy sense of community exists among the people who live there.

Bibliography

Coyote Tales: Stories of the Methow Valley. Liberty Bell High School Class, Toni Hughes, Faculty Advisor, 1974.

Hitchman, Robert. *Place Names of Washington.* Washington State Historical Society, 1985.

Hottell, Diana. "Deke Smith." *Methow Valley News*, Souvenir Issue, Summer 1977.

———. "Marie Risley: She is One of the Few Who Remembers." *Methow Valley News*, June 11, 1981.

———. "Frank Thurlow: Four Generations in the Methow Valley." *Methow Valley News*, Souvenir Issue, Summer 1977.

———. "Cynthia Bailey: Mother of the Methow Valley." *Methow Valley News*, Souvenir Issue, Summer 1977.

Kerr, Mary. "I Remember." *Okanogan County Heritage*, June 1963.

Kikendall, Hazel. Letter describing her personal history in the Methow Valley. Twisp, Washington, summer 1990.

LaMotte, Vernon. Phone Interview. Carlton, Washington, summer 1991.

Magee, Cecile Colwell. "I Remember When Twisp Was Platted." *Okanogan County Heritage*, September 1963.

Majors, Henry. *Exploring Washington.* Van Winkle Publishing Co., Holland, Michigan, 1975.

McAllister, Mrs. Dan. "Twisp in 1901." *Okanogan County Heritage*, December 1964.

Nickell, Walter. *The Way It Was.* Naples, Florida, June 1990.

Steele, Richard F. *History of North Washington.* Western Historical Publishing Co., Spokane, 1904.

Wilson, Bruce. *The Late Frontier.* Okanogan County Historical Society, 1990.

Chapter 13

THE OLD WEST TOWN
OF WINTHROP

The town of Winthrop was born over 100 years ago when an industrious easterner, Guy Waring, arrived at "The Forks," where the Methow and Chewuch rivers converge, and launched the Methow Trading Company.

Before Waring, Indians hunted and gathered in the area, miners camped on their way to mountain riches, and trappers searched for game. Among the first known white people to live in Winthrop were trapper brothers Tom and Jim Robinson who spent the winter of 1886-87 camped at the site of the present baseball diamond. Locals named massive Robinson Mountain at the head of the Methow Valley after these two early woodsmen, as well as Robinson Creek in the Pasayten Wilderness.

Arriving soon afterward around 1887, James Sullivan and his wife, Louisa (Heckendorn) Sullivan, settled an area which included all of what is known as Heckendorn today. James built a cabin where a beautiful spring flowed into the Methow River across from the present Winthrop bridge at the southeast end of town. Sullivan opened a log hotel on his land, charging 25 cents a night for horses and 50 cents for humans. The Sullivan Cemetery bears his name.

In the late 1880s quite an influx of settlers arrived to find homesteads near Winthrop. Well-known pioneers like the Thompsons, Boesels, Filers, James Ramsey, and Ben Pearrygin all settled in the Winthrop area. Walter Frisbee homesteaded the verdant land across the river from Winthrop, where the

Mr. and Mrs. Sullivan were one of the first couples to settle in Winthrop. Photo from the Okanogan County Historical Society, negative 357.

fish hatchery is now.

Early settlers welcomed Guy Waring and his enterprising plans. Laura Thompson described her reaction to Waring's arrival:

> One day in 1891, we passed a distinguished-looking family camped by the river—a gentleman, a lady, a 15-year-old boy with a smile on his face and a very pretty little girl about 13 years old. A few days later friends visited and exclaimed, "Good news! Good news! We are going to have a store." Mr. Waring and family planned to build a store at the forks of the Methow, the true beginnings of the town of Winthrop. At that time there was nothing in Winthrop. Walter Frisbee lived across the river and the Sullivans about one-half mile below. All of us settlers spent every cent we could with Mr. Waring.
>
> —*Okanogan County Heritage*, March 1967.

No wonder Waring's plans pleased settlers. Before his store opened, many people traveled to Coulee City for groceries, a four-day round trip with a wagon team.

How Winthrop Was Named

Waring is the acclaimed founding father of Winthrop but there's a dispute over how the town got its name. Waring's stepdaughter, Anna Greene Stevens, believed Waring named the town for Massachusetts colonial Governor John Winthrop. But according to post office records, Charles Look, Winthrop's first postmaster, named the town after one of John Winthrop's relatives, Theodore Winthrop. Theodore was a Yale graduate, adventurer/traveler and gifted 19th-century author. In 1853 he wrote the book *Canoe and Saddle* which described his trip from Puget Sound over the North Cascades to the sagebrush plains of Yakima, with the return trip by way of the Columbia River. On June 18, 1891, Mr. Look established the Winthrop Post Office in his home one and a half miles below the present townsite. This was several months before Guy Waring arrived on the scene.

The final puzzle piece is a letter from Waring to historian Edmund S. Meany, penned in 1910, describing how the town was named.

> Winthrop was a name selected by the late John
> L. Wilson when a delegate to Congress, for the
> new post office here around 1890 ... I knew the
> late Senator well and asked him how he came to
> select Winthrop for a name. He could never re-
> member but thought it might well have been in
> honor of the memory of Theodore Winthrop.
> —*Exploring Washington*, by Harry Majors.

Letters in the University of Washington library archives written by Waring indicate he tried to change Winthrop's name to "Waring" after he became postmaster in 1892, so it seems un-

Winthrop about 1896. Photo from the Shafer Museum collection.

likely he chose the original name.

From this evidence, it appears certain the town was named
after Theodore Winthrop. *Who* actually chose the name remains more of a mystery, though local historians feel sure
postmaster Look deserves the credit.

The Duck Brand Saloon Story

In 1891, 32-year-old Guy Waring built his Methow Trading
Post near the bridge crossing the Chewuch River at the northwest end of Winthrop. Despite Guy's reputedly puritan nature,
he soon opened a saloon across the street from the Trading
Post. Called the Duck Brand Saloon after Waring's cattle
brand, the new establishment reflected its owner's rigid standards of conduct. Stepdaughter Anna Stevens described
Waring's management strategy:

> He knew that a bar was inevitable at Winthrop
> and felt that one run in a high tone would do much
> to keep out the rough elements which would pro-
> tect the community as well as his family. The
> rules were very strict. Only the best liquor was
> sold. No rotgut such as miners sought was available.

*Winthrop in the 1920s. Guy Waring's Methow Trading Co. is the larg-
est building in the center of the photo, located on the corner of Bridge
Street and Riverside Avenue. It burned in 1928. Photo from the Washington State Historical Society, Tacoma.*

The Duck Brand Saloon. Photo from the Dick Webb collection.

No gambling was allowed. The bartender was only
allowed to talk to customers concerning the orders
he was taking. The bar closed promptly at ten
nightly.

—*Ibid.*

Basically, Waring owned the saloon so he could control local
alcohol consumption. While the bar never made a profit (one
year it lost $680), it was considered respectable. In fact, numerous
church publications cited it as the best run bar in the country.

Waring felt uncomfortable running a saloon no matter how
rigid its rules, and when he and his bartender were arrested in
1910 for maintaining the establishment without a license, he
must have secretly heaved a sigh of relief.

After Waring left the premises, the Duck Brand continued
to have a colorful history. In 1910, the Episcopal Church
rented the building and held services amid the bar rails, chan-
deliers and mirrors of the defunct saloon. It went from a
church to a restaurant in 1912 and the next year became a
schoolhouse. While the flu epidemic raged in 1918, it served
as a hospital and was a center for bandage rolling during
World War I. The Allen Family Bakery and Cafe settled in
for the next seven years. To provide for a town community
center the Winthrop Civic League purchased the Duck Brand
in 1928, promptly deeding the building to the city for tax
purposes. Winthrop's library moved comfortably into the
larger portion of the building which doubled as a community

center. A barber set up shop in the smaller room from 1928 to 1936. (Later the library moved into the barber shop quarters.) Fire almost caused the structure's demise in 1948, and in 1950 it was restored.

In 1972, the original Duck Brand received a well-deserved westernized face-lift and the building's original barn-red color was restored. It continued as the Joyce Shafer Memorial Library and the Winthrop Community Center until 1989 when Winthrop City Hall took over the community center portion of the building. In the late 1980s tourism inspired the town to add a lean-to information center to the library side. An historical marker appears in front of the building now.

In 1992 the library moved to a new site just south of Winthrop. It now shares a residence with the local Little Star Montessori School in a new structure funded by donations.

The restored Duck Brand looks very much like it did in Waring's day. Waring would be pleased to know the place has retained its air of respectability.

Guy Waring promised his wife a home with a view. Being a man of his word, he built a log cabin on a bluff above town where one could view both the confluence of two rivers below and snow-capped peaks beyond. In 1897, Waring's modest little cabin appeared pretentious to other homesteaders, who referred to it as "the Castle."

Winthrop Becomes a Bona Fide Town

In May 1897, Henry H. Greene, Waring's stepson, filed notice for homestead rights on 160 acres of land where the town now stands. He paid $1.25 per acre for a total of $200. A month later, Greene sold the land to the Methow Trading Company. Waring and business associate Earl F. Johnson meanwhile had filed for incorporation of the Methow Trading Company. The company then issued 25 shares of capital stock to Greene in exchange for the land.

The Methow Trading Company platted the town and the Okanogan County Board of Commissioners approved the plat January 11, 1901. Immediately, the Trading Company put the 69 lots in the development on sale. Riverside Avenue, Castle Avenue, and Bridge Street retain the names originally given them on the plat.

What did the shiny new town of Winthrop look like when

Guy Waring's "Castle," now part of the Shafer Museum. Photo from the Shafer Museum collection.

Waring's real estate business began? Where the Trail's End Motel and Bookstore stand, Dick McLean had a general merchandise store and livery stable. The Methow Trading Company stood on the corner near the Chewuch River bridge. The post office was located between the Methow Trading Company and a general store owned by Tom Wills. Winthrop's first school, called the Literary Log House, stood in front of the present city hall, and of course the Duck Brand Saloon rested under the watchful eyes of Waring directly across the street from his trading company.

Three years after Winthrop was platted, David Heckendorn, stepson of early homesteader James Sullivan, platted the town of Heckendorn one-half mile downstream from the first town. Hoping to claim some of the extra business created by the recent mining boom, Chauncey R. McLean opened the Heckendorn General Store.

Besides selling all manner of goods to miners and farmers, McLean ran a commission business in fruits and vegetables to be sold to miners, thereby furnishing an outlet for nearby farms. McLean's shop proved to be stiff competition for Waring, who, according to McLean's daughter, Ruth Davis, "lacked the common touch for getting along with early day farmers and miners who liked to shoot the breeze with Dad while doing their trading."

After many disagreements, Winthrop was incorporated in 1924 to include Winthrop proper, Heckendorn, and Carl Johnson's addition across the river, the last for the purpose of getting lights installed by the Upper Methow Valley Power and Light Company. The residential area just downriver from Winthrop is still called Heckendorn by locals, but it's no longer a bona fide town.

Winthrop bustled with activity in the early 1900s. Pioneers arriving in town around 1909 enjoyed the services of the Methow Trading Company, a grist mill, the Winthrop Market, Methow Valley Stagelines, Will's Store, H.R. Steele's Brick Company, McLean Brothers' Auctioneers, F.F. Ventzke (US Deputy Mineral Surveyor), the Winthrop Hotel, Winthrop Land Company, Star Creamery Company, Winthrop Blacksmith Shop and the photo business of Charles LaRue. By then the first telephone lines reached Winthrop. The lines ran on interconnected barbed wire fences.

Life in Winthrop had become so eventful by 1909 that the town got its first newspaper, *The Winthrop Eagle*, edited by George W. Goode. Three years later, Bill Brinkerhoff bought the *Eagle* and christened his new paper *The Methow Valley Journal*.

Brinkerhoff became one of the Methow's earliest and best promoters. He was quite proud of Winthrop's development potential and in the paper's first issue claimed: "The surrounding country will easily support a town of 3,000. There are approximately 30,000 acres of tillable land. Alfalfa produces three crops with two month's pasture after cutting. The area supported 1,500 fruit trees," wrote Brinkerhoff in the *Journal*. In addition to agricultural riches, he touted local mines of copper, molybdenum and gold.

Brinkerhoff's *Methow Valley Journal* ran for 30 years from 1912 to 1942, despite a competing newspaper in Twisp, the *Methow Valley News*, which is published to this day.

Winthrop's one and only bank, Farmers State Bank, which opened in 1916, has never failed, merged, or been purchased. When President Roosevelt declared a bank holiday during the

Depression, Farmers prevailed, according to Frank Buell, chairman of the bank's board. People in the Methow never had much spare cash, but somehow the local lending institution retained enough capital to keep its doors open. Still solvent and serving customers, Farmers State Bank can be visited at its original location on Winthrop's main street.

G. E. Nickell and sons ran a store in Winthrop from 1914 until it burned in 1927. It was a classic, old-fashioned general store where only non-perishables were sold. For fresh meat one went to the butcher, and vegetables came from one's own garden. At Nickell's enterprise, a clerk measured items on scales, and sold bulk goods by the pound. The market stocked dried beans, sugar, candy, tea, coffee, rice, cured ham and bacon, as well as everything from hog feed to dry goods and shoes. Most of the wares came from afar—West Coast Groceries out of Tacoma, Marshall Wells from Spokane and Seattle Hardware being the main wholesalers to the valley at the time.

Nickell's store won two firsts—the first place to have a gasoline tank in Winthrop, and the first place to have electric lights. The lights, installed around 1915, were powered by 14 batteries which were charged by a kerosene-driven engine with an attached generator.

The federal government built a US Forest Service ranger station in town around 1915. The Okanogan National Forest had been established in 1911, much to the disapproval of miners, stockmen, and homesteaders, since the agency controlled their use of government land. The Forest Service gained more acceptance after issuing 55 summer grazing permits for stock.

Fanned by fears of wildfire in the 1910s, the Forest Service erected fire lookouts on Methow Valley summits. Most are abandoned today, but a few have been staffed regularly in recent times, notably First Butte and Goat Peak, the latter landmark resembling a bold sentry standing guard over the upper Methow.

In the roaring '20s, Winthrop still looked like a rough western town with false-fronted buildings, board sidewalks and hitching rails. But despite its old-fashioned image, technology connected the valley to the outside world. Electricity streamed into the Methow and autos putted on potholed lanes. You could view Hollywood at local motion picture shows and hear the news on the radio. New businesses sprouted up, including the

The power plant just south of Winthrop used by the Upper Methow Valley Power and Light Company. Photo from the Okanogan County Historical Society, negative 3822.

Winthrop Billiard Parlor, which evolved into Three Fingered Jacks Saloon, still a local legend and tourist attraction.

Winthrop Sees the Light

In the early 1920s, Butler J. Woodward, manager of the Upper Methow Valley Power and Light Company (UMVP and L), adopted the job of "bringing the light" to Winthrop. Locals welcomed the kilowatts with open arms. Esther Spurgeon, for example, was thrilled by the new convenience:

> I can't remember anything that changed our
> lives like electricity did. The single bulb in each
> room was no less than a miracle—all you had to
> do was to pull a string. There was no cleaning
> and filling kerosene lamps.
> —*Okanogan County Heritage*, Spring 1986.

Butler's power plant was stationed on the Foghorn Ditch. The UMVP and L rebuilt part of the irrigation ditch, diverted water over a hill, whisked it through turbines and dashed it back into the Methow River. The fossil remains of king-size pipes and dynamo can be viewed just south of the Winthrop bridge crossing the Methow River.

Perched on a bank above the river, the barnlike power plant housed a generator and several generations of mud swallows.

The swallow hordes were a minor inconvenience compared to other challenges the company faced. A local would frequently tease Butler Woodward by saying with a leer, a wink and an elbow to the rib, "Lights are dim, Woody. A cow must be drinking out of the ditch." Of course the real cause of dimming lights was a farmer illegally opening a headgate to water his south forty.

Mother nature got in the act too. "Salmon for dinner" meant a 4-foot fish had gotten tangled in the turbines. During violent storms the "heavens always reserved one good healthy bolt for the electric company," remarked one history buff.

Power could be cut for hours during the long, dark winter. Snow broke the transmission lines and locals spent shivery nights chopping out ice that dammed the ditch. Spring floods threatened to wash away the entire operation. So many farmers helped themselves to extra shares of water in the summer that sometimes a mere trickle remained to turn the turbines.

Nevertheless, the UMVP and L kept cranking out kilowatts until the REA (Rural Electrification Administration) arrived in the valley in the late '30s bringing power to everyone, even farms and ranches outside Winthrop.

Supplying Winthrop With Water

A good water supply to Winthrop became imperative not only for domestic use, but because of the high fire danger inherent in wood buildings, wood stoves and bone-chilling, fire-building winters. Guy Waring's house and store burned in 1893. Five buildings fell to ashes in 1927, including the Nickell home, store and creamery, and Dr. E.P. Murdock's home and hospital. Two years later, Therriault's store, the former Methow Trading Company, burned. Locals lost the little town show hall to fire in the early 1950s, and even the Central School built of rock and brick burned to the ground in 1961.

At first Winthrop townspeople carried water in buckets from wells, springs or the river. Next, Methow Valley Trading Company president Waring piped water from a large spring above town to the "city center." One of the first successful wells was dug at the city park from which point water was pumped through a pipeline into Winthrop. Foss Creveling bought this system in 1944 and installed a storage system on a hill above town. The town of Winthrop designed a brand new water sys-

Winthrop before the restoration, about 1950 or 1960. Photo from the Shafer Museum collection.

tem in 1984-85 which included a new well, new pump, new storage tank and replacement of all distribution lines.

Moving Toward Modern Times

Ask locals about the Depression and chances are they'll just shrug their shoulders. Winthrop barely noticed the 1930s economic collapse. No one lost a lot of money because no one had much money to lose. People raised their own food, bartered for other necessities and took whatever jobs came their way from Grand Coulee Dam construction to crushing ore at the Azurite Mine in the dead of winter.

With the exception of the devastating flood of 1948, the '40s were quiet times in the Methow. When World War II erupted, many local boys joined the service.

Concerned about the stagnant local economy of the 1950s, civic leaders began to talk about tourism and the construction of a highway linking Western Washington city dwellers to the Methow's recreational utopia. Winthrop's economic slump continued through the 1960s, but by then word of the Methow's charms had spread.

By the mid-1970s young people began to settle in the valley in search of a simpler life. Others, escaping the rat race of the city, bought summer homes here. Retirees liked the affordable land prices, scenic views and peace of the Methow Valley.

Some visitors just came to taste the solitude and simplicity of the local lifestyle, leaving after a weekend of rest.

Winthrop's Restoration

Otto Wagner of Wagner Lumber Products Company in Twisp and his wife, Kathryn, wanted to do something for the Methow Valley which they felt had been so good to them. Together they came up with the idea of restoring Winthrop to its former glory as an 1890s frontier town.

The early 1970s was the time to put this bold plan into action because of the soon-to-open North Cascades Highway and the potential for increased tourism in the valley. Although Otto Wagner had passed away, Kathryn had kept the couple's dream alive.

Mrs. Wagner asked her friend, Leavenworth architect Robert Jorgensen, to draw up some plans for westernizing Winthrop. Kathryn and Robert then appeared before the town civic leaders to present their novel concept. Surprised local leaders immediately voiced their support. While the Wagners never considered tourism an important reason for restoring Winthrop, the merchants and the city government surely did.

Kathryn asked each merchant to contribute $2,000 to refurbish their individual places. She volunteered to pay the balance for the town's renovation. All the merchants must join the ef-

The renovated Old West town of Winthrop. Photo by Don Portman.

fort insisted Mrs. Wagner; it had to be a cooperative venture. In less than four months, all 20 local firms had pledged or donated their $2,000 requirement to the Kiwanis Foundation set up to receive the funds. The westernization of Winthrop took off like a shot.

Organizers focused on making the renovation authentic. Toward this end, Mrs. Wagner, skilled builder Jack Wilson and architect Jorgensen researched every aspect of the project. The group took trips to view old western-style buildings and towns. Kathryn traveled all the way to Alaska to see one historical town. Old photos of Winthrop and other classic cowboy towns were collected and studied. "This won't be just a Hollywood stage setting," said Jorgensen. "We want to make the design as authentic as possible in order to preserve the spirit of the valley."

Using Jorgensen's historical sketches, townspeople restored 20 buildings on Winthrop's main street. The old hotel, bank, restaurant, general hardware, service station, grocery, pool hall, tavern, Okanogan County Electric Coop, US Post Office, city hall, library, trading post and liquor store all received a facelift. All main street utilities went underground and wooden boardwalks replaced cement sidewalks.

Twisp artist Chet Endrizzi and a crew of helpers painted all the town's structures in western shades. On the sides of several buildings, Chet painted wall-sized advertisements of early manufactured goods.

"We had an incredible crew of workers and planners," remembered Kathryn Wagner. "It was like one big family. Everyone pitched in. I was fortunate to have top men I could rely on like painter Chet Endrizzi, and Howard Weller, who was a tremendously capable construction manager."

Mrs. Wagner wanted Winthrop's residents to welcome the project as well. "I don't like to call it a tourist attraction," said Kathryn. "This is a living town. People live in it. *They* aren't tourist attractions." Surely a great deal of the project's success stemmed from Mrs. Wagner's concern for the feelings of all involved—the civic leaders, city government, town merchants and residents of Winthrop.

Winthrop Burns and Rebuilds
Winthrop suffered three tragic fires in the 1990s. One nearly destroyed the town. One nearly destroyed a leader's reputation.

The Emporium explodes in the night. Photo from the Methow Valley News.

Another came within seconds of claiming victims. An account of this last fire which occurred at the Outdoorsman store appears in the chapter "Of Floods, Snowstorms and Other Weather Severities."

One of the most damaging fires in Winthrop's history occurred on Friday, November 5, 1993, when the Emporium building on Winthrop's main street suddenly burst into flames. Ammunition exploded, windows shattered, showers of sparks shot into the sky. Sirens screamed as fighters from Winthrop and Twisp raced to the scene. Alerted locals frantically sought water sources to prevent the flames from devouring the whole town. And they succeeded. Although the intense fire reduced the corner store to charred rubble and destroyed several adjoining businesses, it spread no further.

Due to suspicious circumstances, authorities called in the Bureau of Alcohol, Tobacco and Firearms to investigate. Evidence revealed the fire started below Giovanni's Restaurant and Bakery. The bureau ruled it had been intentionally set. The arsonist has never been caught.

By August 1994 the Emporium building reopened for business. Considering the extensive damage and number of separate business locations that had to be completely reconstructed, workers had done the job in record time. The exterior of the new Emporium looked identical to the old facade right down to the bell tower above the Tenderfoot store on the corner.

When fire consumed the 82-year-old Winthrop United Methodist Church less than six months after the Emporium burned, Winthrop citizens began to think their town was jinxed. That the *Twisp* Methodist Church had been destroyed by fire a year earlier added to the tragedy and sense of disbelief.

The fire occurred Friday, April 22, 1994. At 9:30 a.m., Methodist Church Pastor Gordy Hutchins, working in his basement office, suddenly saw smoke billowing into the area. Smoke and flames prevented his escaping via any doors from his office so the pastor grabbed a chair, shattered a basement window and crawled out of the church.

Fire sirens blasted but firefighters arrived too late to save the wooden structure.

When local investigators charged Pastor Hutchins with arson it set off a whirlwind of speculation, suspicion and debate. Although

The Winthrop Methodist Church bursts into flames and burns beyond repair. Photo from the Methow Valley News.

the charges were later dropped and Mr. Hutchins was exonerated, publicity surrounding the incident had already compromised his standing in the community and emotionally devastated his family. Subsequently, Mr. Hutchins left the Methow Valley to become pastor of the Methodist Church in Moses Lake, Washington.

An independent investigator determined the church fire started when a space heater ignited rummage sale items.

After their year of tragedies the Twisp and Winthrop congregations rallied. They voted to consolidate and become the Methow Valley United Methodist Church. They agreed to build a new church halfway between the two towns large enough to accommodate the combined congregations. Carpenters broke ground in July 1995, the congregation consecrated the church December 1995, and regular services began in January.

The Shafer Museum

Perched like a pioneer citadel above town, the Shafer Museum not only houses Winthrop's history but also is itself an historical Winthrop house. One of the main structures at the museum is the original home of Guy Waring, built in 1897. Before being opened to the public in 1948, "the Castle," as locals labeled it, housed a collection of pioneer memorabilia owned by Simon Shafer who obtained the antiques through the barter system.

Simon Shafer ran a grocery store during a time when both the Great Depression and a long-lasting drought handicapped the Winthrop economy. Tough times made money scarce, so Simon accepted goods in lieu of cash payment of bills. Over time, he amassed a large collection, including cars, rifles, washing machines, tools, kitchenware and assorted hand-hewn pioneer objects. Family heirlooms were added to the collection, all of which Mr. Shafer stored in the original Waring place.

Barbara Shafer Duffy and her brothers inherited the museum in 1954. In 1976, Barbara, S.W. (Bill) Shafer Jr., and Alan W. Shafer deeded the museum to the Okanogan County Historical Society. At the same time, an enthusiastic local support group, the Shafer Museum Volunteers, formed to maintain and operate the museum. The volunteers added an outdoor display of turn-of-the-century heavy mining equipment retrieved from the Hart's Pass area. US Forest Service employee Dale Tonseth installed the machinery at the museum site.

The Shafer Store, 1938 or 1939. Left to right: Frank Therriault, Bill Shafer, Harold Rakestraw, and Frances Pennington in the background. The store was located where the Emporium is now. Photo courtesy Barbara Shafer Duffy.

In the summer of 1991, museum volunteers added three new frontier-style buildings to house pioneer artifacts and displays. One building is a replica of a pioneer general store, another is an authentic assayer's office hauled from Mazama, and the third structure simulates one of Winthrop's early businesses, Hall's dress shop.

The following summer, from the Bear Creek Golf Course, volunteers carefully transported the 1885-vintage Oertel log cabin to the museum site. The building, donated by Marian Court, is in excellent shape; an envelope structure built around the original ranch house protected the logs. Museum workers have fashioned the cabin into a pioneer schoolhouse. A mid-1990s addition to "Waring Village," as the exhibit has come to be called, is an office building dedicated to Dr. Jon Malzacher, the county doctor who for 40 years was at everyone's beck and call in the Methow.

The main Shafer Museum building has returned to its original form as Guy Waring's pioneer home. Repairing Waring's Castle proved to be quite a challenge. Early builders had used dirt to insulate the roof and laid the floor logs flush with the ground. Eventually the roof dirt got too heavy and the dirt supporting the floor gave way. Volunteers raised a new roof, jacked up the building, replaced a huge rotted log in the foundation, and reset all the floor logs in cement. Period furniture has been installed and Waring's Franklin stove stands against one wall.

The Shafer Museum is perfectly located. Anyone who wants to understand what inspired the Winthrop pioneers and contemporary civic leaders to dream up grandiose schemes for the town's future should experience the view from the museum yard. It is the best place to see the soft beauty of the valley's lowland hills framed by the snow-covered magnificence of Mount Gardner and the craggy North Cascades.

Bibliography
"The Awakening." *Methow Valley News*, August 31, 1972.

Blackburn, Judy. *Methow Valley News*, April 28, 1994.

____. *Methow Valley News*, August 11, 1994.

Buell, Frank. Interview. Winthrop, Washington, spring 1990.

Davis, Ruth. "Mining Lured McLean to the Methow." *Okanogan County Heritage*, Fall 1974.

Duffy, Barbara. Notes from Wenatchee Valley College Class on Methow Valley History. Winthrop, Washington.

——. "The Shafer Museum." *Okanogan County Heritage*, Spring 1983.

——. and Marjory White. "Winthrop History." January 1990.

Coyote Tales: Stories of the Methow Valley. Liberty Bell High School Class, Toni Hughes Faculty Advisor, 1974.

Majors, Henry. *Exploring Washington*. Van Winkle Publishing Company, Holland, Michigan, 1975.

Methow Valley News. April 8, 1982.

Methow Valley News. June 29, 1978.

Nickell, Walter. *The Way It Was*. Naples, Florida. June 1990.

Perrow, Ron. *Methow Valley News*, November 11, 1993.

Roe, JoAnn. *The North Cascadians*. Madrona Publishers, Seattle, 1980.

The Spokesman-Review. May 16, 1971.

Stevens, Anna Greene. "Life in the Okanogan." *Okanogan County Heritage*, September 1970.

Thompson, Laura. "Laura Thompson Came to Stay." *Okanogan County Heritage*, March 1967.

Wagner, Kathryn. Interview. Twisp, Washington, summer, 1990.

The Wenatchee World. March 17, 1971.

White, Ken. Field Trip to Power Station. Winthrop, Washington, summer 1990.

Woodward, Douglas. "The Lights are Dim, Woodie." *Okanogan County Heritage*, Spring 1985.

Guy Waring and his second wife, Elizabeth (married April 1917).
Photo from the Shafer Museum collection.

Chapter 14

GUY WARING AND THE METHOW TRADING COMPANY

Guy Waring was an ingenious man with an indomitable energy and sense of purpose. He attempted single-handedly to transform the practically unoccupied area around Winthrop into a thriving, prosperous community. Waring started with little money of his own but was so convincing to the rich Bostonians he lobbied that the financiers gave him thousands of dollars to carry out his dreams.

Many Methow pioneers respected Waring and all he did for Winthrop. Others disliked his austere New England ways and the prestige implicit in his Harvard education. Anna Greene Stevens, Waring's stepdaughter, described the opinion some locals held of "The Governor," as she called Waring:

> The Governor was not favored by settlers when
> he appeared. They didn't like his strict principles,
> which he held in such a zealous manner. They
> were sure he was a snob who was trying to show
> off.
> —*Okanogan County Heritage*, September 1970.

There were even threats to his life, according to Anna. Surely the difficulty Waring encountered in some of his business ventures was due to local animosity.

Locals got used to Waring's ways though, and his inventiveness and zest for progress eventually won over many people. In a more positive vein, Anna concluded:

> Before he left the valley he was greatly loved by
> a large proportion of the inhabitants. His many
> kind acts and good which resulted from his resi-
> dence were appreciated. To many he was known
> as the "Father of the Methow."
> —*Okanogan County Heritage*, September 1970.

One instance of Waring's versatility stands out above the others. When a cook from one of the Slate Creek mines acci-dentally shot himself in the leg, a doctor was brought all the way from Chelan 75 miles away. When the doctor arrived he was drunk and his only remedy was to amputate the limb. The injured cook refused; the doctor left angry. Amateur physician Waring to the rescue. Guy meticulously and *soberly* removed the bullet and all the pieces of bone, then bandaged up the miner. The patient's leg healed without infection and he suf-fered only a slight limp.

Another time when a log-rolling accident resulted in a man ripping off his finger, Waring deftly sewed the finger back together. Waring excelled at fixing things and making things happen. It is unfortunate that he lacked the warmth and so-ciability that would have made him popular with locals from the start.

Traveling West

Working in his father's engineering business had not been a satisfying experience for young Guy Waring, so like many Easterners, he'd headed West to seek his fortune. As Anna Stevens remembered, "My Daddy felt the lack of a profession and in the West this proved no handicap."

Waring's travels first landed him on a cattle ranch in Loomis, Washington. At that time the Okanogan territory was becoming a county and Washington a state. With a man named Loomis (for whom the present town is named), Waring opened a trading post but soon became disillusioned with the area be-cause of the influx of so many miners (roughnecks to Waring) during the boom in silver. After returning for a short time to Boston, Waring once more felt drawn to the West. This time he ventured into a different area of Okanogan County, one that was just opening up for settlement—the Methow Valley.

With his wife, Helen Clark Greene, a widow 11 years older than Waring, her three children, Harry, 10, Robert, 7, and

Anna, 5; Waring arrived looking like a peddler with his wagonload of merchandise at the confluence of the Methow and Chewuch rivers. Here he thought he'd found the perfect spot to establish his trading post. In his pocket nestled $4,000 donated by friends in Boston. One estimate of the Methow Valley population when he arrived is 150 people, though Waring, always the optimist, estimated 350 people inhabited the area. Records show there was a permanent agricultural community sparsely scattered throughout the valley's 70-mile length, with concentrations near the mining centers.

Waring Meets the Methow

Waring moved to the Methow Valley in the fall of 1891. Out of necessity the family first lived in a tent which afforded little protection from chilly autumn weather. They had to eat directly from the stove to keep the food from freezing. Waring wasted no time in building a cabin which the family gratefully moved into by November. Next, Waring built his store. With four walls, a roof, but no floor and only a blanket over the door, his shop was neither cozy nor inviting. Waring's shopkeeper complained that during the first winter, temperatures in the store stayed below freezing!

The first store opened in January 1892 with $2,100 worth of merchandise purchased on credit. Customers soon began trickling in. Later that opening month, Waring wrote:

> ... business proceeds and I have not had a day without selling something. Some days only 10 cents worth of candy or a plug of tobacco ... but from now on, as people are getting out of their supplies, business will really be worth something.
>
> —Methow Trading Company Correspondence compiled in Rohn's *Guy Waring and the Methow Trading Company 1891-1936.*

Early in 1892 Waring became postmaster of Winthrop, at which time he moved the post office to his store.

Somehow the family survived that first hard Methow winter with its bitter cold temperatures and tons of snow. In March 1893, just when spring began to lift their spirits, Waring's home and store burned to the ground. The family stoically crowded into a tiny 16- by 20-foot log cabin. Since they lacked insurance and were in debt, Waring left the area to work in Michigan and to find more financial backing. What goods could be salvaged from the inferno Waring displayed in a 12- by 14-foot root cellar and placed under the management of Walter Frisbee, a nearby homesteader, and later Earl Johnson, who was a Waring employee for many years. Johnson tried to sell the $728 worth of undamaged merchandise left, plus run the Winthrop Post Office in the root cellar until Waring returned.

Center of Trade

Unfazed by poor luck, Waring returned to the Methow and hurled himself wholeheartedly into his goal of turning Winthrop into a center of trade. To make his store more accessible to settlers, Waring had a cable ferry built across the river. In 1895, he bought a saloon building for $40. After he purchased the town's hotel, Waring owned every building in Winthrop except the town hall.

Watching prospectors, miners, fur traders and homesteaders arriving in the Methow in the mid-1890s, Waring became convinced "The Forks" offered a great location for a thriving trading business. Back to Boston he went between February and April 1897 to enlist more financial support for his plans to develop Winthrop. Proof of Waring's persuasive powers came when his wealthy associates agreed to invest $17,500 in a

The Methow Trading Company in the town of Barron. Photo from the Okanogan County Historical Society collection.

newly formed corporation called the Methow Trading Company, whose purpose was to "exploit economic opportunities" in the valley. Stockholders elected Waring president of the company, and he made all decisions regarding use of corporate funds.

The heyday of the Methow Trading Company occurred during the years 1897-1915. Capital investment rose from $17,500 to $67,000, and the company greatly increased the services it provided. Opening a store in Twisp was the first step in expansion and a profitable one, as the store did very well in 1897 and was successful for several years thereafter.

Business at the Winthrop store soared due to the mid-1890s mining boom in the Slate Creek District. In 1899 a renewed mining frenzy prompted Waring to open another Methow Trading Company (MTC) outpost at a wild mountain mining community called Barron, located west of Hart's Pass at 5,000 feet. Soon afterward an MTC store and warehouse operated at Robinson, 22 miles above Winthrop and 13 miles east of Barron. This post never paid its way, but it served as a freight and transfer point where the road ended and supplies from wagons freighted from Winthrop could be packed on stock animals for the remainder of the arduous route up to the Barron mines. The long hand of the MTC reached all the way to Pateros where in 1903 Waring established yet another outlet.

Encouraged by the success of the Twisp store, Waring's company delved into a business venture almost guaranteed to succeed—that of a saloon. Moralist that he was, Waring preferred to have *no* bar in town. However, he was savvy enough to realize a competitor's establishment would *surely* be unsavory. With a righteous attitude like that, it is no surprise that Waring's Duck Brand Saloon, which opened for business in 1897, lost money during most of its 12-year history. By 1899, three different managers had thrown in the towel, probably because the bar's operating rules were so strict.

"What else did the Winthrop area need?" asked Waring. Quickly he came up with an answer—"a sawmill to supply the upper half of the valley." By September 1897, this mover had a sawmill producing 1,000 feet of lumber per hour. He erected the mill on a homestead site seven miles north of Winthrop along the Methow River. Neighboring farms being cleared conveniently supplied logs for the operation.

Government Restrictions

Because of its remoteness, the Methow Valley has always avoided strict government control. So when President Cleveland issued an executive order creating the Washington Forest Reserve which included all but the southernmost portion of the Methow Valley, locals, especially Waring, were livid. No matter the order allowed exclusion of land more valuable for agriculture or mining. This was an infringement of local rights, the populace shouted, and besides, there was little timber on the valley floor to protect.

Waring doggedly appealed the order until President McKinley kindly removed most of the Methow from the forest reserve. Already, though, the order had retarded settlement in the Winthrop area, grumbled Waring.

Controversy with the federal government over forest reserve lands delayed Waring's Winthrop townsite claims from his filing date in 1897 until 1901, when his lobbying finally paid off and title was granted. Right off the bat, Waring had realized land would be a worthwhile investment, hence one of the original purchases made by the MTC was Winthrop townsite property. Once the town lots were formed in 1902, they sold better than expected.

"More is better" seemed to be manager Waring's motto for his company's first seven years. He believed the MTC's manifest destiny was to span the entire length of the Methow Valley from the Columbia River to the Cascade crest.

By 1903 company expansion had confirmed Waring's vision. Investments included a store and headquarters at Pateros, branch stores in Winthrop, Twisp and Barron; a sawmill, a saloon and a ranch, plus townsite property and a water power system in Winthrop. It was the most prosperous year since incorporation. The Methow Trading Company had reached its zenith.

After the years of expansion, the MTC was forced to consolidate. First, the Robinson store closed, but it had really just been a transfer point. More serious to company coffers was the loss of receipts from the Barron store which failed in 1905 due to the depression of local mining activity. Like dominoes, the once profitable Twisp and Pateros stores both closed in 1910 at which time the MTC became solidly consolidated in Winthrop.

Guy Waring's Land 5 orchard near Winthrop. Photo courtesy Ken White.

The Apple Orchard Idea

What had extended the company's financial resources to the breaking point and forced consolidation was Waring's grandiose plans of an entirely different nature: He had dreamed of a magnificent apple orchard business near Winthrop.

Waring's apple orchard idea started innocently enough. First he planted 22 acres of winter apples on his 120-acre parcel called the L 5 Ranch. Purchased in 1904 for $1,000, the L 5 Ranch land was ditched, drained and cultivated so that its worth increased to $5,375. Winter apple trees had been planted on 75 acres by 1909, and by 1911 5,000 saplings grew on 100 acres of L 5 Ranch property.

To augment the orchard investment, Waring planted corn between the fruit trees. Never missing a beat, he next invested in a grist mill in Winthrop so the company could grind its own grain. The local media publicized the project to attract settlers.

Financial success of the company depended largely on apple production from 1911 on. Waring had traded merchandizing for orcharding. The good price received for the first batch of apples sold in Boston raised his hopes, but couldn't pay the costs of cultivation and harvesting of the crop.

One researcher believes Guy Waring's 12-year effort to grow apples bankrupted the empire he'd built. MTC reports appearing in 1910 seem to reinforce this theory. One said, "We have put so much money into the L 5 orchard that we find ourselves very greatly in need of ready cash. We have not declared a dividend in over four years." And in another statement, "As fast as money comes into the Methow Trading Company stores it has gone into improvements in the L 5 orchard, planting and cultivating and building it up." (Bruce Wilson. *Late Frontier*. Okanogan County Historical Society, 1990.)

What usually kills Methow orchards financially and physically is weather, and Guy's winter apples were no exception to this rule. Waring blamed lack of precipitation for the fact that his labors bore so little fruit.

> The climate underwent in 1915 an entire change and became a country averaging only five inches of rain and snow instead of fourteen inches, as it had been. This made irrigation necessary and that we could not obtain for the 100 acres of orchard which we had. Thus faded away a brilliant prospect as the drought lasted till last winter.
>
> —MTC correspondence compiled by Rohn in *Guy Waring and the Methow Trading Co*. This statement was made by Waring at a Harvard University Graduation Anniversary, May 27, 1932.

Back to the East Coast

Records of yearly precipitation kept at Twisp and Winthrop support Waring's analysis. Refusing to relinquish his dream, Guy kept his L 5 orchard up at a loss for many years. Later, he sold it at an auction for $1,300, despite the orchard's appraisal at $20,000. The new buyer defaulted in payments and in 1935 Guy Waring's field of dreams was let go for back taxes.

Meanwhile, a $40,000 loan taken out earlier to pay debts failed to save the MTC. Its stores had become unprofitable, real estate speculation had made little money, and the L 5 orchard had drained investments. A demoralized Waring lost control of the company. In 1917 he moved east to Milton, Massachusetts.

This sounds like a sad ending to Waring's superhuman efforts, but on reflection it seems Waring must have enjoyed great power and experienced great joy while attempting his projects, despite setbacks and failures. His own remembrance of Methow times substantiates this view.

> I had a hard but healthful life for most of the time spent on the frontier; but came away with

> pleasant memories of the climate; and with love
> for the beauty of the country.
> —*Ibid.*

This theme occurs again and again in Methow history. The hardships of living here are compensated for by the beauty of the land, and the chance to live in such a place.

Bibliography

Duffy, Barbara. Notes from Wenatchee Valley College Class on Methow Valley History. Winthrop, Washington.

———. "The Shafer Museum." *Okanogan County Heritage*, Spring 1983.

Roe, JoAnn. *The North Cascadians*. Madrona Publishers, Seattle, 1980.

Rohn, Thomas Jesse. *Guy Waring and the Methow Trading Company, 1891-1936*. University of Washington Master's Thesis, 1973.

Stevens, Anna Greene. "Life in the Okanogan." *Okanogan County Heritage*, September 1970.

Waring, Guy. Letter to Prof. Edmund Meany. *Okanogan County Heritage*, Spring 1978.

Wilson, Bruce. *The Late Frontier*. Okanogan County Historical Society, 1990.

. . .

OWEN WISTER AND HIS METHOW VISITS

Before writing his sensational novel, *The Virginian*, Owen Wister had come to Winthrop to visit his college friend, Guy Waring, both in 1892 and 1898. On his earlier trip he hunted mountain goats and bagged a trophy. Six years later he brought his bride and they spent their honeymoon charming and being charmed by the Methow Valley and its people.

Several years after Wister's Methow visits, his book, *The Virginian*, hit the stands. It was the nation's first true western novel and an instant coast-to-coast success. In 1902, its publication date, *The Virginian* became the best-selling book in the US. Before the end of that year, it had been reprinted 14 times. Gary Cooper starred in Paramount Pictures' film version of the book. Overnight, Wister became world famous.

Many people believe Wister gathered material for his famous novel during his honeymoon in the Methow. According to local legend, Milton Storey, long-time bartender at the Duck Brand Saloon, was a model for the main character in *The Virginian*. Storey did have a reputation as a fierce gunfighter. One famous tale about Storey started with a difference of opinion over a card game. When the other "fella" drew his gun, Storey leaped to the bar to grab his own gun. Without turning around, Storey shot over his shoulder, using the reflection in the mirror behind the bar to aim at his opponent. The two gunfighters' shots sounded as one. When the smoke cleared, Storey was minus two fingers on his pistol hand and his opponent was dead!

Wister spent 10 years in the West and his masterpiece was a composite of all the observations he made during that time. Still, much of what he saw and heard in the frontier town of Winthrop undoubtedly ended up in his book. He probably based the baby-switching episode in *The Virginian* on a real prank a couple of rascals pulled one night at a Methow Valley party. In Wister's version the hero of the novel takes revenge on his aloof sweetheart, who ignores him at a social gathering, by switching the blanket wraps of a dozen babies ensconced in a separate room from the party-goers. Arriving home, the parents were shocked when they unwrapped the wrong offspring!

Storekeeper/farmer C.R. (Dick) McLean and miner Pete Bryan pulled off this exact same stunt in the Methow, and in all likelihood Wister heard about their prank during his Winthrop visits.

Bibliography

Duffy, Barbara, and Wilson, Bruce. "When You Call Me That Smile." *Okanogan County Heritage*, June 1965.

Roe, JoAnn. *The North Cascadians.* Madrona Publishers, Seattle, 1980.

Wilson, Bruce. *The Late Frontier.* Okanogan County Historical Society, 1990.

Chapter 15

MAZAMA:
MORE THAN A SMALL TOWN

Mazama: It's the smallest town in the Methow Valley. In the year 2001 at the Mazama junction (downtown Mazama) there's a general store, two outfitter establishments and several nearby lodges. But it is more than just this little town. To locals, Mazama is an area that encompasses the entire upper end of the Methow Valley.

Tucked up against the high foothills of the North Cascades, minutes away from the Cascade crest, Mazama is the most pristine of Methow areas. The land is heavily timbered, the homes hidden in the trees. Hiking trails into the Pasayten Wilderness start here. Lost River, Goat Creek and a myriad of other clearwater creeks pour into the Methow River at Mazama.

The peaceful beauty of the area belies its recent tumultuous history. Early day settlement of this locale closely resembled that of other areas in the valley. Settlers cleared the forest and farmed the land. They built the Early Winters irrigation ditch to water their crops. They built schools and socialized with neighbors. But in the early 1970s the Aspen Corporation of Colorado announced plans to build a destination ski resort in Mazama, igniting a passionate struggle between pro- and anti-development groups. Though the players changed along with the development goals, the struggle continued into the new millenium.

Mazama Gets Mail

Mrs. Minnie Tingley established the first Mazama-area post office in her home in June 1900. Residents at the time called their settlement Goat Creek after the major creek that flows southward from Goat Peak. The government post office found both the name Goat Creek and Goat Peak unacceptable but local civic leader Guy Waring suggested what he believed to be the Greek word for mountain goat—Mazama. Despite the fact that "Mazama" is probably derived from an Aztec word meaning deer, everyone agreed to this name.

Methow Indians called the Mazama area "N'tat-goos" which a researcher interpreted to mean "picking service berries," but this name never apparently gained favor with white settlers.

Twice a week, the mail arrived at Minnie Tingley's home. In summer it came via hack and horse; in winter by horse-drawn sleigh. Minnie always offered a steaming bowl of soup to the faithful mail carriers, giving special care to those who stomped in extra miles on snowshoes. After a few years, Angus McLeod took over Minnie's job. For more than a decade he ran the post office in a commercial structure he built which housed a general store and rooms for rent.

A Sample of Mazama Settlers

Zora and Hazard Ballard

Because of its proximity to Hart's Pass, many miners settled in Mazama. Prime examples were well-known Slate Creek miner Hazard Ballard and his wife Zora who homesteaded in the Mazama area.

Hazard and his brother Charles came to Okanogan County in the late 1880s to find jobs surveying and packing. Zora arrived in the upper Methow in 1892 with her parents, Henry and Caroline Johnson. Zora and Hazard married in the early 1900s. At that time Hazard was packing for a survey party exploring mountain passes in search of a railroad route from Spokane to Bellingham. Spunky Zora accompanied her husband on his forays into the mountains. One time the pair rode horseback down the Skagit canyon to Marblemount. According to Zora, she was the first white woman to make the journey.

After Hazard discovered the Azurite claim on Mill Creek and bought some adjacent claims, the Ballards spent much of their time in the Hart's Pass area. Zora helped Hazard and his brother

Zora and Hazard Ballard, Mazama miners. Photo from the Okanogan County Historical Society.

build a horse trail to their mining claims and she scrambled up steep canyon walls to post location notices of the brothers' claims.

Early-day investors in the tourist industry, the Ballards purchased a hotel at Robinson, a way station on the road to the Hart's Pass mines. Hazard advertised his hotel in the Methow Valley News as a "sportsman's paradise" located on the "Slate Creek route."

Hazard and Zora moved from Robinson to Lost River in 1916 and stayed there for the rest of their lives. Hazard packed equipment and supplies for miners but also kept his hand in the tourist business by packing campers, hunters and fishermen into the high country. Never losing his zest for the mining life, Hazard discovered and developed the Gold Hill Mine over the ridge from the Azurite. He also owned and operated the Rockview Sawmill for a time.

In their older years, the Ballards became some of the Methow's first snowbirds, spending their winters in Arizona and their summers back at Lost River.

Zora chose to stay at Lost River after her husband died in 1938. She continued to operate the couple's pack train business with her brother Roma Johnson. Because of her community involvement, she never felt isolated at her remote home even when the flood of 1948 took out the road and bridges between Lost River and Mazama. Zora died in 1956. Both she and Hazard are buried in the Sullivan Cemetery in Winthrop. The present-day Lost River Resort is located on the Ballard property.

Alva Welch and the Rattlesnake House

The famous "Rattlesnake House" (later part of the Shafer ranch) was built by Alva Welch, a pioneer whose background was quite different from the Mazama miners. Originally an Iowa farmer, Alva got involved in the Seattle building trade. He became a master craftsman and his home with its siding, overhanging windows and fine woodwork testifies to his carpentry skills.

Noticing his talent, many of Alva's neighbors hired him to do woodworking projects. Since there was little cash on hand, Alva bartered his work for some service a neighbor could offer. Besides woodworking, Alva logged and raised about a dozen dairy cows to support his family. Once a week he went to Winthrop to sell cream either at the cheesemakers or the Okanogan Creamery.

The original Mazama road ran directly in front of Alva's house. The Welches crossed the road and climbed down a 100-foot embankment to fetch water from a spring and shallow well. The spring functioned as a refrigerator to keep their milk cool.

Born in 1912, Alva's son Gordon attended a one-room log school at Goat Wall. The long walk to school for Gordon turned miserable in early spring when the deep winter snow began to melt. He'd break through the crust and end up "post-holing" all the way home.

Gordon saw many Indians near his home when he was a child. Every year, late summer, 100 to 150 Indians migrated to Mazama. They'd camp near the confluence of Early Winters Creek and the Methow River (an area that is now part of the Early Winters campground). Gordon watched the women and children gather berries along the creek, while the men caught fish then smoked the catch on large log racks. The women made pemmican by mixing berries with fish.

Finally the Welches became discouraged by the difficulty of eking out a living in Mazama. In 1934 they decided to leave. They hoped to make enough money elsewhere to enable them to return to the area later. But disaster struck after the Welches left. Four feet of snow collapsed their barn roof, killing a horse. The family never returned to Mazama.

Mazama resident Grace Devin gave the Rattlesnake House its threatening name. One day many years ago, Grace went on a horseback ride with daughter Betsy, about 3 years old, and son Steve, about 7 at the time. Smokey Woods, a wrangler for packer Jack Wilson, accompanied them on the adventure. Passing by the Welch homestead the kids heard the chilling sound of a rattlesnake right next to the abandoned house. Without hesitation, Smokey hopped off his horse and boldly dispatched the snake with a rock. The Devins were astonished. "Our eyes popped out," said Grace. At that moment she named the Welches' place the Rattlesnake House, and it has been known as that ever since.

Jack Wilson: Mazama Packer and Modern Pioneer

Jack Wilson became a Methow Valley legend in his own time. A tough, trim, long-legged, craggy-faced man, he looked the spittin' image of a classic cowboy. Jack was a great horseman, packer, trapper, fisherman, wilderness adventurer and story-teller—a Methow-style Renaissance man. He taught himself everything he ever needed to know. When he wanted to learn some skill, he simply read up on it. Friends say Jack was not afraid of anything.

At the age of 8, Jack decided to strike out on his own. His formal education ended with the third grade. After leaving his family home in Edmonds, he jumped boxcars and rode the

The Alva Welch house still stands in Mazama, summer of 1999. Photo by Don Portman.

rails. A career in construction beckoned him before he came to the Methow Valley. He worked as a foreman both on construction of the Golden Gate Bridge and Grand Coulee Dam. Later, he served as rigger superintendent in the Kaiser Shipyards in Portland, Oregon.

On one big construction job, Jack was captivated by a fetching co-worker named Elsie. He told a friend she was the best-looking gal he'd ever seen and he was bound to marry her. Elsie found her rugged individualist suitor attractive too and soon agreed to be his bride.

While Jack worked on the Grand Coulee Dam project he'd sneak up to the Methow for visits. He fell in love with the place and in 1946 Jack and Elsie bought the Early Winters homestead, purchased a pack string and riding stock, and began building a resort.

First, Jack figured out how to build one cabin. Based on this learning experience, he then built the rest of the guest houses, barns and corrals, doing all his own carpentry and masonry. Soon his 100-acre homestead had turned into a working dude ranch and construction-expert Jack had also become an expert packer.

Jack began packing into the Pasayten Wilderness when it was still called the North Cascades Primitive Area. In those days, people considered this vast reserve lying north of the Methow Valley untamed country that needed to be civilized, according to Steve Devin, Mazama resident and Jack's good friend. Staffed guard stations existed in the backcountry, phone lines trailed through tree branches, and packers carried chain saws to cut out downed timber.

Jack never advertised his business. He didn't need to. Through word of mouth, patrons quickly discovered his competent packing service and the Wilsons' comfortable resort. Sometimes, Jack led groups of 20 or more people from the Wilderness Society into the backcountry. These big excursions forced Jack to borrow nearly every available horse in the valley.

Many famous people like Justice William O. Douglas, Edward R. Murrow, Governor Dan Evans and eight US Senators joined Jack on pack trips. Jack introduced the Haubs, future owners of Sun Mountain Lodge, to the wonders of the Methow backcountry. He did the same for Otto and Kay Wagner, owners of the Twisp lumber mill.

Jack developed a friendly relationship with all of his clients and they in turn became great fans of their infallible wilderness guide. "People loved going with him because he was such a mountain man," said Steve Devin. "He understood nature. People spent the whole day with Jack and they'd constantly be entertained by learning so much about wildlife and wilderness skills. Plus he was a very professional packer, very safety conscious. Everyone went single file on the trail. Jack meticulously planned every facet of the trip."

Jack and Elsie loved kids but couldn't have any of their own, so they invited boys to work for them in the summertime in exchange for room and board and outdoor education. "It was like an early-day Outward Bound," said Twisp dentist Bob Maves, who attended the Wilsons' unofficial youth camp. "The young men learned lots, worked hard, fished their hearts out."

Making fire without paper was one of the many survival skills Jack taught at his outdoor school. Once it was learned, Jack expected his disciples to flawlessly demonstrate the skill. Periodically, he'd put students on the spot by having a pop quiz in paperless combustion.

Steve Devin recalled being 13 years old when he worked for Jack on pack trips, scrubbing dishes, rowing guests in rubber rafts to fishing spots on Hidden Lakes and rounding up the horses for the day's ride. "Everything had to be perfectly done," said Devin. "He (Jack) had the longest crooked pointer finger in the world. If you did something wrong that long finger made a big impression!"

Kids found Jack hard to keep up with in more ways than one. He walked so fast he could cover four miles an hour in the woods! His upper body would lean forward and he'd take a 4-foot stride. All the boys had to trot to keep up with their lanky leader.

If packing was Jack's sociable side, trapping was his solitary self. And he appeared to enjoy and excel in the lonelier activity as much as he shined with a crowd of friends or tourists.

Jack began trapping three years after buying the upper Methow property. For the next 15 winters he snowshoed alone into the North Cascades, setting his traps and spending hundreds of nights at an old trapper's cabin at Lone Fir Campground. There was no North Cascades Highway then—no easy route out if he ran into trouble in this isolated, avalanche-prone area.

224

Jack was competent and confident and he possessed the stamina to withstand long days snowshoeing in the cold. He'd trudge in 10 miles to Lone Fir the first day, stay overnight, then the second day run the trapline to Washington Pass five miles away and a 1,500-foot gain in elevation. Next, he'd trap five miles up Cutthroat Creek and return to the cabin the third day. Early the following morning he began the long trek home. One day of rest at home would ready Jack for a repeat performance.

Jack Wilson with a well-known sparkle in his eyes. Photo by Josef Scaylea.

To snare weasels and martens, Jack hung horsemeat at the end of a limb inclined against a tree, then placed a trap just beyond the bait. He doused the whole thing with skunk oil scent which he insisted was irresistible to game.

Jack stocked the Lone Fir cabin during the fall hunting season. In a protected basement area, he covered his food with a mattress to prevent freezing. A fired-up wood stove kept the place comfortable even at minus 25 degrees.

But what Jack remembered best was not the toasty comfort of the little shelter, but the adventures he had during his wintertimes in the wilderness. Once it took him from 6 o'clock in the morning to 11 o'clock at night to reach home. Rain falling on top of 4 inches of new snow had created "Cascade cement" conditions. Jack figured his snowshoes weighed 30 pounds while carrying their heavy snow burden. When his snowshoes grew this heavy, he had to attach leather straps to the webbing so he could use his arm strength to help lift them out of the snow.

Despite the dangerous conditions prevailing in the high Cascades midwinter, Jack seldom felt afraid. A cougar followed him once. Another time his snowshoes got stuck in heavy snow right smack in the center of an avalanche chute at Washington Pass (Number 10 chute, it's now called), but these were only passing adrenaline rushes.

For Wilson winter was a time for quiet discovery. "Everything that moves in the wintertime leaves its sign in the snow," Jack said. "A black eagle dove after a rabbit one time. He left a perfect set of wing prints as he took off ... without the rabbit."

Despite the huge amount of time Jack spent walking, riding and snowshoeing, he somehow managed to do an incredible amount of reading. "He read everything he could get his hands on," recalled Steve Devin. A subscription to the *Wall Street Journal*, which he read religiously, kept Jack well informed. He loved debating current affairs and politics, his favorite topics of discussion. "He expressed an opinion on everything," claimed Steve.

Books and his own field observations taught Jack natural history. Friends say Jack knew the Latin and common name of every wildflower you'd ever see. His knowledge of wildlife was so great the state Game Department often sought his advice.

Jack was also a civic-minded man. He spearheaded a successful campaign to convince owners of priceless property around Pearrygin Lake to sell their land to the state for a state park. Due to Jack's lobbying, the Paul Heatons sold their beautiful 430-acre parcel to Olympia for a paltry $12,000. The estate became Pearrygin Lake State Park, one of the most popular recreational sites in Washington.

Jack served as president of the association promoting the North Cascades Highway, a development which more than anything else has made tourism a mainstay of the Methow Valley economy.

Mazama Landmarks

From the earliest times upper valley residents have wanted a center where they could meet and socialize. With this goal in mind, pioneers built the Rockview Community Hall in November 1915. To help defray costs of construction, they held a basket social and dance. Each basket of homemade goodies sold for $22, rather a hefty price for the times.

The Mazama Community Center where present residents share

Volunteers keep the Mazama Community Center, built in 1921, in fine shape. Photo by Don Portman

holiday meals, run meetings, offer classes and hold all sorts of special events, was originally built in 1921 as a school. Previously Mazama homesteaders donated cabins to serve as schools.

The Great Depression brought benefits to Mazama. The government located a CCC camp at Early Winters, building cabins at the site to house workers for the Works Progress Administration. The WPA hired fine craftsmen, who were otherwise unemployed during the Depression, to build the Early Winters Ranger Station in 1937. The buildings have a unique architectural style and are now included in the National Register of Historic Places. When completed the station became headquarters of the Pasayten District. So much Forest Service activity was going on in the area that Mazama needed a ranger district all its own.

Bibliography

Blonk, Hu. "For Ex-Trapper, Cascade Road's a Luxury." *The Wenatchee World.*

Devin, Doug. *Mazama: the Past 100 Years.* Peanut Butter Publishing, Seattle, 1997.

Devin, Steve. Phone Interview. Mazama, Washington, summer 1990.

Duffy, Barbara. "Zora Ballard and Anna Ballard." Okanogan County Heritage, March 1999.

Hart, Richard. Letter to George Turner regarding Mazama's name. July 1999.

Maves, Robert. Phone Interview. Winthrop, Washington, summer 1990.

"Pearrygin Land Sold." *Okanogan County Heritage.* Scrapbook Entry, Spring 1990.

Wagner, Kathryn. Interview. Twisp, Washington, summer 1990.

Chapter 16

MAZAMA SKI WARS

For more than 25 years, opponents fought for and against a downhill ski area in Mazama. Battles raged in boardrooms, at public meetings, in county commissioners' offices and in federal courtrooms.

The ski area controversy resembled a tennis match: Developers proposed a resort plan, environmentalists objected to the proposal; developers made another proposal, environmentalists objected, and on and on. One development team would give up and leave the fray but a new group always arrived with new plans and new investors. Though the environmental team remained the same throughout, new members joined in to inject fresh energy and environmental zeal. For so long it seemed the ski wars would never end. Then in December 1999, everything changed.

Following is an abbreviated account of the Mazama ski wars. Many details of this complicated controversy have been left out. But I hope the reader can get a sense of how this issue divided the Methow and held the community in its powerful grip for so long.

The Prequel

Jack Wilson, owner of Early Winters, a small Mazama resort, thought he'd like some winter income to supplement his successful summer business. He scoped out the hill behind his cabins on Early Winters Creek and decided it would provide a nice little ski run for his resort guests. After sharing his brainstorm with Doug

Devin, a neighbor with experience in the ski business, Jack had second thoughts about the project.

Devin felt Jack's hill, only 100 feet high, just didn't cut it. The two pored over maps and soon hit pay dirt. For just around the corner from Jack's little hill, they identified a north-facing snow-hugging slope with 4,000 feet of vertical rise. The mountain's name was Sandy Butte.

Devin researched Sandy Butte's potential as a downhill ski area. He looked at snow depths, temperatures, and weather conditions. He found out that over 1,000 acres of private property at the base of the mountain might be for sale. To help finance the ski hill, developers would need to purchase this property for guest accommodations and real estate sales.

Devin's research convinced him that Sandy Butte could make a great ski hill. Along with some community leaders and ski industry people, he formed the Methow Valley Winter Sports Council. In early spring of 1968, the group took various measurements of the mountain and confirmed Devin's positive assessment. At about the same time, Dorothy Shafer asked Devin if he wanted to buy her ranch at the base of Sandy Butte. Devin enlisted a group of Crystal Mountain, Washington, investors willing to "bank" the land for the time being, then sell the property later to developers.

At the end of 1969, the Winter Sports Council met with the Forest Service to explain their plans. The Forest Service agreed that Sandy Butte had potential as a ski area.

In 1972, the North Cascades Highway opened. Before that time, the Methow had been a dead-end valley with Mazama at the end. Now it was just the beginning—the first stop for tourists coming from the west who had visited the North Cascades National Park. Many people of Washington state had never heard of the Methow Valley much less Mazama. But once the highway opened, and word got out of a possible ski hill development, the area became famous.

Aspen Knocks at Mazama's Door

In the early '70s the Colorado-based Aspen Ski Corporation came to Mazama. The ski business was growing, resorts were booming and Aspen thought the time for expansion had arrived. Of 300 potential sites for ski area development, Sandy Butte caught Aspen's eye. Twenty-nine-year-old Jerry Blann of

Aspen's planning department contacted Doug Devin, checked out the mountain, and decided it was one of the best projects he'd seen. Aspen put Blann in charge of the project. He moved to Mazama, hired a cadre of consultants and began environmental and technical assessments of the area.

In 1974 Aspen bought options on 1,200 acres at the base of Sandy Butte for a resort.

When the press began publicizing Aspen's intentions,

Doug Devin and dog Scooter.
Photo courtesy Grace Devin.

a major land rush began in Mazama. Savvy investors, aware of the prices paid for real estate near ski resorts, purchased property in the upper valley. Many buyers came from Aspen, Colorado.

Birth of the MVCC

While Jerry Blann measured Sandy Butte for its possible ski-hill attributes, Maggie Coon, a person with a very different frame of reference from Blann's, was also doing research in the valley. Maggie came to the Methow to assist the Forest Service in preparing a planning report. The valley charmed her and she decided to stay.

She met Vicky Welch, local goat rancher, who shared Maggie's environmental philosophy. Maggie, Vicky and others concerned about future development in the valley formed the Methow Valley Citizens Council (MVCC) in 1974.

According to one member, Isabelle Spohn:

> The MVCC was a coalition of young environmen-
> talists who were loath to give up their newly found
> haven and were concerned about the impacts of a
> large resort in the Methow and long-time residents
> who felt threatened and offended by plans for a large
> resort in their valley.
>
> —*Isabelle Spohn Report, 1998*

Isabelle, herself, was one of the newcomers who feared losing what she'd found in the Methow. She recalled:

> Shortly after moving to Mazama in the late '70s, my
> enchantment with the isolated beauty of the upper
> Methow was disrupted with the realization that a
> huge ski development was planned right outside my
> picture window.
>
> —*Ibid.*

Like many baby boomers, Isabelle had seen a lovely place where she'd once lived turn overnight into a packed suburb. Isabelle's feelings were echoed by many others moving into the valley. They had left a hectic life in a big city or a monotonous suburban existence. The peace and beauty of the Methow brought the hope of a lifestyle they could love and respect.

Isabelle felt it was psychologically better to "do" something about the proposed resort rather than simply complain. She related:

> My first contact with MVCC was in attending a
> hearing on the proposed county zoning ordinance in
> the late '70s. I was struck both by the eloquence of
> Beulah LaMotte, lifelong resident, spokeswoman for
> MVCC, and president, and by the verbal attacks
> against environmentalists. Although I had never
> taken part in any political or environmental action
> before, I resolved to become a part of the MVCC.
>
> —*Ibid.*

The MVCC wanted to prevent the impacts that a large ski development would have on the Methow. The proposal conjured up a picture of the Methow subdivided into small lots. MVCC members worried that wildlife habitat would be lost with development, that the Methow's pure air and water could become polluted. They feared land speculation would raise taxes and encourage farmers to sell off their land, fostering residential sprawl. MVCC members saw the Methow as perfect just the way it was, while the developers saw a ski resort as a dazzling jewel which could only enhance the Methow's natural beauty.

Aspen Leaves for Greener Pastures

Federal legislation soon interfered with Aspen's plans. Though the bottom half of Sandy Butte had been logged, the top third was an unroaded area, hence a candidate for wilderness designation. Until Congress passed the Washington Wilderness Bill (which didn't happen until 1984), ski area plans could not go forward.

In 1977, Aspen dropped the ski project, citing economic factors, opposition by environmentalists and government delays. Instead, Aspen headed to British Columbia, Canada, where they developed Blackcomb Mountain ski area next to Whistler Resort. When Aspen left, local Sandy Butte supporters were disheartened but nowhere near ready to give up their goal.

Methow Recreation Inc. and
Hosey Engineering Combine Forces

After Aspen left, Doug Devin formed Methow Recreation Inc. (MRI) and applied for a Forest Service permit to build the ski area. The Forest Service launched an environmental impact statement using data supplied by MRI.

In 1983, MRI felt they needed help and a partner. They found Harry Hosey of Hosey Engineering. MRI needed the financial and permitting expertise of Hosey's group to expedite what was now called the Early Winters project. Hosey's group vigorously entered the proceedings. Hosey's relatives provided a loan to help pay Aspen for 1,200 acres at the base of Sandy Butte. The Hosey family then spent thousands for consultants and attorneys.

The US Congress passed the Washington Wilderness Bill of 1984, which meant the Forest Service could proceed with the permitting process for skiing on Sandy Butte. Later that year, the Forest Service published its Final Environmental Impact Statement (EIS) on Early Winters along with its decision to issue a permit for the ski hill. Although developers rejoiced, MVCC appealed the EIS and permit.

MVCC Focuses on Environmental Impacts

Facing their new adversaries in the ski hill controversy (MRI and the Hosey group), MVCC members got to work. They divided up the issues, then gained expertise on these issues by communicating with government agencies, attorneys and scientific experts, plus researching scientific reports. An example of the type of involvement necessary on these issues was related by Isabelle Spohn, who became concerned about possible air-quality deterioration resulting from resort development. Neither MVCC nor the state and federal agencies in charge had adequately addressed this issue. Isabelle explained her concerns:

> Having moved to the Methow partially because of my interest in nature photography, I also could not help but notice what happened to smoke in the Mazama area during the winter. Ellis Peters' place was right across the field from my window, and each morning the smoke traveled a couple of feet above his chimney, settled down around the house and the surrounding acreage and stayed there for hours until the morning inversion had lifted. In addition, I noticed an increasing haze over Winthrop during the years I traveled from Mazama into town. I wondered what several thousand wood stoves or fireplaces in the proposed ski resort could do to the air in Mazama during those winter inversions.
>
> —*Ibid.*

Isabelle became a volunteer air-quality expert for MVCC. Her research turned up some glaring omissions. Isabelle recalled:

> After reviewing the Draft Early Winters Alpine Winter Sports Study (DEIS), I was left with the impression that air-quality deterioration due to resort development was not taken seriously. After calling the Washington Department of Ecology, I discovered that the federal Environmental Protection Agency was the agency with jurisdiction in this matter, and I developed a correspondence with them in an attempt to understand the complicated regulations. In addition, I discovered that the DEIS on Early Winters had never reached the desks of the air-quality personnel in either the DOE or EPA. This began the development of what was to be a winning point for MVCC's lawsuit on this EIS, the adequacy of the air-quality analysis and its impact upon the Pasayten Wilderness, which eventually progressed to the Ninth Circuit Court of Appeals and US Supreme Court.
>
> —*Ibid.*

The Worst of Times

Mazama became big news in the 1980s. Major newspapers throughout the state plus TV stations from Spokane and Seattle carried stories about the proposed resort, the controversy surrounding the proposal and the community clashes the proposal caused. The press focused on the divisions within the community; in the Methow, it seemed, everyone was taking sides on the issue.

During the early 1980s a group called Mazama Neighbors for the Early Winters Ski Hill came into being. The group supported development and actively promoted their cause with "Ski Early Winters" bumper stickers, advertisements, press releases and public meetings. But things turned bad after a compromise could not be reached regarding resort size at a meeting between MVCC lawyers and the Hosey group. An anti-MVCC campaign sprang up. Some local businesses displayed MVCC buster signs in their windows and, behind their store counters, kept "hit lists" of MVCC members they planned not to serve. These actions only deepened distrust and heightened tension between the two groups. Living in the Methow at the time, one could not help but be disheartened by the political climate.

Courtroom Drama

MVCC, the Sierra Club and the Washington Environmental Council in December 1985 brought suit against the Forest Service for the inadequacy of the Early Winters EIS and for issuing a special use permit for skiing at Sandy Butte. The US District Court dismissed the appeal in 1986, but in 1987 the US Ninth Circuit Court of Appeals reversed the decision, ruling the EIS inadequate. Finally the case came before the US Supreme Court in 1989. Representing MVCC and the other groups, David Bricklin argued against a large ski resort at Early Winters. The high court left intact part of the ruling determining the EIS was inadequate which meant a supplemental EIS had to be done.

Isabelle Spohn.
Photo by Albert F. Spohn.

Under the Equal Access to Justice Act, litigants can recover legal costs if they prevail against a government agency. Since the federal magistrate awarded MVCC more than $260,000 in legal fees and expenses, the environmental group claimed victory.

MVCC Gains Allies

Several events outside the courtroom also encouraged the environmental side. Newspapers in the late '80s prompted sympathy for MVCC when they reported the proposed resort would have 4,000 units accommodating up to 12,000 guests at build-out. To many people, the vision of 12,000 visitors packed into Mazama was mind-boggling since the entire population of the Methow Valley totaled only 3,500.

A group called Friends of the Methow (FOM) formed about this time to bolster the environmental cause. Some FOM members owned land in the Methow, some lived elsewhere, but all cared a great deal about controlling growth in the area.

One prominent member was Maggie Coon, a founding member of the MVCC and homeowner in the Methow, who had taken a job with the Nature Conservancy in Seattle.

Also at the end of the '80s, the designation of Sandy Butte as a possible habitat for the endangered spotted owl halted all development activities on the mountain until the issue could be settled.

Hosey Steps Down, Merrill Steps In

In the late 1980s, the Early Winters Resort partnership gained an influential ally. Mary Ferguson, President of R.D. Merrill, a wealthy timber family firm, was impressed by the development plans and she convinced R.D. Merrill to invest $300,000 in the project and guarantee a loan for $4 million.

As it turned out though, some of the Merrill windfall was spent frivolously. Harry Hosey, manager of the resort project, began a spending spree; he bought expensive furniture, took trips paid for out of the partnership's pocket and moved to a fancy new office.

Finally the Hosey group went totally broke. In August 1992, it lost the entire project (stock, land and plans) through foreclosure to its lender, R.D. Merrill. For $800,000 (plus the $4 million loan they'd guaranteed), Merrill bought all of the Early Winters' project's assets. Theirs was the only bid at the Okanogan County Courthouse foreclosure sale on February 3, 1992. Merrill got the

land held by the Early
Winters' partnership
and a Piston Bully
snowcat. The rest of the
investors came out
empty-handed.

**A Memorandum of
Understanding**

Merrill now led the
troops for Mazama de-
velopment. Hoping to
end the ski wars, Merrill
representatives met
face-to-face with a
cross section of valley
people to hear what the
community wanted to
see happen at Early
Winters.

*Maggie Coon, left, and Vicky Welch. Photo
by Richard Murray, from the 1980s.*

Ron Judd, part-time Methow resident, professional negotiator
for the AFL-CIO, and president of Friends of the Methow
(FOM), saw the opportunity here to end the seemingly endless
controversy over a ski hill through compromise. He approached
R.D. Merrill and set up meetings between Merrill and their
partners, Lowe Development Resorts, and the MVCC board of
directors.

In September 1993, MVCC/FOM and Merrill/Lowe signed a
Memorandum of Understanding (MOU) which would allow the
Wilson Ranch Planned Development to proceed. This relatively
small development (located in the area of Jack Wilson's original
resort) was to serve as a sample of the type of larger development Merrill intended to pursue. Plans for further development
would wait until the public had had a chance to size up the Wilson Ranch.

In the MOU reached among the groups, Merrill agreed to 10
provisions. Most gratifying to those who had fought so long
against a downhill ski resort was the developer's promise to
abandon forever the use of property for lift-served skiing on
Sandy Butte. In addition, Merrill granted MVCC/FOM the right
of first opportunity to purchase the property should the corpora-

tion choose not to develop it. Merrill agreed to certain mitigating measures for air quality and for mule deer migration corridors and consented to replace the name of Early Winters with another name. The project received the new name Arrowleaf which came from arrowleaf balsamroot, the wild sunflower that grows in abundance during the Methow springtime. In return, along with several other concessions, environmentalists agreed not to challenge the Wilson Ranch planned development. However, the MOU stipulated, "This agreement shall not affect the right of FOM or MVCC to challenge any aspect of a proposed planned destination resort."

A member of the Merrill family, Charlie Wright, came to the Methow to lead the development team. After Wright arrived, Merrill dove into the Wilson Ranch development, opening the elegant Freestone Inn in 1996 with 12 guest rooms and a dining room. In front of the lodge builders created a lake from an old gravel quarry. The Early Winters cabins (originally owned by Jack Wilson) had been refurbished earlier.

Meanwhile Merrill's plans for development had expanded and a new MOU became necessary to address these changes. As the number of units Merrill proposed for the larger resort development crept upward, MVCC board members became increasingly uncomfortable. By February 1995, MVCC had agreed to 689 units, if in turn, Merrill complied with certain performance standards the groups agreed upon. Merrill also promised to reserve a percentage of real estate sales as matching funds for an environmental center. MVCC was prepared to sign an updated MOU, but before all items could be agreed upon, Merrill and Okanogan County released the Draft Environmental Impact Statement (DEIS) in December 1995. A second MOU was not signed.

DEIS Reveals Impacts

Merrill's detailed plans for Arrowleaf as spelled out in the DEIS called for the following features: 690 dwelling units; 239 wood-burning stoves; an 18-hole golf course and a club house; a tennis center; equestrian center; heliport; shopping center; restaurants and convention center; and a sewage treatment plant. To a prospective tourist, the resort proposal probably sounded ideal. But for many MVCC members, the plan was a rude awakening.

Merrill's DEIS brought to light certain environmental impacts which some MVCC general members had not considered before and could not accept now. Other members felt the DEIS document itself was flawed. They pointed out that the DEIS ignored significant impacts of the development and left out certain mitigation measures such as that for deer migration. In addition, various government wildlife and fisheries scientists submitted strong negative comments about both the DEIS and the proposed project.

Specifically, MVCC wanted a reduction of units from 690 to 250 (which would be the legal number of lots allowed if the property were to be subdivided). Members pointed out that the units could be clustered more to provide open space, wildlife habitat and a deer migration corridor. They objected to the estimated 2 million gallons of water per day required by the golf course. They objected to the chemical fertilizers and pesticides the golf course would require.

Despite disappointments on both sides of the issue, neither

The Freestone Inn. Photo by Bob Spiwak.

group had given up on negotiations. In May 1996 after hearings on the Draft EIS had ended, MVCC president Jim Doran wrote Charlie Wright encouraging renewed negotiations:

> There is a danger of a much stronger resistance to your plans emerging from within our group if the vacuum from our broken-off negotiations persists. I am personally committed to bringing the MOU back into focus and hopefully completion. We have all put too many months' energy into it to let it die.

Charlie Wright for his part had hoped MVCC would agree on substantive issues and promote the project as an environmentally sensitive resort development. However, MVCC felt this type of support coming from their camp wouldn't be possible at this stage.

Meanwhile, Merrill wanted to launch Phase 1 of the Arrowleaf Resort which consisted of the golf course, 20 townhouses, a restaurant and a meeting facility. State law would not allow a final EIS on only one phase of a development so Merrill released the entire EIS which included all phases of the resort.

Release of the Final EIS in May 1996 took MVCC by surprise; negotiations between environmentalists and Merrill had not ended. Also MVCC still had concerns about the adequacy of mitigation measures and Arrowleaf's plans for future phases of the resort. With legal deadlines looming, MVCC had to decide to appeal the Final EIS or lose its right to future challenges of environmental issues. Without any finalized agreement with Merrill forthcoming, MVCC leaders decided their only option at that time was to appeal.

In December 1997, Superior Court Judge Carol Wardell found the EIS inadequate in areas of water quantity and water quality, in particular the effects of the golf course chemicals on water quality. The judge required Okanogan County (which had approved Arrowleaf's EIS in 1996) to provide additional information regarding available water and pesticide management for the golf course. The county approved an addendum to the EIS in 1998.

OWL Challenges Water Rights

Meanwhile the Okanogan Wilderness League (OWL) along with the Sierra Club Legal Defense Fund had challenged water rights for both the Wilson Ranch phase of Arrowleaf already completed and the larger resort still in the planning stage. OWL

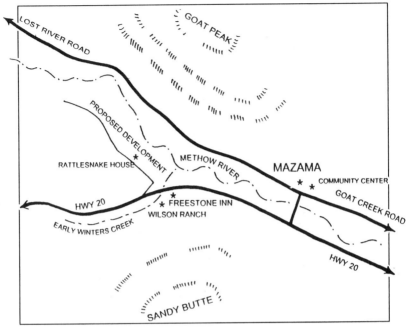

Mazama area and proposed Arrowleaf Development.

challenged Merrill's conversion of old agricultural water rights
from ranches in the area to year-round domestic use for the resort and golf course. They argued that the state Department of
Ecology couldn't allow this conversion if it harmed existing water
rights including a certain volume of water (instream flow) required in the river for endangered salmon.

Strengthening OWL's position, the state Department of Ecology disputed some of Arrowleaf's key water rights in an October 1999 report. The DOE concluded that several groundwater
rights could not be changed from agricultural use to resort use.
They also found that two other water rights associated with the
1,200-acre project had not been "beneficially" used since 1977
and had therefore been relinquished. According to state law a
water right can be lost if it has not been used for a certain
amount of time. Stunned by the report, developers said they
would vigorously appeal the DOE's interpretation of the law.

Merrill Drops Resort Plans
To the astonishment of Methow residents, R.D. Merrill an-

nounced on December 7, 1999, that the company would abandon its $20-million seven-year effort to build the Arrowleaf Resort complex.

Why at this point did Merrill scrap its plans? The company blamed water issues, specifically state Department of Ecology delays in issuing a decision on water rights for the resort. The DOE warned it could take up to a year to make a final decision on water rights critical to Arrowleaf's further development. A year was too long to wait according to CEO Charlie Wright.

The DOE defended its delay. The department couldn't favor Arrowleaf over the 40 other Mazama water rights applications that were ahead of the resort's. The DOE also insisted that an agreement between county, state and federal agencies on local water rights and endangered fish must be in place before the DOE could process applications in the Methow Valley.

In December 1999, the future of the Arrowleaf land was in limbo. The land had been legally divided into 50 twenty-acre parcels. A buyer could subdivide a 20-acre piece into 5-acre lots. But the division into tiny parcels wasn't necessarily the land's fate.

Charlie Wright informed the Methow Valley Citizens Council and Friends of the Methow that his company would recognize the environmental groups' right of first opportunity to find a buyer for the 1,200-acre site.

The environmental groups' right to buy the land in the event Merrill cancelled development plans had been part of the Memorandum of Understanding between Merrill and MVCC/FOM. The agreement gave environmentalists 60 days to find buyers for the property and 90 days after that to seal the deal.

Soon after Merrill's announcement, MVCC and FOM asked the Northwest office of the Trust for Public Land to arrange for a conservation purchase of the property. Craig Lee, director of the Trust's Seattle office, and Charlie Wright met to discuss the potential purchase. The 60-day deadline passed with little fanfare. Rumors abounded but no sale had been finalized.

Resort Site Preserved
A year passed and uncertainty still remained. Then early in January 2001, the announcement came: the Trust for Public Land had bought the Arrowleaf property for $15.165 million.

TPL financed the deal by selling several parcels of the land and borrowing the balance from the environmental community.

While the Trust had divided the property into five saleable parcels ranging from 143 to 232 acres, only three acres of each parcel could be developed for a home site, leaving the rest in open space. Conservation easements would preserve 99 percent of the land for wildlife habitat and public trails. Bicyclists, skiers, hikers and equestrians would be welcomed on Jacks Trail, while River Run Trail (in a riparian area) would be limited to skier and hiker use.

Charlie Wright said his company would continue to own and manage the Freestone Inn, nearby cabins and other facilities at the Wilson Ranch development. Wright's family kept an 80-acre piece of land with four home sites on the Arrowleaf property.

Nearly 30 years after they began, the ski wars ended. Mazama would not host a downhill resort serving 8,000 to 10,000 skiers per day, nor a resort of 650 housing units, a retail village and golf course; nor would the 1,200 acres so long a source of contention be sold in 20-acre parcels or 5-acre lots. After 30 years of controversy, all of the land, except for a very small percentage, would be preserved.

Gleaning the Good: The Methow Conservancy

Despite the enduring animosity between environmentalists and developers, the controversy over land use in Mazama has had many positive results. A noteworthy example is the Methow Conservancy. Formed in 1996 as a non-profit land trust, the Conservancy resulted from the merger of two entities—the Methow Land Trust and the Methow Valley Environmental Center. The Merrill Corporation, which had originally supported the Environmental Center during negotiations with MVCC, helped fund the new organization by providing a low-interest "seed-money" loan in 1997. The "seed money" has allowed the Conservancy to hire staff and develop programs.

Dedicated to land conservation and stewardship of the Methow Valley's natural, historic and scenic resources, the Methow Conservancy can already claim many accomplishments. The state of Washington Interagency Committee for Outdoor Recreation awarded them a $500,000 grant to purchase conservation easements on property adjacent to wetlands and streams in order to protect open space. The Conservancy has also worked on conservation easements with many private landowners. Ranging from large ranches to riparian river bottom to Mazama commercial properties, the group has arranged for the protection of several thousand acres in the valley.

In addition to conserving the Methow landscape, the Conservancy wishes to foster a strong sense of community. With this goal in mind, the group continually sponsors lectures on the valley's natural history and has held workshops on irrigation efficiency. The organization produced a "Good Neighbor Handbook," a guide to living lightly in the Methow. Members have organized a successful scrap metal drive and joined in a hands-on wildlife and ecology education program for fifth through seventh graders. It's become the lead organization in the Small Diameter Wood Initiative, a Forest Service community-building grant to promote a sustainable forestry industry.

Developers, environmentalists and all the rest of us want to preserve the resources that make the Methow Valley a wonderful place to live. The Methow Conservancy has taken on the challenge to protect the Methow's resources that all of us treasure.

Bibliography

Devin, Doug. *Mazama: the Past 100 Years.* Peanut Butter Publishing, Seattle, 1997.

Hicks, Lee. "Arrowleaf wins County Approval." Methow Valley News, August 22, 1996.

_____. "Arrowleaf Judge to Leave Bench." Methow Valley News, November 20, 1997.

_____. "Arrowleaf Resort Has New Management Structure." Methow Valley News, June 10, 1999.

_____. "Resort Water Rights Disputed by Ecology." Methow Valley News, October 28, 1999.

_____. "Merrill puts an end to Arrowleaf proposal." Methow Valley News, December 9, 1999.

_____. "Arrowleaf demise raises many questions." Methow Valley News, December 16, 1999.

_____. "Trust for Public Lands to attempt Arrowleaf purchase." Methow Valley News, December 30, 1999.

_____. "Arrowleaf Site Sells." Methow Valley News, January 3, 2001.

Mehaffey, K.C. "Arrowleaf Resort Gets Second Go-ahead." The Wenatchee World, July 13, 1999.

_____. "Arrowleaf Plans Scrapped." The Wenatchee World, December 8, 1999.

_____. "Methow Land Buy is Final." The Wenatchee World, January 9, 2001.

Methow Conservancy staff. "The Methow Conservancy: Fostering land and community stewardship," 1999.

Spohn, Isabelle. Personal research. Twisp, Washington, 1998 and 1999.

The Valley Voice, News from the Methow Valley Citizens Council. Fall 1996.

_____. Spring 1997.

_____. Summer 1997.

Chapter 17

CATTLE RANCHING IN THE
LAND OF PLENTY

Until the mid-1910s the Methow Valley was a land of plenty, blessed by an abundance of rain and snow. Early ranchers raised cattle on rich pastureland they neither planted nor irrigated. Stock feed was free, there for the taking—an untapped gold mine far more valuable and accessible than the illusive gold buried deep in the surrounding mountains.

Pioneer Alice Rader believed the Methow offered ideal moisture conditions for cattle ranching in the early days. Her family homesteaded in the Carlton area beginning in 1888, and for the next eight years the Rader ranch was well endowed with water. Here is Alice's description of the early days when precipitation made stock grazing easy in the Methow.

> At first there were no irrigation ditches and
> farming depended on the natural supply of water
> which was more plentiful in those days. There was
> always 5 to 6 feet of snow every winter. The
> streams filled with water every spring as well as
> there being many natural springs. Cattle grazed on
> bunch grass that grew 3 feet high in those days.
> This was later cut for winter hay as well.
> —*Okanogan County Heritage*, Winter 1975-76.

The Methow was cow heaven; its rich grasses attracted ranchers like a magnet. Word spread of the plentiful rangeland found here, and soon homesteaders appropriated nearly every section of bare ground in the valley and eventually in the dry rolling hills above.

When drought came, the honeymoon ended for most of the hill farmers. Without precipitation they starved out. Their choice was to move to town nearer to the river, or leave the Methow. It took 10 to 15 years for drought to chase the farmers out of the high, dry hills. They knew the weather pattern would change, and they kept hoping it would be sooner, not later.

The ranchers who had sunk roots in safer ground near dependable water sources stayed and made it through the hard times. When weather conditions raised the specter of disaster, Yankee ingenuity literally saved their "hides." The Thurlow family fell into this category. They arrived here first and refused to be ousted when times got tough. They encountered obstacles and suffered setbacks but overcame them all.

Home on the Range With Mason Thurlow

Much of the Thurlows' success was due to their basic nature, or the nature of cattle ranchers in general. Lucille Thurlow summed up the positive attitude that kept the family going through tough times:

> Cattlemen above all others, I think, have faith.
> They say, "This year is not too good, in fact,
> things are pretty bad, but next year will be better."
> They have the faith of Job.
> —*Methow Valley News*, Souvenir Issue, Summer 1977.

The Thurlows had arrived in the Methow in 1887 when only fur trappers and prospectors roamed the valley. Frank Thurlow, Mason Thurlow's son, said those were rather wild days, the earliest inhabitants being "tough old hounds" and adventuresome. "Some people carried a Bible in one hand and a six-shooter in the other," said Frank.

Mason Thurlow and his family ran the first cattle ranch in the Methow. They began with 35 head of stock in 1888, setting them out to graze on the lush fields of their 160-acre homestead above Beaver Creek. At first things went smoothly. Winters were mild and the cattle could graze even in the coldest months of the year. However, these halcyon times were short-lived. A killer winter smashed into the Methow Valley in 1889-90. Snow buried the grass so deep the cattle couldn't get down to it, and few ranchers had stored enough hay to see their stock

*Hay derrick used to hoist and stack hay in the early 1900s. A massive
haystack protected the crop from bad weather. Photo from the Okanogan County Historical Society.*

through the stormy season. Thurlow herded his cattle to the
south slopes of nearby hills where he shoveled snow by hand,
uncovering wild hay to feed the hungry animals. Later, he
cooked grain, then doled it out to the starving beasts from his
saddle horse. Many died, despite Mason's efforts.

The cruel winter wiped out nearly the entire cattle population
in the Methow Valley. When the worst had passed, the ranchers took what was left and began to rebuild their herds. But
they'd learned a lesson. To prevent future stock losses, the
ranchers started to store hay.

Though Mason had arrived when moisture was still abundant
in the valley, he'd had the foresight to obtain water rights on
Beaver Creek. He dug an irrigation ditch by hitching a heavy
log behind his horse and pulling the log behind him. Next, he
rode to Ellensburg to buy 20 pounds of alfalfa seed—the first
alfalfa to be planted in the Methow Valley.

Thurlow also introduced the first plow to the valley, lugging
it by wagon up the arduous Chiliwhist Trail from Malott. With
this smart new piece of technology, he broke up five acres of
land and hand sowed it to alfalfa. No harrow being available to
cover the seed, Mason invented a device to do it. Lashing willow brush together, he created a sheaf which he then dragged

back and forth across the plowed land, nicely covering the seed.

Once the alfalfa grew thick and tall, haying became a huge event at the Thurlow Ranch. All the men in the area gathered at the homestead to help. Using only manpower and horse-power, they cut, raked and piled up all the hay. Hired men earned $2 per day for 10 hours of work, not extravagant pay. As a fringe benefit, however, the workers received room and board and the meals were reputedly sumptuous and scrump-tious. Women spent entire days in the kitchen cooking huge feasts for the crews and washing dishes afterwards.

Ever since Mason Thurlow sowed those first fateful seeds, alfalfa raising has been an integral part of cattle raising in the Methow. Easy to grow, prolific, and rich in nourishment, this legume has spelled success for valley cattle ranchers. And even for locals who don't raise stock, the fields upon fields of sweet-smelling alfalfa are always a welcome and comforting sight.

The US Forest Service Serves the Ranchers

When the US Forest Service became established in the Methow, it offered ranchers summer range rights on public lands to augment stock range available in the valley. In the early '20s, for example, 2,000 head of cattle grazed on the Cub Creek range each summer. Thurlow ran his cattle on deeded and Forest Service range in the Alder Creek and Booth Canyon areas around Mount McClure south of Twisp. Other government ranges were in the Wolf Creek area, Little Bridge Creek, Eightmile Creek and parts of the upper Twisp River.

Once stock migrated to distant grazing grounds, cattle driving became a Methow occupation. Ross Filer recalled his cattle-driving days in the upper Twisp River area with the gusto of a man born to be a cowboy.

> We put hundreds of cattle up on the range. We camped up there on the range all summer. We had Canyon Creek, Lime Creek, North Creek, War Creek and the Twisp River.
>
> At first the cattle are wild, you fight them all the way. The second year you don't have to fight them. The third year they practically go by them-selves.
>
> Riding herd, driving those cattle, doing that, was my pleasure. That was my heaven. You got hot and you got cold and you worked hard. But it

was still the easiest work in the world.
—*Methow Valley News*, April 14, 1977.
In the Methow Valley real cowboys rode home on the range. They lived rough and tough lives and they loved it!

Getting the Goods to Market

Some people feel the Methow's remoteness is its greatest attribute. But this seclusion can be a hindrance when one's goal is getting goods to the marketplace. What made cattle raising a reasonable proposition in a place so hampered by transport problems was that the produce could move itself to the market ... almost.

Cattle buyers from Seattle or Ellensburg traveled to the valley to purchase stock in the early days. Ranchers, such as the Thurlows and Nickells, sold to these buyers, then organized group cattle drives to send their stock to the shop. Before the railroad came to Wenatchee, making *it* the destination, cattle had to hike to Ellensburg. It was a long, hard trip for the animals and perilous too, for they were often forced to swim rivers on the way—though sometimes they lucked out and hopped a ferryboat ride.

To catch the train in Wenatchee, Methow cattle traveled by way of Alta Lake and Antoine Canyon to Chelan, then a stock trail from Chelan to Wenatchee. This rugged, narrow route

Haying time on the Thurlow Ranch, early 1900s. Photo from the Shafer Museum photo collection.

often took up to nine days each way.

Cattle could be shipped to Wenatchee once steamboats chugged on the Columbia, but this wasn't the perfect solution, since loading the four-legged passengers was difficult and only 40 or 50 head could squeeze on a boat at one time. Once the railroad extended to Pateros, cattle could be driven a shorter distance downvalley to the Columbia, then shipped to Wenatchee by train.

Despite circuitous routes to market, cattle raising appeared to be a winning prospect in the Methow right from the start. At 3 or 4 years old a steer was mature enough to be sent to market. A rancher would receive 3 to 4 cents per pound for his stock.

The Thurlows built up their herd until it was over 500 strong. Each year, they'd drive a huge bunch to Wenatchee—possibly 200 to 400 head of cattle—and load them on the train. "No, it wasn't fun," said Frank Thurlow, Mason's son. "It was rainy and wet and snowy, or else it was hot and dry." Frank often rode the caboose and took the cattle all the way to the stock-yards in Seattle.

By the 1930s roads and automobiles revolutionized cattle driving and cowboys became truck drivers in some cases. Cattle were either trucked to the railroad station or motored all the way to Seattle.

The Miller Family Ranches

The Rose Miller Place

William Miller was a logger, a miner and a Methow Valley homesteader. He spent his logging days in Sedro Woolley, then mined Canyon Creek up towards Hart's Pass. The land east of the mountains appealed to Miller and in 1907 he claimed a homestead on land in the Rendezvous area.

His wife Rose along with 4-year-old son George, left the coast to join William on the new homestead. They traveled by train to Wenatchee, chugged up the Columbia by steamboat to the mouth of the Methow River and then by wagon to the Rendezvous.

When his father died, George at 14 became head of the Miller family, which now included five siblings. He quit school to run the farm but according to son Carl, George's eighth grade education at Grafford Hall taught him more than Carl's entire high

The Rose Miller Place in 1970. Photo courtesy Carl Miller.

school education.

The weekly cream check and selling some steers and surplus hay kept the family going, supplemented by Rose and son Tom traveling the Methow playing fiddle for grange dances. They couldn't afford to eat their own cows so they ate venison from July to January until the deer got "poor" (no longer fat and healthy). But it got drier and drier and harder to farm, so George decided to work away from the ranch for extra cash. He broke horses, drove a team that ran a saw, competed at rodeos and began a long career as a packer.

Later, the Rendezvous homestead became known as the Rose Miller Place.

The Beaver Creek Ranch

With money he saved from packing, George bought a ranch on Beaver Creek in 1942. He ran 400 head of stock year-round on 4,000 acres of deeded land in the Pipestone Canyon and Balky Hill areas. He grew 350 acres of alfalfa and corn for silage, rotating the crops to keep the land fertile.

By this time George had a family of his own: his wife Mary Dammann and four boys: Wayne (Swede), Ross, Carl and Claude. George managed his ranch with the help of his sons and several boys who lived with the Millers because they couldn't get along with their own folks. A hardy woman, Mary often worked all morning harvesting alfalfa with the boys, cooked lunch, washed dishes, stacked hay all afternoon, then cooked dinner for the crew. This was while keeping the house orderly and the garden weeded.

Like other ranches in the valley, the Millers lagged 50 years in technology. No one owned a tractor; teams of horses did the work. Mowing alfalfa took two teams of horses. For the "smart job" of mowing, an older person had to be in charge. A 9- to 10-year-old worker drove the dumprake team, which raked the mowed hay into windrows. The overshot stacker team, which gathered up the windrows and put the hay on a stacker, demanded the skill of a 15- to 20-year-old worker.

Despite the antiquated farming methods, George could grow anything anywhere. He grew feed on 50 irrigated acres but also squeezed good alfalfa crops out of dry sections of land.

While farming with his family during the '40s and '50s, George ran pack strings into the backcountry. In the fall he packed hunters into the hills and supplies to firefighters. He devised a method to pack 20-foot timbers on pack mules to lookout sites and for 12 years transported mining machinery to the Glacier Peak mines.

When it looked like his sons would eventually leave home to seek their fortunes elsewhere, George decided to sell the Beaver Creek ranch. The place was just too big to run alone. He sold it to a Texan—Tex Cloyd—who soon discovered the ranch demanded way too much work. Tex then sold the land to the state Game Department.

Following in His Father's Footsteps

Like his dad, Claude Miller has chosen the life of ranching and packing. He raises cattle for the market and packs customers into the Pasayten and Sawtooth wildernesses.

Claude owns a small ranch on the Eastside County Road. He keeps some horses there but his cattle graze on public land. Some local ranchers, such as the Thurlows, Stokes, Campbells and Christiansens, still own property large enough to grow feed and range their cattle, but these families are more the exception than the rule.

Like many local ranchers, Claude leases both state and federal land. He farms some of the family's original Beaver Creek ranch, which is now owned by the Washington Department of Wildlife, and gives a percentage of his harvest back to that state agency.

Cows on the Moo ... ve

Claude's cows while away the winter months in the warmer basin area near Malaga on the Columbia River. (Other ranchers send their cattle to Moses Lake.) The animals graze on waste products left after the corn harvest. The calves are born in January and along with the rest of the herd get to fatten up until May when they're trucked to the Methow. For about a month, they graze here on state-leased land. At this point the 5- to 6-month-old calves are videotaped, put on a futures market and marketed to feed lots nationwide. The seller (Claude) guarantees the calves will weigh 500-600 pounds by fall when they will be sold.

When the grass in the high country is at its richest and most nutritious the cattle move to Forest Service land Claude leases in the Thompson Ridge area and Wolf Creek up to Gardner Meadows. A rider spends the summer with the cows, keeping them on the move yet contained in the leased area.

This arrangement, while good, still has its pitfalls. A couple from Lummi Island arrived at the Winthrop Forest Service office frightened and exhausted one Sunday in July 1999. They'd just hiked all the way out from Gardner Meadows in the dark after a very large, chocolate-colored bear with a hump on its back had harassed them by braying and roaring 150 yards from their camp. Concerned for the safety of other campers, the Forest Service flew two wildlife experts and a paramedic to the scene where the grizzly-looking bear had been sighted.

When the rescuers met other campers at the trailhead they learned that an obnoxious domestic bull had bothered the campers all night. Perhaps Claude Miller's bull felt lonesome and was just bellowing at the moo ... n!

After a summer spent in the Forest Service hills, the calves are rounded up and corralled on Thompson Creek. They spend October back on state land. Claude sends his calves, fattened to about 600 pounds, to an Iowa feed lot called Iowa Beef Processors, the biggest beef processors in the U.S. There the calves gain 3 pounds a day until they weigh 900 pounds, at which point they head to the slaughterhouse.

Methow Cows Sell Well

The number of cattle living in the Methow year-round is about 1,500. Another 2,000 to 2,500 live here part-time.

These days 90 percent of the cattle raised in the valley are Black Angus—a leaner, more muscled breed than most. The feed lots want Black Angus since consumers now demand lean beef.

Methow beef is considered excellent. Cows grow well in the Methow Valley and hence sell well once they're grown. Their exceptional growth may be due to the cool temperatures and high elevation where they graze all summer. Claude's cows love the high altitude meadows below Gardner Mountain. They hate to leave the sweet alpine fescue grass that grows there. Calves grazing on the fescue weigh 100 pounds more than those grown in sagebrush country. The animals get fatter when they're comfortable—not panting and hot.

Price of Cows

Methow cows may be well fed and well liked by buyers, but the business of raising cattle here is not always profitable. It used to be better. In 1962 a steer calf sold for $1.10 per pound; in 1997, 80 cents per pound. While prices are down, costs are up. The cost of transporting the cows to all their various havens has risen. Wages are higher. Then there's inflation. According to Claude Miller, he couldn't afford to raise cattle if his wife hadn't worked for the PUD (utility) all the years he's been ranching.

Bibliography

Duffy, Barbara. "Pioneer Girl." *Okanogan County Heritage*, Winter 1976.

Filer, Ross (with editing by Diana Hottell). "Driving Cattle, That Was My Heaven." *Methow Valley News*, Souvenir Issue, Summer 1977.

Hottell, Diana. "Frank Thurlow: Four Generations in the Methow Valley." *Methow Valley News*, April 21, 1977.

——. "Frank Thurlow." *Methow Valley News*, Souvenir Issue, Summer 1977.

____. "George Miller." *Methow Valley News*, September 10, 1981.

Kerr, Charles and Mary. "Mason Thurlow: Beaver Creek Pioneer." *Okanogan County Heritage*, Fall 1973.

McMillan, Jim. "Mason Thurlow had Many Firsts in the Valley." *Coyote Tales*, 1974.

Mehaffey, K. C. "Authorities think culprit was a bull, not a bear." The Wenatchee World, July 20,1999.

Carl Miller. Interview. Winthrop, Washington, summer 1997.

Chapter 18

SAWMILLS AND LUMBERMEN

Early Mills Serve Locals

When pioneers came to the Methow they found a vast forest resource. Glorious red-barked ponderosa pines with trunks tall and straight grew in open forests. There were old-growth stands of Douglas fir, tight groves of lodgepole pine, and even some cedar grew on wetter sites in the valley.

The Methow's untapped forests provided pioneers with lumber for homes, furniture, wagons, fences, bridges—every useful structure people want and need. There was abundant wood for cooking, and wood to feed fireplaces to warm the settlers during the long chilly winters.

The pioneers' resourcefulness matched the vastness of the timber resource. When log shelters lost their luster, settlers erected sawmills, produced boards and built box homes. They all welcomed this refinement in building materials. Here's Laura Thompson's story of one of the first sawmills in the upper valley.

> One of the important developments was our first sawmill. Two neighbors came to see if they could build a sawmill on Thompson's ditch because we had a splendid source of waterpower from the bench above our cabin. The water wheel was soon in place and the mill went into production. Men brought logs and donated labor to get lumber. Settlers and their teams made quite a traffic hauling

Rockview Sawmill in the upper Methow Valley. Photo from the Dick Webb collection.

all the green lumber their horses could pull.

It would be hard to have you understand what a change that sawmill made in this valley. Some of us were foolish enough to build box houses in exchange for our warm log cabins. Many built floors for their cabins. All settlers benefited from the sawmill. The lumber was not first class but it was nice to see a board, get a board, have a board.

—*Okanogan County Heritage*, March 1967.

Charles Randall and John McKinny operated the sawmill Laura Thompson described. It was located above Wolf Creek, close to McKinny Mountain.

In the early 1900s small sawmills serving locals popped up wherever people wanted to settle and there were trees to cut. Logs came right from the sawmill site, and most, if not all, of the lumber was used right in the area as well.

Lumber mills soon became an integral part of the local economy. A Great Northern Railway Company report from 1910 listed the following sawmills in the Methow: Rockview, Thompson Creek, Twisp Valley, Gold Creek, Texas Creek and Brewster Summit. Sawmills provided not only a source of lumber for local use, but a source of jobs and supplementary income. When the Wetzel Mill opened in 1920, many people sold their cows and went to work at the mill according to one source, an exchange which probably occurred more and more often as the logging industry grew in the Methow.

The Fender Mill Near the Weeman Bridge

George Fender was one of the first logging magnates in the Methow. In 1910 he got his toes wet in the business when he joined C.N. Burton to operate the Burton-Fender Sawmill near Patterson Lake. After this rural mill had served its purpose, Fender whisked the equipment to Twisp where he installed it at his new Fender Lumber and Box Company, the first commercial logging and sawmill operation in the valley.

To furnish raw materials for the Twisp company, George built a lumber mill near the Weeman Bridge. Workers hauled rough lumber from the upper valley mill to the Twisp mill, where the wood was planed. By 1929, most of the wood was cut into box "shook" for apple boxes and other apple industry uses.

The 15 to 20 employees of the Fender Sawmill in the upper Methow lived in a small community surrounding the mill, or in their own homes nearby. Single men stayed in the bunkhouse and ate at the cookhouse courtesy of the company. For years, Mrs. Alma (Ma) Tait slung flapjacks and bacon for the lumberjacks, charging 90 cents a day for her home-cooked meals. When she raised the price to $1.05, the men almost went on strike.

No doubt these early loggers needed Ma's hearty fare. They worked in pairs, using crosscut handsaws nicknamed "misery

Fender Mill pond located downriver from the Weeman Bridge. Photo from the Washington State Historical Society, Tacoma.

whips." Horsepower helped them skid and load logs. Before the technical advances of the '30s, Howard Weller recalled skidding 40,000 to 50,000 board feet per day, using teams of horses. Drivers hauling logs to the mill in the 1920s often experienced an adrenaline rush, since roads were steep and rough, while the hard-tired trucks they drove were low-powered with poor brakes.

The mill ran from spring to fall, but lots of logging was done in the wintertime, because it was easier for horses to drag logs over the snow. Since winter days in this northern latitude are short, loggers worked by lamplight before dawn and after dark. Often, they labored in unbearably cold weather. Bill Stewart recalled a 48-degree-below-zero day when two horses dropped dead with frozen lungs.

Fender Mill loggers experimented with log driving on the Methow River in the late 1920s. Workers cut the trees in the wintertime, hooked them up to horses, then the horses dragged the logs to the banks of the Methow River. Here men stacked the trunks and secured them in place with a key log. Logs were decked on the riverbank all the way from Goat Creek to Early Winters Creek. When the Methow's level rose in the spring, loggers kicked the key log loose and tons of would-be lumber tumbled into the frothy water en route to the Fender Mill.

A frame or "boom" made of four-by-fours, 8 feet long and lashed together, barged the logs to the mill, 10 miles downstream. Logs starting their float trip in late April might not appear at the Fender Mill slough and pond until late June.

Herding logs on the Methow River. Photo from the Dick Webb collection.

Once in the water, men riding the log raft herded logs with peaveys and pike-poles to keep the resource floating along. Bill Stewart, whose job it was to keep the logs moving, often had to rescue rogue logs hung up on shallow bars. Sinking deep into

Logging near Mazama, 1925-26. Photo from the Dick Webb collection.

cold, rushing water, Bill would ride his horse out and work the log loose with a special hook. It was dangerous work, Bill claimed. "Some horses swim so low all you see are their eyes and nose above the water."

Indian Ed Walsh chose his own aquatic skills over that of his steed. According to Stewart, "He swam to the logjam just like a beaver. The cold water didn't bother him."

Near the Weeman Bridge the logs detoured into a ditch, which plunked them into a log pond near the mill. The pond was formed by an earth and gravel dam with a headgate on it so irrigation water could flow to farms below. (This later became known as the Rockview Ditch. Still in use today, it irrigates most of the Big Valley Ranch.)

Propelled by high water and forceful current, many logs failed to be arrested by the log-boom diversion at the mill. Workers would watch helplessly as logs sailed onward to Winthrop. "Lost so many that we finally gave it up as a bad job," said Stewart.

A method invented for winter log transport to the Fender Mill proved more precarious than herding a logjam on the river. To get logs down from Grizzly Mountain and nearby summits, the Fender inventors built a mile-long, 4-foot-wide log chute which plunged down a canyon near the original Boesel homestead about five miles north of Winthrop. Loggers sent water down the chute which created a frozen slide for logs to descend. After logging above with crosscut saws, the men had

The Twisp-Wagner Mill. Photo from the Shafer Museum collection.

to wrestle the trees into the chute. When the logs crash-landed, workers loaded them on sleds and delivered the timber to the mill.

The chute idea had promise—speed of log transport being the greatest benefit—but problems with the program soon surfaced. The method was costly and dangerous, according to historian Barbara Duffy. One day her husband, Paul, was walking up the chute—that being the easiest route to the top where he worked—when a log skated down the chute, slammed into him and smashed his leg. Paul's co-workers rigged a homemade stretcher and lowered Paul down. By luck a school bus came by, drove him to the mill, and then to a doctor. Paul survived the assault, but everyone soon agreed the chute was too hazardous. After one winter in the early 1930s, loggers abandoned it. One can still find remnants of the chute in Boesel Canyon.

On weekends, Fender Mill singles released tension built up by their dangerous, demanding jobs. Said Walt Hanan, "Every Saturday night was all personal business. We'd get a fifth of moonshine and go down and have a good time at the Rockview Dance Hall halfway between Winthrop and the Fender Mill." You had to beware of the local brand, however; Walt went blind for three days once after drinking some of that $10-a-gallon valley firewater.

The Fender Lumber and Box Company went bankrupt in 1936 and the Wagner Lumber Company of Okanogan purchased it in 1939. Wagner operated the mill for one season at the original site.

Otto Wagner and the Logging Revolution

By the time Otto Wagner bought the defunct Fender Mill, tractors, instead of horses, skidded logs. A revolution in logging practices had been launched and Wagner embraced the new technology. Otto constructed a brand new mill, and in 1941 the Twisp-Wagner Lumber Company opened for business.

The new Twisp mill caused a sudden demographic change. Eventually, the mill employed about 400 people. Like a magnet, the job openings attracted workers from up and down the valley. Men who had worked at the Fender Mill in Mazama moved to Twisp. People who had farms and needed extra income moved to Twisp. Due to these relocations, the population of Twisp soared in the early '40s. Many large farms were cut up into smaller farms and bought during the influx of mill workers and families.

"Mr. Wagner was aggressive and developed a very progressive outfit," said Howard Weller, first logging superintendent for the Wagner Mill. Bunkhouses for men and barns for horses became a thing of the past. Soon logging crews commuted by bus instead of buggy to logging sites. The two-man misery whip was banished to the attic and modern power saws buzzed the tree boles. During Wagner's time, large, efficient tractors and rubber-tired skidders replaced horse-drawn rigs. Instead of loading logs on a wagon by horsepower, frame loaders mounted on a truck did the job. The large, solid-tired pokey trucks (top speed 20 mph) made way for modern trucks. The Wagner Mill claimed fame as the first mill in Washington state to have a rubber-tired loader and a D-9 cat in road construction. These technical advances took place over a period of about 30 years.

The local lumber industry literally opened up the backcountry with road building. The Wagner Company either built or rebuilt every road on the Methow forest. Howard Weller claimed the far-reaching business opened every major Methow drainage: Fawn Creek, Goat Creek, Finley Canyon, Benson Creek, the Loup area, Chewuch River, Falls Creek, Eightmile Creek, Cub Creek, Ramsey Creek, the Twisp River and all the others. They built several major valley bridges, such as the main Chewuch River bridge seven miles north of Winthrop, and the Falls Creek bridge.

The Wagner crew selectively logged the Methow forests. At first 80 percent of what they cut was pine. They chose many of the choicest old-growth trees, but saved some to reseed for future harvests.

When Otto opened his Twisp mill, rough-cut lumber was produced and sent to the Okanogan mill which he also owned at the time. Later the local mill produced mostly fruit boxes, the majority of which were sent to Okanogan and the Columbia Basin. Cardboard boxes stole the fruit-box market in the '50s, so the Wagners switched to selling regular lumber.

The Wagner Mill was central to Twisp's economy and it gave locals a sense of economic security. Everyone recognized the mill as one of the major employers in the valley. Every day and night people living near Twisp heard the big whistle signaling a change in the mill shift. For many, the whistle was a comforting sound; it reminded them that there was work, that locals had jobs.

Biles Coleman bought the Twisp mill in 1969. Later, Crown Zellerbach purchased the mill. It was never quite the same as when the Wagner family owned it.

Otto and Kay Wagner Move to the Methow

Otto Wagner's father, Ernst Wagner, was a Wenatchee orchardist. The first apples ever exported from the USA grew in Ernst's Chelan County orchard. Ernst chose Australia as his export market, then to ensure his business venture, Ernst took his whole family there by boat. Young Otto got his first taste for commercial enterprise by selling apples down under.

The lumber business snared Ernst by chance. After receiving some timber on the Loup Loup as payment on a debt, he decided to build a mill on Loup Loup Creek. A settlement soon developed at the site which included a sawmill, box factory, cook shack, commissary, bunkhouses for single men and homes for families. About 150 men worked at the mill.

Otto managed the mill for his father for about five years. Then one summer morning in 1931 the entire scene became an inferno. Roy Graves described the intense heat at the scene in the book, *The Late Frontier*, by Bruce Wilson. Graves recalled that within minutes the whole camp burst into flames. Workers

Early day skidding crew. Photo from the Dick Webb collection.

ran for their lives. It was so scorching, they couldn't even peer over the hill crests—where they had fled for safety —to the valley below. Pieces of tin roof floated like leaves in the air.

Otto and Ernst rebuilt the mill in Okanogan which Otto managed until disaster struck again in the same searing form. All was not lost, however, for Otto had already expanded elsewhere. Since competition for timber had been so stiff in Okanogan, Otto had purchased the Twisp mill in 1939. So when the Okanogan sawmill burned in 1946, Otto simply changed his focus from the east side of the Loup Loup summit to the west.

Kay Wagner, Otto's wife, admitted they started the mill here as much for personal reasons as financial expediency. They were introduced to the Methow when Otto's sister invited them to visit the valley. From Okanogan, over the summit they came. At Patterson Lake they camped, fished and fell in love with the valley.

For the next couple of years, Kay came here weekends looking for land. The Leedy place five miles out the Chewuch Road looked perfect to her, and for several years Kay tried to purchase it. Finally, Mrs. Leedy sold her small dairy farm to the Wagners.

On their new land, Kay and Otto built a beautiful, classic, white farmhouse, surrounded with white fences. Arabian thoroughbreds pranced in the meadows. They bred Labradors and Weimaraners and raised a registered herd of Herefords. They bought the adjacent Methow Valley Ranch, the Trunkey

place and Cub Creek Ranch, which provided grazing land for
a commercial herd of stock.

With the help of a manager, Kay ran the Wagner's big
ranch. Otto paid the bills by running the mill. Mild-mannered
Otto was a successful mill owner and a well-liked employer,
but eventually he tired of supporting his ranch by mill earnings, longing instead to spend time relaxing and enjoying the
fruits of his industry. The Wagners decided to sell the big
ranch keeping 100 acres where they planned to build a new
home. Sadly, the original "classic" farmhouse later burned.

After Mr. Wagner passed away, Kay built a home which
has become one of the Methow's most renowned landmarks.
Bob Jorgensen, the architect of Winthrop's renovation, designed Kay's home and her close friend, Jack Wilson, built it.
The design and layout of the house, barn and other buildings
in the complex are unique. Kay's house has six, windowed
sides to take advantage of all the mountain views. An octago-
nal barn with a water tower houses fire fighting equipment. A
four-sided manager's house completes the scene.

To create the ultimate in tranquility, Kay raised the dam on
Ramsey Creek, creating a seven-acre pond populated by ducks
and geese.

Bibliography

Duffy, Barbara. Notes from Wenatchee Valley College Class on Methow
   Valley History. Winthrop, Washington.
Hottell, Diana. "Bill and Martha Stewart: Sharing Their Memories of the
   Valley." *Methow Valley News*, December 13, 1979.
——. "Stanley and Edna Darwood." *Methow Valley News*, November 17, 1977.
——. "The Wellers: A Sparkle in Their Eyes." *Methow Valley News*,
   April 26, 1979.
——. "Mary Demmitt: The Long and Tricky Road From Chancellor."
   Methow Valley News, June 3, 1982.
Johnson, Abbie Williams. "Life in the Upper Methow." *Okanogan Valley
   Heritage*, March 1968.
Kittrell, Glenn. Interviews. Twisp, Washington, summers 1990 and 1992.
Thompson, Laura. "Laura Thompson Came to Stay." *Okanogan County
   Heritage*, March 1967.
Wagner, Kathryn. Interview. Twisp, Washington, summer 1990.
Weller, Howard. "From Horses to Helicopters." *Okanogan County Heri-
   tage*, Spring 1988.
Wilson, Bruce. *The Late Frontier*. Okanogan County Historical Society,
   1990.

Chapter 19

IRRIGATION AND ORCHARDING

Keeping the Methow Green

Touring the Methow Valley during the dry season, one encounters unexpected streams of greenery crossing arid hill-sides and paralleling dusty roads. The lush vegetation, which appears so out of place in its parched surroundings, grows alongside irrigation channels fed by waters diverted from rivers and creeks. The channels are constructs of pioneers, who saw the need for extra water to grow their crops, even before the years of drought. Many of the original waterways still serve farmers, ranchers and orchardists today.

Between 1900 and 1910, farmer associations developed 20 irrigation systems which would benefit everyone for the rest of the century. Using only horse and human power, the settlers carved ditches through rocky soil, and constructed flumes to carry the flow across cliffs.

According to pioneer Walter Nickell, three ditches built near Winthrop around 1910 turned "what would have been star-vation ranches into at least a living." These were the Chewuch, the Fulton and the Foghorn ditches.

To irrigate their dry acres, Bear Creek farmers initiated the Chewuch Ditch in 1910. Their efforts succeeded in bringing river water to their crops a year later. First they hired surveyor Fred Ventzke to map a 12-mile channel beginning at the north fork of the Methow River (as the Chewuch was called in

1910), then passing through the upper part of Winthrop and continuing to a proposed finish at Bear Creek.

Farmers built the Chewuch Ditch the hard way, recalled Blossom Hanks, one of the Bear Creek pioneers who promoted the ditch project. Using only picks and shovels, horses and scrapers, each landowner attacked his allotted section of ditch construction. For the intake tunnel, which required extensive rock work, farmers used explosives. People donated their labor and lumber for flumes, along with explosive powder for blasting rock.

Since all the farmers worked simultaneously on their assigned sections, the entire length of the ditch was finished at the same time. As water first whirled down the Chewuch channel and spilled into Bear Creek on May 10, 1911, the farmer-canal-builders whooped and cheered for joy. Everyone who participated in the project received shares in the company.

One person suggested the ditch be called the "North Fork Ditch." But Guy Waring thought the Indian name for the stream feeding the ditch would be more appropriate, since many natives hunted and fished the area which was rich in wildlife. When Indians visiting Waring's trading post made reference to the North Fork in their language, the last syllable sounded like a grunt to a white man. To Waring's ears, the native word sounded like "Che-wuch" and the ditch company claimed that name.

The Fulton Ditch, named after a Bear Creek homesteader, followed a route similar to the Chewuch Ditch; it delivered water from the Chewuch River above Winthrop downvalley to Bear Creek ranches. However, the Fulton took a lower course

Keeping the Methow green. Photo by Steve Barnett.

The Fulton irrigation ditch, shown in 1910, passes right through Winthrop. Photo from the Shafer Museum collection.

passing right through the town of Winthrop. Today from the patio of the Duck Brand Cantina, guests enjoy the refreshing sight and sound of the Fulton Ditch which flows below the restaurant during the summer months.

Pioneer Walter Frisbee launched the Foghorn Ditch when he took water rights out of the Methow River in 1888 to irrigate his ranch across the river from Winthrop. The Foghorn Ditch traveled down the west side of the Methow River, making water available to 1,300 acres of ranchland, about half of that under irrigation by 1909. Alfalfa, grain and apples were the main crops fed by the Foghorn. Later this ditch supplied water for Winthrop's first power plant and now it fills the federal fish hatchery ponds.

A Great Northern Railway report, dated May 1910, listed the amazing number of Methow ditches either in use or planned at the time. In addition to the ones just described, there were the Skyline, Wolf Creek, Burke-Lehman, Banker-Wetsel, Ramsey, Rockview, Pope, Bolinger and Barkley ditches, plus the Methow Canal Company Ditch. Methow ranchers irrigated 12,000 acres, the report claimed, 400 of which were orchard-bearing acres.

Lord Blythe and His Grandiose Canal

The legendary Thomas "Lord" Blythe dreamed of transforming all the undeveloped land from Twisp to Carlton into orchards and farms. He believed the one essential ingredient needed to

Thomas "Lord" Blythe (fifth from right) developed a huge irrigation system in the Twisp-Carlton area. Photo from The Wenatchee World.

realize his vision was irrigation water. Thus, Blythe's Methow Canal Company was born, and the largest irrigation project ever attempted in the Methow Valley was set into motion.

Everyone called Blythe a "Lord" and he surely looked the part as he promenaded the streets of Twisp with his gold-headed cane in hand, and wearing a black suit, dark tie and fashionable hat. Son of a Scottish duke, the courtly Blythe was not officially a lord but a remittance man—a person living abroad who receives an allowance from aristocratic family coffers but has no chance of inheriting the family fortune.

Instead of fretting over lost opportunities, Blythe sailed the seas to seek his own fortune in the American West, first as a cattle baron. While experimenting with this career, Blythe was often seen riding the range in his imported coach with mohair upholstery and beveled glass windows, a rig which made the cowboys cringe!

Blythe landed in Twisp in 1905 and financed a canal intended to irrigate 2,000 acres on both sides of the Methow River. A Methow Canal Company bulletin (1909) described the ambitious route of Blythe's ditch. Water was diverted at the mouth of Poorman Creek (where it flows into the Twisp River) several miles above Twisp. From there, two miles of flume (wooden ditches on legs) had to be built to a point opposite Twisp and 100 feet above the town. Here the flow divided;

part traveled across the Methow River by way of a redwood bridge trestle to the east side, then headed downriver for 11 miles, while on the west side of the Methow River the ditch just continued downstream 10 miles beyond the division point.

To make the ditches, heavy plows, rooters and Martin ditchers dug, drilled and pushed out dirt and rocks. When the work was finally done, there was still one problem—not enough water flowed from the Twisp River to fill both ditches.

With premature expectations, people had started planting orchards in the early 1910s, using water wagons to irrigate young trees. Some places received water from Blythe's ditch by 1917, and their saplings thrived on the nourishment. Soon, however, many orchard trees grew large and their thirst for water could no longer be quenched by the trickle from Blythe's ditch.

To make matters worse, the dry years started. The coup de grace came in 1918 when a mile of flume flipped over one night, dashing Blythe's dreams to pieces. Broke, the disappointed lord relinquished ownership of his grandiose canal.

Meanwhile, the orchardists and farmers of the area, seduced by their first sweet taste of irrigation water, wanted more, so in 1919 landowners formed the Methow Valley Irrigation District (MVID) and laid plans to water lands on the east side of the Methow River between Twisp and Carlton. To accomplish this feat, the district talked the state into loaning them $80,000.

First locals constructed a dam on the river near the Methow Valley State Airport (former Intercity Airport). Next, a mammoth coal-burning steam shovel, the biggest piece of machinery Methow people had ever seen, began scooping up earth to create a canal. Starting at the airport, the mechanical beast chewed a path 3.5 miles cross-country to a rocky area where human labor took over. At this point, workers hand built a wooden flume traversing rocky spots until the terrain leveled out. An easy one-half mile more of ditch building connected the new diversion to a portion of Blythe's old ditch that was still serviceable.

By 1922, water flowed down the new ditch to thirsty eastside orchards. Nearly 20 years later, directors of the MVID, Vernon LaMotte, Ed Thompson and Charlie Nelson, went to the state Conservation and Development Department and convinced officials not only to cancel the $80,000 debt owed by

From 1900 to 1910 local farmers built 20 irrigation systems. Photo from the Okanogan County Historical Society, negative 2999.

the district, but also to lend them a second $80,000 to replace a mile of dilapidated flume. Once more the state agreed. This time the district repaid the loan.

In the 1920s, despite efforts by the cooperative MVID, Carlton orchardist Vernon LaMotte remembered a scarcity of water in the west-side canal by August and September. The Twisp River which fed the canal just didn't have enough water in it to fill the ditch late in the season. Vernon recalled that in the summer of 1924, only one trench of water flowed in his dad's entire orchard. Every two hours Vernon changed that single trench, camping out all night among the apple trees to keep them growing.

The situation was relieved in 1926 when the Washington Water Power line came up the valley and a pump was installed two miles below Twisp on the Methow River. For 10 years the pump supplemented the natural water flow, buying time until heavy winter snow fell again in the valley.

A Sampling of Early Methow Orchards

Jim Robinson, a trapper in the Robinson Creek area, decided it was time to put down roots—fruit tree roots to be exact—so in 1888 he planted 200 fruit trees, reputably the Methow's first orchard, and started irrigating his land across from the town of Methow.

Another vanguard of the local apple-growing business was Peter Averill, an immigrant from Michigan, who set out a cornucopia of apple varieties on his 15 acres in the early 1900s. He planted all his favorites from "back East" plus some new ones: Northern Spy, Wolf River, Missouri Pippin, Rhode Island Greening, Bell Flower, Delicious, Winesap and Jonathan apples.

Averill realized that irrigation and juicy apples go hand in hand, so he and neighbor James Caddy masterminded a 2-mile-long irrigation project that diverted water from the Methow River to their orchards. To get the water around a vertical bluff en route, the partners assembled a flume which hung like a cradle from the rock cliff. One-half mile below the McFarland Creek turnoff on the east side of the river, one can see holes drilled in the rock face where Averill and Cady placed the steel supports for their flume. A short section of flume still hangs by a thread from the cliff wall.

George Edward Nickell raised the first orchard in the Twisp area, said daughter Katie Nickell Mattison. Her dad lashed a stack of little fruit saplings behind his saddle and transported them by horseback from the Okanogan Valley. "I remember eating the first apples from those trees," said Katie. They grew

The Averill-Cady flume hangs by a thread above the Methow River.
Photo by Don Portman.

The Fulton Ditch flume. Photo from the Okanogan County Historical Society, negative 2991.

old-fashioned types of apples unheard of today, like Ben Davis and Northern Spy. "Snow apples were the best; I can still taste them," she reminisced.

Guy Waring attempted the first commercial orchard in the Winthrop area on his Land 5 Ranch. His apple trees managed to reach bearing age, but it was a struggle due to dry weather and lack of irrigation. For several years, Waring packed, shipped and sold his crop. He often hauled his apples to Pateros on bumpy wagon roads and one wonders how bruised the crop got in transit. Waring finally gave up his ambitious apple enterprise, but one still can see remnants of the legendary Land 5 orchards, shabby and stunted from lack of moisture.

In the early 1900s, pioneers planted orchard after orchard in the Twisp River Valley and in other Methow areas where fruit trees might flourish. Apples were the number one choice, but many farmers raised a sampling of other fruit varieties as well. Emma Rader Pidcock's farm near Twisp offered a mouth-watering menu of cherries, apricots, peaches, pears and plums, as well as apples.

Once their irrigated orchards began to bear, the Mason Thurlows were visited by all their neighbors, who loaded up their wagons with the delicious, bountiful fruit. The Thurlows stored their apples in pits and cellars and brewed their own delectable brand of cider. After the juice fermented and turned hard, the old cider barrel became a very popular place. Thurlow's apple arbors included Russets, Northern Spy, Ben Davis, Yellow Transparent and Red Astrakhan.

W.A. Bolinger, who seemed to have a finger in every pie, including fruit varieties, owned 100 acres of orchard near the town of Methow. He shared his apple enterprise with Lord Blythe of the Methow Canal Company fame. To water their fruit trees, the two entrepreneurs organized the 5-mile-long Bolinger Ditch in 1910.

Bolinger erected his own packing shed in the 1920s and each winter he and his wife took off for Texas in search of apple buyers. In Texas, Bolinger observed some beautiful stone homes which later served as models for the landmark house he built of boulders in the town of Methow.

From the very start, successful orcharding in the Methow Valley depended on the availability of water. Methow orchardists who irrigated their trees saw their crops thrive and apples grow big and sweet. Those who couldn't irrigate were doomed to disappointment, once the natural moisture flow dwindled in the valley.

Vernon LaMotte: Raising a Small Orchard

On a brilliant sunny day in the summer of 1992, Vernon and Beulah LaMotte relaxed in the shade of their backyard while the Methow River rolled right on by their Carlton place. They were relishing a well-deserved break from orchard work. At that time, the spirited couple still raised 20 varieties of apple trees and they still made an income selling their apples. But even small orchards like the LaMottes' demand lots of labor and they'd been growing apples since 1941—Vernon since he was a kid. So they were ready to lighten the load. These two appeared physically fit from a lifetime of activity, and their family stories, laced with humor, proved their wit was fit as well. The orcharding life in the Methow agreed with the LaMottes.

Vernon's dad, Hector LaMotte, owned a 10-acre orchard in the Carlton area around 1920. His fruit trees were growing, but slowly, their growth limited by lack of water. When ditch water became available in 1921, Hector jubilantly dug trenches and turned it on. Ten-year-old Vernon's job was to change the irrigation so all the trees received an equal supply of water.

In 1922 his dad built a small apple-packing shed, several 4-by-5 fruit bins and a 16-foot slide board to push the apple boxes along. Like Hector, many Methow orchardists built private packing sheds at the time. One landmark packing shed built in 1919 still stands in the center of downtown Twisp. Growers also made their own boxes in the early years. Locals bought box shook (box parts) at the Twisp lumber mill and assembled the boxes at home.

Vernon's family lived away from the orchard site except for the five-week apple-packing season, when the LaMottes camped right amid their apple trees and packed their apples by hand. Vernon's mother did the sorting. His father handled the full apple boxes and stamped the produce. They hired one extra person to do the packing. Vernon got a legal holiday from school, but the work he did at home making apple boxes and picking apples proved harder than schoolwork, he said.

Vernon's folks raised an orchard and packed apples for 20 years, from 1922 to 1942. Several times a week during pack-

Vernon and Beulah LaMotte in the family's orchard, 1992. Photo by Stephanie Rowatt.

ing season, the mail truck would pick up Hector's boxes and haul them to Pateros to be placed in cold storage.

A lot of country kids remember their childhood chores as tedious, choosing never to repeat them once they have left home. Not Vernon. In 1941, for $5,000, he bought his present 10-acre place on the west side of the Methow River near Carlton. Vernon knew his new purchase would produce, since west-side orchards had the best drainage, the best soil, and a reputation for producing the best fruit. He grew mostly Delicious apples —Reds and Goldens.

Once Vernon had purchased an orchard, he needed to hire help—not such an easy task at the time. According to Barbara Duffy, whose family had an orchard near Twin Lakes, "Orchardists always had three crews—one coming, one leaving and one working." They were called (not unkindly) "wino crews," said

Barbara, because "they weren't very dependable." Everyone had a wino crew story, and Vernon was no exception.

Vernon's search for a seasonal crew always began rather inauspiciously at the Pateros jail. After hobnobbing with the jailer, he'd leave in the company of four winos fresh from the slammer. "Those men were good pickers and good thinners," Vernon testified. "When they worked, they worked well." Staying power, however, was not their forte. And "wino" was an accurate description in most cases, since the majority guzzled down all their earnings.

The first stop after jail was the grocery store where Vernon purchased several days' worth of food for the men. LaMotte also provided a cabin and bedding for all his employees. Workers with their own cars were risky, Vernon learned, because when they'd depart, their cabins were apt to be left completely

In the early 1900s, the Twisp River valley was a land of orchards. Photo from the Dick Webb collection.

empty, any worthwhile items owned by the employers having
been stealthily packed up and hauled away.

To get to know their help better and establish a homey atmosphere, Vernon suggested to wife Beulah that she cook family-
style meals for the crews. Beulah willingly complied, but always
felt odd listening to the dinner conversation which consisted
mainly of a comparison of various jails employees had known!

Carlton apples like the LaMottes' became famous for being
"good keepers." Possibly the cool Methow air and crisp early
frosts instilled hardiness in the stock. The snappy, long-lasting
upper-Methow apples were much coveted by the lower-river
growers and Columbia River orchardists, whose apples
wouldn't keep as well, nor fetch as high a price. Wenatchee
produce companies could store Carlton apples all the way into
June. The apples would still taste luscious and they'd still sell
well. In the early days, Methow apples weren't even attacked
by worms, according to historian Walter Nickell. No one
needed to spray until 1925 and then only for mites, he recalled.

Orcharding was a profitable business in the Methow for
many years. Beginning in the 1930s it seemed like everyone
here raised orchards. Everyone thinned in June and picked in
the fall. If someone *didn't* own an orchard, it's likely they
sorted or picked apples for someone else. During the height of
apple growing in the Methow, from 1940 to 1968, LaMotte
heard truck motors chugging by his place all day from 6
o'clock in the morning until 10 o'clock at night. There were a
total of 850 apple-producing acres in the Carlton area alone
during the heyday of Methow orcharding.

Two events in the 1960s turned this economic upswing into
disaster. The first change was in technology. Researchers invented CA, or controlled atmosphere, a process that puts apples
to sleep and keeps them fresh. As a result of this preservation
method, the famed longevity of Methow apples no longer mat-
tered. All apples became "good keepers" in CA conditions. The
coup de grace occurred in 1968 when at dawn on Christmas
Day, 50-below-zero temperatures greeted anxious orchardists.
Their worst fears were realized the following spring, when the
frozen cambium layers in the trees shut off the flow of sap and
the trees could grow no leaves.

The freeze of December 1968 devastated the apple orchards
in the Methow. Barely a tree remained unscathed. Many grow-

ers didn't bother to replant. Many sold their orchard land
which was then put to other uses.

LaMotte claims only large orchardists can turn a reasonable
profit now. In the Methow (circa 1999) there are still viable
orchards but mostly small ones. Vernon estimates the largest to
be about 75 acres. About 40 acres of apple trees still bear fruit
in the Carlton area. A peripheral glance around Vernon and
Beulah's place proves apples continue to thrive in their neighborhood. Anyone who doubts this must try a "crispy Twisp" apple
come fall, on sale at local stores and the farmer's market in
Twisp. These moist, munchy morsels exude a simultaneous tart-
ness and sweetness that could only be created in the Methow's
apple-flavor-perfecting climate.

Ditches in Jeopardy

People couldn't remember a year when there was so much snow
in the mountains. So much snow stored in the high country meant
abundant water available for summer irrigation. Yet in the spring
of 1999, many Methow Valley ditches remained dry. The Skyline
Ditch, the Wolf Creek Ditch, the Eightmile, Buttermilk, Aspen
Meadows and Early Winters ditches—all remained closed. Federal agencies in charge of the 1973 Endangered Species Act
(ESA) had ordered ditch operators to keep their headgates closed.

The federal agencies identified the ditches as potentially harmful to spring chinook salmon, steelhead trout and bull trout—fish
listed as endangered or threatened under the ESA. To divert
water, the ditch operators needed authorization from the National
Marine Fisheries Service (NMFS), the US Fish and Wildlife
Service and the US Forest Service.

Other ditches in the valley were potentially harmful to the fish
as well but only those ditches that conveyed water across Forest
Service land needed a special use permit to operate, hence NMFS
found it easy to target these first. All the aforementioned ditches
originated on land in the Okanogan National Forest.

The Forest Service seemed sympathetic to irrigators, but had to
suspend permits to be in compliance with the ESA. They promised to reinstate the permits as soon as they received biological
opinions from NMFS. The biological opinions would specify
mitigating actions each ditch must take to minimize impacts on
endangered fish, and they'd set target flow levels that would have
to be maintained in streams for spawning fish.

The Forest Service claimed that NMFS had failed to issue its biological opinions on time. NMFS countered that it needed more information on instream flows before it could write the opinions.

What seemed clear in all this confusion was that the ditch users had to reduce the amount of water they used. The ditch managers had to come up with plans to conserve water lost through leaks and evaporation as well as plans to prevent fish from getting trapped and killed because of the water diversions. Some ditch companies installed fish screens for the first time; some replaced old screens with new screens. By mid-July after mitigating measures had been taken all the ditches opened except the Skyline and Wolf Creek which both needed more extensive improvements.

Wolf Creek Runs Dry—Skyline Lines the Ditch

The Wolf Creek diversion normally flows into the Patterson Lake reservoir and from there down to irrigators. Even without any water diversion from Wolf Creek allowed during the first half of the 1999 summer, Patterson Lake still acted as a reservoir since several natural streams drain into it. Hence, irrigation water was still available to ditch members, but only to a point.

The irrigation district had an agreement with Sun Mountain Lodge that stipulated irrigation water would be turned off when

No water flows from this irrigation system on the Wolf Creek Ditch, July 15, 1999. Photo by Don Portman.

the lake was drawn down to a certain level. The reason for this cut-off point is that Sun Mountain pumps its water from Patterson Lake and the lodge's water system fails if the lake is drawn down too far. Because Sun Mountain is one of the Methow Valley's largest employers, it seemed everyone, including irrigators of the Wolf Creek Ditch, wanted to protect the lodge's water source.

On July 23, Patterson Lake dropped to the cut-off point and all irrigation from the lake was stopped. Ironically, just a few days later, the ditch company diverted water from Wolf Creek into Patterson Lake for the first time in 1999. (This diversion was finally allowed by the federal government after ditch workers had installed a new fish screen .) However, the amount of water that could be diverted into the lake at this late date was so small that irrigation could not resume for the remainder of the summer.

The Skyline Ditch, which diverts water from the Chewuch River, normally irrigates 60 parcels of land along the West Chewuch Road. The summer of 1999 was the first since 1903 that the canal had been dry. With a new fish screen in place, finally the Forest Service allowed the Skyline to reopen in mid-July, with the stipulation that only one-third the normal amount of water could be diverted. Irrigators turned on the headgate and watched the water flow 1.8 miles down the earthen canal. Without even reaching the first user, all the water seeped into the parched soil. It was a sad moment.

Then to the rescue came federal and state workers and local citizens. Armed with enormous lengths of thick white plastic, the volunteers lined more than half the 6-mile-long canal to prevent water from leaking out. It was a temporary fix which would not work for long, but the action nourished a sense of optimism and spirit of cooperation that was sorely needed.

Meanwhile, the Wolf Creek District filed an appeal with the Portland regional office of the Forest Service alleging that failure to issue a timely ditch permit during the 1999 season created a loss of property rights. The Skyline and Early Winters ditches made similar appeals.

Life After Mitigation

Even after mitigation measures were taken, fish screens installed, ditches patched and replaced, the question remained:

How much water could irrigators count on every year and how long could they irrigate each season? To plant seeds, grow alfalfa, raise cattle, put in a garden or keep an orchard, irrigators felt a certain amount of water had to be guaranteed.

NMFS answered this question when the agency issued the long delayed draft biological opinions in July 1999. And the answer was "no guarantee." The biological opinions set minimum target water flows for local streams used for irrigation. According to irrigators, NMFS set the flows impossibly high. Steve Devin, Early Winters Ditch president, said the target flows "appeared to be aimed at shutting down the valley."

NMFS' longer-range goal was to develop a basin-wide Habitat Conservation Plan (HCP) to enhance fish recovery which would include every irrigation ditch in the valley. Officials estimated the HCP would take several years to complete.

As a result of the irrigation shutoffs, several alfalfa growers expected to write off up to 60 percent of their potential crops. Already worried about the 1999 season's losses, alfalfa growers, orchardists and other ditch users were even more anxious about the future. Irrigators argued that they were excluded from meaningful participation in developing the biological opinions. Without having a voice in the matter, they had been ordered to carry out NMFS' decrees: Doing this became more painful to irrigators after they learned from local biologists that NMFS had almost no scientific evidence on which to base their decisions.

"No doubt things needed to change," claimed fish biologist Jennifer Molesworth. "Local ditches needed to reduce water wasted through inefficient irrigation systems. They needed to install fish screens or repair old ones. But it's hard to support such a hard line (taken by NMFS) when fish are killed in such great numbers at the dams, through fishing, and through habitat destruction downstream. Compared to these other losses, the loss of fish due to irrigation in the valley is very small." (Interview, Winthrop, August 1999.)

Bibliography

Duffy, Barbara. Notes from Wenatchee Valley College Class on Methow Valley History. Winthrop, Washington.

Hanks, Blossom. "62 Years in the Methow Valley." Okanogan County Heritage, September 1966.

Hanron, John and McCreary, Ann. "Ditches Still Dry as NMFS Sets Target Flows." Methow Valley News, May 13, 1999.

Hanron, John. "Ditches Get Work Orders." Methow Valley News, May 27, 1999.

____. "Some Ditches Receive Money, Priority Status." Methow Valley News, June 3,1999.

Hicks, Lee. "Ditches: Some Movement, Much Uncertainty." Methow Valley News, June 10, 1999.

____. "A Big Week but Just a Beginning." Methow Valley News, June 17, 1999.

____. "Wolf Creek Plan Could Have Gates Open by July." Methow Valley News, June 17, 1999.

____. "Sun Mountain Expansion Uncertain." Methow Valley News, July 1, 1999.

____. " 'BOs' are delayed for federal diversions." Methow Valley News, July 8, 1999.

____. "Irrigators Shocked at Biological Opinions." Methow Valley News, July 15, 1999.

____. "It's Crunch time." Methow Valley News, July 15, 1999.

____. "Wolf Creek Irrigators cut off as Patterson Lake Drops." Methow Valley News, July 29, 1999.

____. "Crop losses on just a few ditches reach six figures." Methow Valley News, August 5, 1999.

Hottell, Bill. "Katie Mattison." Methow Valley News, Souvenir Issue, Summer 1977.

LaMotte, Vernon. Interview. Carlton, Washington, summers 1990 and 1992.

McCreary, Ann. "Ditches Facing Closed Gates as Paperwork piles up." Methow Valley News, April 29, 1999.

McMillan, Jim. "Mason Thurlow had Many Firsts in Valley." Coyote Tales, 1974.

Methow Canal Company Bulletin, USDA, 1909. Okanogan County Heritage, Winter 1976.

Molesworth, Jennifer. Fish biologist, Forest Service. Interviews. Winthrop, Washington, July and August 1999.

Nickell, Walter. The Way It Was. Naples, Florida, June 1990.

Partridge, Michelle. "Water, water everywhere, but ditches still are dry." The Wenatchee World, July 16, 1999.

Pidcock, Emma Rader. "Pioneer Life in the Methow Valley." Okanogan County Heritage, June 1969.

Robinson, Tom and Jim. Robinson Brothers' Diary. Barbara Duffy History Notes, Winthrop, Washington.

Schmidt, Jesse. "Walter Frisbee, Versatile Winthrop Pioneer." Okanogan County Heritage, June 1971.

USDA Bulletin on Ditches, 1909. Okanogan County Heritage, Winter 1976.

Wilson, Bruce. The Late Frontier. Okanogan County Historical Society, 1990.

Chapter 20

SHEEPHERDERS, SHEEP RANCHERS and SHEEP RANGES

The Rise and Fall of Local Sheep Allotments

Cattlemen had the entire Okanogan County rangeland to themselves before 1900. Sheep entering the scene at the turn of the century soon created competition for grazing space. The cattlemen resented the number of allotments eventually claimed by the sheepmen, and they feared that sheep would overgraze public lands.

The cattlemen's fears were well founded. In a short time, the national forest lands surrounding the Methow Valley were, in fact, severely overgrazed. The reason for the range abuse, however, was not so much the type of stock browsing as the huge number of browsers allowed on public lands.

Around 1902, permittees William and Hank Didra drove 1,500 sheep into the Salmon Meadows area east of Tiffany Mountain. Their band of sheep was the first ever to graze west of the Okanogan River. After this modest start, sheep grazing allotments increased exponentially. By 1910, Chelan National Forest (now the Okanogan National Forest) hosted 32,274 sheep. For comparison, only 4,403 cattle roamed the range simultaneously. Soon new driveways leading to untapped backcountry meadows were opened to sheep, and by 1917 the woolly wanderers were 75,000 strong on local forest lands.

Fortunately, during the first decade after sheep were introduced, US Forest Service management segregated the range allotments of sheep and cattle. Hot tempers cooled and feuds between livestock owners were mostly avoided.

After the peak grazing year of 1917, foresters woke up to the impacts created by so many voracious foragers and began to make reductions in the number of sheep allowed on government lands. In 1941, 32,000 sheep grazed. By 1949, the government awarded permits for less than half that number. By 1963, the population had plummeted to 5,000 sheep.

Raising Sheep the Lehman Way

"If you loved mountains, it was not bad work," said Carolyn Hotchkiss, recalling the days in the 1920s and '30s when her family ran a sheep ranch in the Methow Valley.

Frank Lehman, Carolyn's father, owned a ranch two miles north of Twisp on the east-side road. Most local range users wintered their stock in the open country near Ephrata, Vantage, Ferry, Sunnyside and Yakima, then imported their sheep to higher elevation Methow meadows for a nutritious summer vacation. Unlike the majority, Frank preferred living in the Methow during all seasons, and wintering his stock at home on his Methow ranch. It made more work for him, since he had to raise alfalfa for winter feed, but Frank thought it was worth the extra labor to live here.

Lehman's band totaled about 1,300 ewes. After the lambs were born in early spring, his livestock numbers doubled. The Lehman band lived an idyllic life. Early spring and late fall the sheep pastured the low hills around the ranch. In winter they huddled together feasting on stored alfalfa and grain. Come summertime they'd hike up the Early Winters' sheep driveway to munch on high country cuisine. The only members of the band who stayed home during the summer crusades were the rams. While the ewes romped in meadowland, the males got a breather from breeding.

Lehman mixed breeds to improve his stock. He raised mostly white-faced ewes that produce the best wool and bred these to heavier black-faced Hampshire rams renowned for their excellent meat. This coupling created a good crossbreed.

Every year Lehman sold the offspring. When his ewes produced a good crop of lambs, Frank accompanied them by rail cross-country to the giant stockyards of Chicago. He'd travel to Seattle to sell a smaller crop of lambs.

Carolyn remembered best the adventuresome days riding the sheep driveways. Lehman's driveway wound up Early Winters Creek in Mazama near Sandy Butte. When Lehman drove his stock in this area, no North Cascades Highway existed to give the security of nearby civilization. No charming country inns provided a respite from bad weather. It was wild, untamed country. In fact, the local wildlife caused Lehman much grief over the years. Bears were abundant in the area, and bears are partial to sheep meat.

On the plus side, the Early Winters' stock driveway offered spectacular scenery for the drivers and sheep thrived on the vegetation of the area. The stock browsed in the morning, then at noon took a nap. One day during the afternoon siesta, Carolyn left camp on horseback to view Liberty Bell Mountain. Another day she climbed Storey Peak near Mount Gardner. Somewhere in the Early Winters area, there's a camp named after this sprightly young miss who loved to adventure in the mountains—Camp Carol, it's called.

Lehman raised and trained Australian sheep dogs, "highly bred, very intelligent dogs," said Carolyn. "They knew more than the men about driving sheep." One dog Carolyn particularly loved had two "glass eyes" which meant they had a natural whiteness to them. If that dog was herding from behind and a man gave the hand signal ordering him to the front, the clever canine would leap up and run over the tops of the sheep, arriving in seconds at the front of the pack.

Two other helpful pets tagged along on the long highland hikes—the

Carolyn and her mother, Hazel Lehman, arrive at sheep camp with the milk goats. Photo courtesy Carolyn Hotchkiss.

Lehman's milk goats. The goats joined the entourage partly because of Frank's thoughtfulness; his crew of local sheep-herders all loved drinking fresh milk on the trip. The goats' other duty was to keep predators away, which apparently they did very well.

Horseshoe Basin Herder Ted Bolin

In the late '30s and early '40s Winthrop woodsman Ted Bolin herded sheep in Horseshoe Basin, a beautiful, rolling meadowland located at the northeast tip of the Pasayten Wilderness. He was responsible for two bands of sheep, about 1,000 ewes and sometimes 1,300 lambs, so the total was over 2,000 head of stock.

Ted kept the sheep constantly on the move all summer, because "they make short work of an area of pasture," he claimed. Thus the herders and their charges would move to different parks in the area. Ted himself stayed 21 days at Ditch Camp in Horseshoe Basin, but he bedded the sheep down in a new place every night. "Sheep want to move when the feed's getting low," said Ted. "They tell you! Plus you need to keep the grass healthy for the future."

Ted relished the sheepherding lifestyle. "Oh it was a good life," he reflected. "Back there the air was fresh. The fishing was good. You'd see wildlife like bighorn sheep that wandered down from Canada." According to Ted, the sheep he herded seemed pretty pleased with their lot as well. "When evening came and the sheep had their bellies full, they'd just bed down. They basically just want to eat and sleep," he said.

Of course the job had its problems, the biggest problem being predators. Coyotes weren't the worst threat, at least not at night. A coyote won't usually invade a flock once they've been gathered and "tucked in," said Ted. But bears barged in where coyotes feared to tread. Bears began to haunt the herd around early September each year. "A 30-30 was good medicine," said Ted. To protect his flock, a herder sometimes laid his sleeping bag right alongside the slumbering sheep. In bad weather that meant only a tarp over the herder's head.

Once a bear gets a taste of lamb, he's addicted, claimed Ted. That bear will follow the herd forever for a second helping of his favorite dish. In the summer of 1939 or 1940, a grizzly killed 60 sheep in Horseshoe Basin. "Only a grizzly could have

A flock of sheep on the driveway. Photo from the Shafer Museum collection.

got away with so many because they're so smart and they bury their kill," said Ted.

Bolin recalled one night when *he* tangled with a marauding bear. The sheep were bedded down near Ted's tent, when he heard them start to "rumble" or make a thunder-like sound with their hooves to warn of a bear charge. Ted ran out in his stocking feet. A bear had a ewe down 50 yards away. Ted's nearly deaf dog was nowhere to be seen. Ted crept up as close as possible and fired at the bear. Infuriated, the intruder roared toward Ted, who split for the tent. Ted moved so fast he bypassed the tent door and had to run a lap around the tent. He knew the tent would not save him anyway; the bear could follow him right in.

At this crucial moment Ted's dog entered the fray and a nasty battle ensued between bear and dog. After much growling and gnashing of canine teeth, the bear retreated. The ewes calmed down, but Ted had meanwhile grown permanent goose bumps and his hair stuck straight out from the back of his neck all night.

Wayne Luft: The Lifestyle You Get to Love
Wayne Luft retired from sheepherding after many years on

the driveways but he never lost his lust for the sheepherder's way of life. Every time he'd see a band of sheep come through the area, he'd still want to join the crew and walk the high mountain route that circumnavigates the Methow Valley. "You have a heck of a time getting it out of your system," said Wayne.

Wayne worked during the heyday of sheepherding here, when wool still fetched a good price and the US Forest Service awarded a generous number of grazing permits. Beginning around 1925 and during the following decade, Wayne remembered times when 30 bands (up to 2,000 sheep per band) ranged in the mountains of the Sawtooth and Pasayten areas during a single season.

Wayne grew up hanging around sheep camps in the 1930s. The lifestyle suited him from the start. In the mid-'40s he grazed sheep on a huge circuit ringing the Methow Valley. Sheep were shipped by train to Pateros, where they began their epic summer hike.

First the sheep got their legs in shape scrambling up to Alta Lake. As the snow receded, Wayne herded his charges up to the Sawtooth Range. He reached the high meadows by the time they opened up around July. Wayne drove the ewes and lambs from one grassy, flower-decked valley to the next, until the sheep circled around the head of the Methow Valley and headed into the lush pastures of the Pasayten. The journey continued trans-Pasayten to the Methow highlands all the way back to the Columbia River at Brewster.

Luft walked the entire distance of this Methow circle tour. "Pack horses carried supplies, but the sheepherder walked the driveways," said Wayne. Sheep wander into heavy brush and rough terrain on the trail, places a horse can't go, but people can, he explained.

The ratio was one herder per 3,000 sheep for the whole distance. "Sheepherders would have the sheep scattered for miles and miles, but they knew where they all were," said Wayne. Even so, he added, a herder could lose 100 or more sheep per season. Some strayed and were never found. Others were snatched by predators.

Wayne admired the sheepherders he knew. One old Scot sheepherder named Bob Kier was a master craftsman. He gathered wool caught on barbed wire and sheared the wool off dead sheep. Then with his fingers, he spun the unwashed wool to create beautiful patterned sweaters and caps.

"The sheepherders I knew were real dandies," said Wayne. The same could be said of Wayne himself.

Helen and Gus Smith:
The Trials and Tribulations of Sheep Ranching

Whenever you'd see Gus or Helen Smith on their sheep ranch above Twisp, they'd be out working. Not hard, not fast, not like someone just trying to get a job done, but in a relaxed and steady manner. They seemed to enjoy the process of work as well as the product of their labors. "If you don't work, you won't be satisfied with yourself," Gus said.

Gus and Helen raised sheep for 30 years on their 600-acre Alder Creek ranch. There was no need for the couple to lead their sheep up a rough stock driveway, for the Smiths owned enough land to graze their stock all summer, and to raise alfalfa for winter feed.

There were always plenty of chores to do on the Smiths' ranch. "Those sheep work a person," said Gus. The Smiths built miles of sheep-proof picket fence, a project that took three years to complete, and half of Gus' time mending it once it was completed.

The hardest time of the year for sheep ranchers is during lambing, said Gus. For 24 hours a day the ewes must be watched. Ewes can have a difficult time giving birth. Some years, for some reason, most of the lambs are born upside down and backwards. To top it off, some ewes are "mutton-headed," said Gus. He explained the term: Ewes often stubbornly refuse to mother one of their own offspring. If a ewe has two lambs, one female and one male, she'll usually refuse the female. Encouraging the ewe to accept the second sibling often fails. So the rancher tries to graft the orphan to another mother.

The second hardest time of the year is when the sheep are sheared, recalled Gus. Every year, the shearer from Moses Lake appeared at the Smiths' ranch to fleece the sheep. It was the Smiths' duty to ready and steady the sheep for the shearer, plus they helped stomp down and compress the wool into huge 8-foot burlap bags weighing 200 pounds each. Once they'd finished the physical tasks, they had to arise at 4 a.m. to transport the goods to market. One year they drove to Moses Lake

Gus and Helen Smith at their sheep ranch near Twisp, about 1987.
Photo courtesy Gus Smith.

to sell their wool to the Portland Pendleton Mills, famous makers of expensive wool sportswear. Sometimes buyers came all the way from Massachusetts for Washington wool.

Predators created as much havoc on the Smiths' Twisp ranch as they did on the backcountry ranges. Coyotes were the main culprits, Gus claimed. One year in the 1970s coyotes killed 32 sheep, mostly lambs, some yearlings, and even a few ewes.

The Smiths' watchdog provided a first line of defense against predators. If the dog sensed a coyote it made a ruckus and woke up Gus, who would tear outside rifle in hand and shoot skyward. During that worst year, Gus snared eight or nine coyotes in traps and shot some as well. Gus doctored many lambs left barely alive after an attack. "I patched up one lamb whose neck had been bitten clear through," recalled Gus.

Despite their mutton-headed nature, Gus is fond of sheep and defends them against critics. Their wool is valuable, said Gus. It resists acids, and it's flame resistant to a degree, and will smolder rather than burn.

Sheep control barnaby thistle, Gus added. When he ran his sheep up the Lookout Mountain Road, they'd chew thistle in preference to grass. In the fall when the barnaby bore its insidious seed pods, the sheep would gobble up the harvest and prevent reseeding.

"After you're around sheep, you really notice quite a difference in personalities," said Gus. "Sheep are like people—for 100 sheep you get 100 different personalities." Gus got along with 90 percent of his flock, but "there were usually 10 old bearcats that would just as soon fight you as look at you," said Gus. "Just troublemakers, not in tune with the crowd."

Gus and Helen quit raising sheep in 1984. "It just wasn't profitable anymore," said Gus in the summer of 1991. "There are still some small bands of sheep raised in the valley," he added, "but it's hard to make much money now sheep ranching in the Methow. The price of wool is low, and a fat, 100-pound lamb might only sell for $47—not a good deal for the seller."

Sheep ranching in the Methow was never a real profitable venture, one suspects, but it seems some folks are naturally cut out for the job: Gus and Helen in particular. Both recalled the trials of sheep raising, but their recollections were peppered with a large dose of humor and seemed utterly free of regret.

Sheep Ranching in the 1990s

In the early 1990s, Mike Buchert, Tonasket, was the only rancher to have permits for ranging sheep in the high country surrounding the Methow Valley. Every spring some of Buchert's sheep traveled to Horseshoe Basin in the Pasayten Wilderness. Every other year, Buchert sent a band of his sheep, numbering about 1,200 ewes, to the high meadows of Hart's Pass. On alternate years, some of his livestock were driven into the Sawtooth Range. Their route went up West Fork Buttermilk Creek to the green meadows of Merchants Basin, then out Foggy Dew Creek.

By the year 2000, Buchert was still the only permittee for the Methow high country. Under the name Cascade Sheep, Buchert and a partner still ranged 1,200 ewes and lambs but now only in the Gold Creek and Buttermilk Creek areas from early May to mid-July.

Mike Buchert is a grandson of legendary pioneer sheep rancher Victor Lasamiz. Lasamiz was a teenager in the early

1900s when he began herding sheep. A descendant of Basques, inhabitants of the western Pyrenees of France and Spain, Victor Lasamiz inherited his ancestors' capacity to raise sheep.

As a young man on his own, Victor moved to Okanogan in 1910 and immediately bought a band of sheep. His timing was perfect. The Forest Service at the time welcomed stock grazing on national forest ranges and Victor seized the opportunity this policy presented. He ran more sheep than most sheepmen at the time—seven bands at the peak, or about 10,000 of his ewes, browsed on public allotments. The difficulty of finding good help raising sheep prompted Lasamiz to switch to cattle ranching after 1949.

Now Mike Buchert carries on the family tradition, raising sheep in the Okanogan Valley and ranging them in the Methow Valley backcountry.

Bibliography

Bolin, Ted. Phone Interview. Winthrop, Washington, fall 1991.

Bauman, Christina. Forest Service. Phone interview. Twisp, Washington, February 2000.

Buchert, Mike. Phone Interview. Tonasket, Washington, winter 1992.

Gaylord, Mary. Notes on sheep grazing in the Okanogan National Forest, gathered from Forest Service records. Twisp, Washington.

Harris, P.T., Forest Supervisor. "Outline of Grazing History, Okanogan County, Washington." April 4, 1941.

Hottell, Diana. "He Packed for the Sheep Drives." *Methow Valley News*, February 19, 1981.

——. "Helen and Gus Smith, Sheep Ranchers." *Methow Valley News*, June 30, 1977.

Smith, Gus. Phone Interview. Twisp, Washington, fall 1991.

Wilson, Bruce. "Cow Country: A History of Okanogan Livestock Industry," *Okanogan County Heritage*, June 1963.

Chapter 21

THE DEPRESSION YEARS

The Methow Valley Was the Best Place to Live

When quizzed about the Depression years, Methow Valley octogenarian Nedra Horn shrugged, adding mischievously, "Well, things were always tough here, so we hardly noticed the difference." Most of the Methow's population during the Great Depression would have agreed with Nedra. Severe drought plagued the Methow in the late 1920s, jobs were scarce, pay was poor. However, the bank crash of 1929, bankruptcies, and suicides due to lost fortunes—these were news items from "back East," a world away from the Methow's isolated farming community.

Self-sufficiency was the Methow's saving grace during the Depression. No tattered hoboes stood in breadlines here. People made their own bread and preserved their own produce. Everyone had a garden. There were chickens in the yard and eggs in the hen house. Many people raised milk cows and cattle and served meals "fit for kings" with butter, cream and beef gracing the table during the Depression's darkest days.

Local grocery lists were brief and varied little from one shopping excursion to the next. Only sugar, flour, salt, coffee, and tobacco had to be purchased, and occasionally dairy products. Prices for grocery staples were reasonable even considering the times. Sugar cost $4.90 for 100 pounds, flour $1.35 for about

50 pounds, butter 30 cents per pound, milk 6 cents a quart and coffee 18 cents a pound. Merchants sometimes received no money for groceries but instead traded their store items for stock, eggs, hay or firewood.

During the Depression, the state took a survey and discovered that the Methow was the best place to live in Washington during those hardest of times. People were admittedly poor according to the famous survey, but they had learned how to be self-reliant with virtually no money.

When a family was down and out, the survey concluded, the community banded together to offer a helping hand. Historian Walter Nickell remembered one early Methow pioneer, Laura Garrett, who said the time she most enjoyed living in the valley was during the Depression of the 1930s "when there was no money, and everyone helped each other." Nickell reminisced that Methow folks were bolstered during the Depression by "close family ties and a small close-knit community, where everybody was your friend and each person thought he was a big duck even though it was a small puddle."

Most valley people adhered to a neighbors-helping-neighbors ethic during the Depression. Ken White said his family felt comfortable and well-cared-for during the Depression but that some other families were impoverished at the time.

> We had clothing, a good home, electricity, water, incredible amounts of the finest food. That wasn't the way many other kids lived. There were so many tragic families living here. Kids just living in wretched conditions.
>
> —Interview, Winthrop, Summer 1990.

The Ray White family unofficially adopted several young men who were friends of Ken's brothers. Ken elaborated:

> There wasn't enough food at their homes and no jobs, so these boys came to live at our home. My folks fed them and they had a system worked out so they could make a few dollars to pay for their clothing and tobacco by cutting wood.
>
> —Ibid.

Even in the Methow, the ranks of the poor swelled as the Depression lingered. People forgot their pride, sometimes even their honesty when they desperately needed something a neighbor could donate or loan. Living in her house by the side of

*Chickens in the yard and eggs in the hen house. Photo
courtesy Carolyn Hotchkiss.*

the road, Hazel Kikendall welcomed a parade of borrowers and
"keepers" knocking at her door during the Depression. Here's
Hazel's recollection:

> People stopped day or night for "what have
> you." I recall them asking for veggies, fruit, the
> loan of a lantern and tools, or a 'bug' (a candle in
> a can to keep a driver's hands warm). There were
> transients and hangers-on with no definite depar-
> ture date. Most people were appreciative. We also
> lost things. We never could keep a certain type of
> garden fork. Someone tried to rob the bee hives
> one night, but the bees took care of that. One fall,
> someone dug our winter potatoes.
> —Autobiographical letter on Methow history, Summer 1990.

Wild game became an important part of the local diet during
the Depression—a resource unavailable to the needy denizens
of big cities. Yet hunting was a mixed blessing—an economical
food source for hunters but a source of hardship for the
owner of the hunting grounds. Hazel recalled deer season in
the late 1930s.

> The hunters were not too selective. If they
> couldn't find a deer, your livestock would do. We

lost some and so did my folks who also lived in
the Wolf Creek area.

—*Ibid.*

Though hunters often shot what they shouldn't have, far
worse were the desperadoes who set out to steal stock. A horse
thief ring existed, Hazel claimed, and her father lost a horse
taken from his pasture and transported out of the area by
truck. Hazel herself lost a saddle horse and her neighbors had
one stolen out of their barn at night. Fortunately, a local
tracker with the skill of an Indian foiled the thieves by tracing
one horse to the Beaver Creek area and one near Winthrop.

Despite the positive state survey, the self-sufficiency of locals
and the generosity of neighbors, the 1930s were still a time of
tragedy, and the decade left emotional wounds that would never
completely heal. Because of economic and personal disasters,
the Stokes family had to give up the Beaver Creek ranch
they'd worked for 11 years. "My formative years were in the
Depression," Jay Stokes said. "It scars you, something like
that. I still find myself pinching pennies. Working 10-hour days
for a buck fifty would brand anyone." (*Methow Valley News*,
October 15, 1981.)

Landing a Job During the Depression

During the '30s one took any decent job offered even though
most were of short duration, related Jay Stokes. "Working out"
(away from one's own ranch) was a necessity then, said Jay,
whose own resumé during the Depression included driving
cattle, lambing in the basin, skidding poles with horses, clearing the Loup Loup right-of-way with horsepower, and being
official "smoke chaser" on call to fight fires.

Ken White corroborated Stokes' view of the Depression era
job market. "During that time it was a diversified deal," Ken
said. "When the cream check wasn't enough, Dad would work
out carpentering, plus we'd sell a few beef cows."

Valley orchardists, who were lucky enough to have irrigation
feeding their trees during this dry decade, continued to produce
and sell their hardy Methow apples. But even some fruit growers would moonlight to earn extra cash.

The Forest Service was a dependable employer during the
Depression. Not only would one's paycheck from the government eventually arrive but some of the jobs offered were once-

in-a-lifetime adventures. Esther Johnson discovered the thrill of
a Forest Service occupation in the late '30s when she and her
2-year-old son accompanied husband Keith to his fire lookout
post on Milton Mountain near Mount Gardner. A storm came
up from the south, remembered Esther:

> Wind, lightning and heavy rain made the win-
> dow shades flap up and down like wings. The
> house was on a tower 50 feet high. Storms passed
> over us about every two hours all night, first the
> lightning, then the thunder, then the wind. My
> boy and I were in bed with our heads covered
> most of the night.
>
> When the lightning would strike very close, the
> thunder would be so loud it would deafen one, and
> it would shake the tower like a giant hand held
> hold of it. The radio aerial wires would light up
> like sparklers at the Fourth of July celebration.
> —*Okanogan County Heritage.* Spring 1986.

Several other Methow couples also eked out a living by staff-
ing Forest Service lookouts in the Depression. At least in
Esther's estimate, the job had more pluses than minuses, since
the following summer she accompanied her spouse to North
Twenty-mile Lookout, this time with her 3-year-old son in tow
and a new baby boy only 3 months old!

When the gargantuan government-sponsored Grand Coulee
Dam project got under way in the early 1930s, Methow men
flocked to the area to find temporary employment.

The CCC to the Rescue

Within days of Franklin D. Roosevelt's inauguration in 1933,
the Civilian Conservation Corps came into being, combining
two of the new president's favorite causes—conservation of
natural resources and employment.

Because of the vast federal forestlands surrounding the
Methow Valley, this area hit the jackpot when it came to CCC
projects. In the Methow, the CCC built trails, roads, camp-
grounds and fire lookouts. They helped control erosion, fought
fires and re-seeded land.

Picture the Methow Valley with huge CCC camps like minia-
ture cities located up the Methow's drainages. There were camps
at Boulder Creek, Foggy Dew, Eightmile, Robinson Creek and
a huge one up War Creek. "At the Eightmile Ranger Station

the government created a small CCC city," claimed Ken White, "where everything was supplied for workers—housing, food, cooks. They had their own doctors and dentists!"

The CCC crews worked furiously in the Methow backcountry, accomplishing a stupendous amount in a short time. They converted hundreds of miles of Indian, prospector, and trapper trails into hiking trails in the national forests. The CCC even laid out an airstrip in the center of the Pasayten Wilderness, (at the time called the North Cascades Primitive Area). Many fire lookouts atop county peaks were CCC-constructed, as were most of the government warehouse facilities. The original ranger stations, homes, and warehouses at Early Winters and Winthrop are all examples of CCC architecture.

In the Methow Valley, the Corps left an impressive road construction legacy as well. Widening the Hart's Pass Road in 1933-34 was one of their biggest challenges. The ubiquitous CCC either built, rebuilt or extended the Chewuch Road, the road from the Chewuch River up Boulder Creek winding around Tiffany Mountain, the Eightmile Road, roads up Poorman, Libby and Buttermilk creeks and a road from Gold Creek to the Chelan divide.

Local men employed by the Forest Service or contracted by the Forest Service directed the CCC teams. Camps and teams could arrive from anywhere in the United States. The recruits might be shy kids with "barely enough peach fuzz to shave," or, according to CCC camp director Bill Lester, "a bunch from the Bronx, meaner than junkyard dogs." When Bill arrived at Robinson Creek to start his first CCC camp director's job, a pack of disgruntled tough guys greeted him:

> These men had beat up three of us foremen. I had a truckload of them building roads. One day I showed them how to use an axe and saw. The next day there wasn't an axe or saw or nothin'. They'd thrown them all over Dead Horse Point.
>
> I lined them up and told 'em, "If there's anything gone tomorrow, I'll throw *you* all over Dead Horse Point!" After that I didn't miss nothing!
>
> The next bunch were Midwest farm kids that couldn't find a job. (There was a drought back there then.) They were nice kids.
>
> —*Okanogan County Heritage*, Fall 1989.

What about local men? Was the CCC an indispensable

source of employment for the Methow, during the Depression? According to local CCC veteran Bob Crandall, "Okanogan County was a rare item because there was work to do." For a while Bob picked fruit here for 30 cents an hour, an excellent wage considering the times, he claimed. "Sometimes there was work but no money, but at least one could earn food and a roof over one's head," said Bob. And perhaps just as impor-

The Depression years had little effect on Ken White whose greatest joy was always found exploring nature. Photo courtesy Marjory White.

tant, the Depression was gentler on wage-earner egos here. As Bob put it, "Even if you didn't have much, folks around here still made you feel wanted and worthwhile." (*Okanogan County Heritage*, Winter 1983.)

According to Crandall, in the Methow Valley you could survive even without a job, but the CCC became an irresistible option. When the CCC came, Ken White estimated about 90 percent of the young people in the valley joined. If you joined, you'd leave home and live in one of the huge camps. Two brothers and two friends of Ken's worked for the CCC.

Ken believed the CCC was a godsend to the Methow Valley. Too young and independent to join the CCC himself, Ken nevertheless observed the workings of the relief organization in the valley and his admiration was unbounded. Ken summed up his CCC support:

The CCC actually made money for the country.

CCC Camp at Gold Creek. Photo courtesy Hazel Holloway.

> Millions of dollars of wonderful work done for the
> smallest amounts you can imagine, plus it made
> millions of young men stable citizens and kept
> them out of jail. It was one of the most positive
> things ever done for young men here and for the
> nation. The CCC fixed their teeth, took care of
> their health, got them clothing plus paid $1 a day!
> So that's how the Depression was smoothed out.
> Can you imagine thousands and thousands of
> young men going to seed suddenly finding them-
> selves well fed and with their young friends out
> building trails?
>   —Interview. Winthrop, Summer 1990.

CCC alumnus Bob Crandall said it this way: "It meant everything to me. The CCC built up confidence in people, particularly in youngsters at a time when they needed that confidence.
That's what determined their later lives, I believe." Bob used
funds saved from his CCC job to buy land near Winthrop.
"The CCC gave me a start in life; I owe my life to the CCC.
It's that simple." (*Okanogan County Heritage*, Winter 1983.)

Methow Moonshine

The CCC was seductive to the young, the strong and the unemployed. But what if one owned a ranch that had to be
tended even when it failed to fully support a family? What if a

person was older, or not so vigorous, or just not a joiner? One option for extra income if the CCC didn't beckon was moonshine, and many local ranchers supplemented their inadequate incomes during the Depression by producing illegal liquor. Customers were plentiful here.

Bootlegging and moonshining began the minute Washington state banned liquor in 1916. Federal prohibition in 1920 merely gave both occupations a big boost.

Because of its size and remoteness the Methow was a particularly safe and hospitable place to produce and sell alcohol. How could government agents catch a culprit red-handed in the back forty of a Methow ranch?

Charley Barcelou produced home brew up Texas Creek during prohibition. Other folks were doing the same thing up every side canyon and creek in the Methow, but Charley was different, a customer claimed; his moonshine was good because he was fussy about it.

Charley's fail-proof method of whiskey manufacture was to keep his corn mash or fruit mash in big tubs for seven to eight days to work itself into alcohol. He kept the filter scrupulously clean and filtered the mash through charcoal and several thicknesses of flannel and silk. "No one gets poisoned that way," he said. "You got to run it slow. If you boil it fast you boil the mash. What you want is to keep it slow so you get alcohol before the water goes up in steam." (*Methow Valley News*, October 4, 1979.)

Charley's brand must have been potent since (as the story goes) the leftover mash could even make a hog sick. One time Charley dumped some used cracked corn into a hog's trough and his pig gobbled it up. "That pig was drunk for two whole days," laughed Charley. "He was a white pig and his ears turned bright red." (*Ibid.*) Charley tried to exercise the pig back to a sober condition but the porker refused to move and slept off the binge instead.

Since some producers were far less conscientious than Charley, many Methow moonshine patrons probably got as ill from the alcohol as the hog got from the mash. Charley observed that one moonshine still exposed to the elements had blowflies and yellowjackets 2 inches thick all over the surface of the tub's contents.

A locally famous lady named Bessy Sharpe ran a profitable

bootlegging business in Mazama. In the late 1920s and early 1930s Bessy supplied the local Rockview Dance Hall with illicit elixir. Her delivery was quick and easy; she'd just drive her pickup behind the hall and discreetly sell liquor right from her truck. After delivering the goods, Bessy returned to her other business at the Chicken Dinner Inn in Mazama, which historian Barbara Duffy presumes was a speakeasy.

There were plenty of dance halls in the 1930s, related Ken White. There were dance halls both in town and out in the country—like the Rockview Hall that Bessy serviced. The drinking and brawling scenes in those days could have come right out of an old western movie, Ken claimed. "In the '30s fistfights started every night. You went to any dance and there would always be guys outside duking it out. Of course my brothers drank and liked to get in brawls even though they might lose. They weren't thinking too clear—thought it was great fun to get beat up!" (Interview. Winthrop, Summer 1990.)

Gold Mines in Depression Times

Gold mining provided scary, dangerous, mountain-locked jobs, but the pay at the Azurite and Gold Hill mines during the Depression was the best one could get in the Methow Valley.

President Roosevelt's recovery plan nurtured the Azurite Mine by increasing the price paid for gold from $20.67 an ounce to $35. With visions of profits the American Smelting and Refining Company (ASARCO) signed a 25-year lease on 36 gold and silver lode claims and six mill sites near the Hart's Pass area. Profits from gold never panned out for the company, but lots of locals found jobs at the Azurite, earning enough income to support themselves and a family living back home.

The semisuccessful Azurite claims induced miners to bore out the other side of the same mountain, creating the Gold Hill Mine. Large ore veins must cut through the entire peak, people believed. This optimistic assessment led Hazard Ballard (who, with brother Charles Ballard, had developed the Azurite Mine) to organize the Gold Hill Mining Company in the mid-1930s. The success of the mine hinged on construction of a mine-to-market road, a means of transporting ore from the Gold Hill Mine west to the Skagit Valley and its final destination, the

Tacoma smelter. Transporting men and equipment into the mine site by pack train from Lost River in the Methow was not economically feasible in the 1930s, but promoters had high hopes that the so-called Ruby Road to the coast would soon get the go-ahead.

By 1939 the Gold Hill Mine had made no impression on the global gold market; it could claim only one shipment of ore to a Kellogg, Idaho, smelter. But in the Methow Valley, the mining company had a sizable economic impact. Close to 4 million shares in the company were sold at 10 cents a share and most of those shares were bought by local people. "Times were such," said Bob Crandall of Winthrop, "almost anything'd look good. To buy mining shares was like buying a lottery ticket. In the '30s and '40s when people were told they wouldn't be able to save more than $5,000 in a lifetime of work, they thought, 'What the heck' and took a chance on hitting it big." (*Okanogan County Heritage*, Winter 1985.) Gold Hill stock became so common people used it for currency in Winthrop.

Many shareholders were sorely disappointed when they never got a dime back on their investments. Warren Badger's father had bought 22,237 shares to finance Warren's college education. About the only person who came out on top was miner Dick Horn, who said he sold his shares before they became worthless and "earned enough to pay for two outhouses."

Despite the Gold Hill's sorry showing in the stock arena, the mine provided something essential during the time it was active. "It was a bonanza for people who needed work," said Bob Crandall. Wages were $5 to $8 a day, a respectable amount in the Great Depression era.

A Final Note
Walter Nickell tells a familiar, friendly tale that seems to sum up the situation in the Methow Valley during the Depression. The story concerns Walter's nephew, Dale Dibble.

> In Dale's early teens in the mid-'30s, he believed, and still does, that there is no place better in which to grow up than in the Methow Valley. Nobody told him it was not standard to have holes in your shoes and in your pants at the knees. Nobody told him most people painted their houses....
> Then one summer around 1935 there was an

epidemic in the cattle herds. It was so serious the state imported veterinarians from Seattle to inoculate the cattle. As a 15-year-old, he was talking to these veterinarians on the Albert Boesel place before the Weeman Bridge. One of the vets said, "This Methow Valley is a very depressing place." Dale was shocked that he could say such a thing about such a wonderful place. The veterinarian said, "Look at these homes. I do not think any of these people know what paint is." It goes to show ... beauty is in the eyes of the beholder. Both saw the valley from two completely different perspectives.

—*The Way It Was*. June 1990.

Sure, people living in the Methow during the Depression were poor. But most didn't know it, and if they did they managed to ignore it and survive.

Bibliography

Duffy, Barbara. Interview. Winthrop, Washington, summer 1990.

Gibbs, Allen G. "CCC Accomplishments In Okanogan County." *Okanogan County Heritage*, Winter 1983.

Hottell, Diana. "Charley Barcelou: He Did It Right, He Did It Clean, It Was Prime Goods." *Methow Valley News*, October 4, 1979.

——. "Jay Stokes: Farming Beaver Creek Has Been the Stokes' Center of Focus for Generations." *Methow Valley News*, October 15, 1981.

——. "Rise and Fall of the Gold Hill Mine." *Okanogan County Heritage*, Winter 1985.

Kikendall, Hazel. Letter describing her personal history in the Methow Valley, Twisp, Washington, summer 1990.

Lester, Bill. "Bill Lester." As told to Edith Nelson. *Okanogan County Heritage*, Fall 1984.

Nickell, Walter. *The Way It Was*. Naples, Florida, June 1990.

Smith, Richard. "The Winter I Spent At the Old Azurite Mine." *Coyote Tales*, Spring 1974.

Spurgeon, Esther. "Keith and Esther." *Okanogan County Heritage*, Spring 1986.

White, Ken. Interview. Winthrop, Washington, summer 1990.

Wilson, Bruce. *The Late Frontier*. Okanogan County Historical Society, 1990.

Chapter 22

FIREFIGHTERS FROM THE SKY

The Smokejumper Base between Twisp and Winthrop is deceptively quiet during winter and spring, the Methow's wet seasons. Then suddenly one dry summer or fall day there's a fire bust and the place erupts with frenzied, purposeful activity—planes landing, helicopters hovering, parachuters packing, cooks cooking and firefighters coming and going around the clock. It's a place ready to mobilize in minutes. With a fire, time is of the essence.

A Novel Idea

The need to get firefighters to fires faster was what made local Forest Service officials receptive to the novel idea of smokejumping in the late 1930s. When a fire ignited in the high country of the vast Pasayten Wilderness (known for its big fires), a crew might need to walk a day, a day and a half or sometimes all night just to arrive at the site. By the time the fighters reached the fire, they'd be worn out, and the blaze would be roaring out of control.

The innovative officials were racking their brains trying to figure out ways to get men to fires quickly, both to prevent huge burns and worker burnout. Already, they'd tried dropping tools free-fall from planes or dangling from small parachutes to lighten the load employees had to carry in, but this mostly resulted in broken tools. Later, they had better luck dropping food rather than tools to isolated fire crews. While the food itself was not rated exceptional by the recipients, at least it arrived intact.

In 1939, the Okanogan National Forest was chosen to be the site of the first US experimental parachute jumping project. The reason this honor fell to the Okanogan was due to its renowned "air mindedness." In addition to parachuting tools and dropping dinners, this national forest had used planes since 1927 for fire finding after lightning storms, and by 1932 local fire crews were flying in and out of the Pasayten Airstrip to deal a quick blow to fires in this far north region. Then, too, leaders of the local Forest Service were gung ho for the smokejumping project, while other regional officials reacted to the proposal with dismay. "Simply too dangerous," said a USFS manager from Region One. "Jump from planes? A preposterous suggestion," came the cry from some offices.

Meanwhile, in the Methow Valley, the federal agency began to investigate the new firefighting technique. Through research, locals discovered parachute jumping precedents had already been set. Right at that time the Russian military was attempting mass parachute jumps. After studying jumping logistics literature received from the Russians, locals decided the method might work for fighting faraway forest fires. They contacted the Eagle Parachute Company in the Eastern United States, and hired some professional jumpers. By 1939 an airplane sat primed for action at the Intercity Airport.

Before men actually stepped from airplanes into empty space, cargo chutes with sandbags attached were dropped into timber stands. The chutes and sandbags survived the flight fairly well so the Forest Service tried dropping men into open areas around Winthrop. Next, men parachuted into high meadows to a choice drop-spot near Tiffany Mountain which locals christened Parachute Meadows in remembrance of the event. Finally, they fell into timber which guaranteed a gentle landing, when on descent, a parachute hitched onto a tree, dangling the chuter like a marionette.

No serious injuries resulted from the 60 live jumps during the 1939 experiments. This demonstrated to the satisfaction of Winthrop Forest Service officials that the procedure could be done safely. The jumpers also proved they could land near a

Francis Lufkin: premier smokejumper. Photo from the Okanogan County Historical Society, negative 3476.

marked spot; many times they dropped right on the bull's eye. Elated by the phenomenal success of the project, local foresters decided to support smokejumping on an extensive scale. Hence, from 1940 on, smokejumpers dropped from the sky to land right at the site of a fire.

Francis Lufkin: Premier Smokejumper

Francis Lufkin started as a support man during the 1939 experimental smokejumping project. His job was to rescue professional jumpers when they hung helplessly from trees, then transport them back to the base. One day, after the pros had successfully jumped 54 times, supervisors invited local man Lufkin to take the plunge. At that point, Lufkin had had no previous instruction but he'd witnessed a lot of jumps. He remembered vividly the cuts and bruises some jumpers received on their heads. On the other hand, as a ground person he made $135 a month, while parachuters earned a hefty $191 for the same amount of time. At the tail end of the Depression, this jump in salary to Francis outweighed the risks involved in jumping from a plane. Francis accepted the offer.

Lufkin recalled, "They told me about pulling the ripcord after a count of three, to get my body in a good position, not to wait too long, and that's about it." Despite teasing from friends trying to test his courage, Francis wasn't much afraid of the jumping part. More fearful to him was the unavoidable airplane ride—his first—and in bad weather to boot! In his own words, here's how neophyte Lufkin felt moments before the jump.

> Well, it was a long step out of that airplane, I'll guarantee you that. But it really didn't bother me much. The airplane scared me more than anything. Just the way it moved in the air in downdrafts and updrafts. Besides that particular day it had been raining and I jumped right among the clouds.
>
> —*River Pigs and Cayuses,* 1984.

It turned out that Francis Lufkin had the "right stuff" for smokejumping. On his premier drop, he landed right on target at the Intercity Airport. The next year Francis became a member of the first elite smokejumper crew stationed at Winthrop's soon-to-be nationally famous smokejumper base. Besides Francis, the original crew consisted of only three other members—two pro jumpers from California and a local man, George Honey.

On August 10, 1940, when a blaze broke out near Bridge Creek, Francis made the first bona fide firefighting jump in this region. After this real-life test of the new technique, Lufkin declared smokejumping an unqualified success.

> I used to walk for hours or days to get into a fire. It took less than 15 minutes in the airplane to get to this one and we had it out before the trail crew reached us—a total of seven or eight hours. A year or two earlier a similar lightning strike expanded into a 100-acre fire that cost $44,000 in materials and man hours to put out.
>
> —*The North Cascadians,* 1980.

Lufkin went on to become a legendary figure in the world of smokejumping. In 1941 he directed the establishment of the North Cascade Smokejumper Base. After being promoted in 1945 to aerial project foreman for the Okanogan National Forest, Francis strove to improve both smokejumping equipment and technique, receiving three awards for advancements he made in the field.

Lufkin insisted all the jumpers under his supervision receive a high level of training and become highly skilled. Partly due to his vigilance, the North Cascade Smokejumper Base maintained an exceptional safety record. Lufkin himself minimized the inherent dangers of smokejumping. According to this veteran jumper, one has a greater chance of getting hurt falling off a horse than jumping from a plane. To most people the thought of stepping out of a plane is heart-stopping, but looking back over his years of jumping, Francis remembered not so much fear as fatigue.

> I guess it's dramatic to some people but to a
> firefighter ... it's just lots of dirty work, plain hard
> labor that takes all the sap out of you. The main
> job is to go put the fire out ...
> —*River Pigs and Cayuses*, 1984.

Bill Moody's Famous Fall

Despite Lufkin's assessment of the job, smokejumping is fraught with hazards and smokejumpers must be brave men and women. A jumper can pull the ripcord of his parachute before being free of the plane. Instead of alighting butterfly style, gently into a tree, a parachuter can be clipped by branches, snatched by a snag, banged into a tree trunk, or dragged across rocky terrain like a grated carrot. And there's the ultimate smokejumper nightmare—chute malfunction.

It was this last hazard that Bill Moody faced during what he called his "once-in-a-lifetime-jump" November 1, 1964. Bill recalled it had been a long, warm, dry September and October, and there were many fires blazing in the Okanogan that fateful fall day. Moody and some other jumpers were headed for Jack Creek this side of the Loup Loup Summit.

Right from the start things went wrong. The wind was far too strong and the first man to jump, John Lester, got socked with a gust that buffeted him backwards, split his helmet and gave him a concussion. Bill was still worrying about his friend's calamity when it came his turn to jump. He stepped from the plane, and the wind immediately grabbed his chute. Something was amiss; he was falling far too rapidly. Instead of billowing into a balloon shape, his chute formed a "Mae

West," a condition where some of the lines end up on the out-side of the chute, so it splits in the center and resembles an enormous bra.

Zooming downward, Bill threw out his reserve parachute, a 24-foot-diameter circular nylon canopy. But the wind taunted him again by blowing the reserve right back at his face. He tried again, same thing. A third time—no luck. His body by now was skimming the tops of the trees. At the last minute Bill tried one more toss of the reserve chute. "Let the fourth time be the charm," he prayed. Miraculously, the chute filled just enough to slow his descent. He tumbled down on top of an old rotten log that cushioned his fall. Moments later, his hair-raising descent forgotten, Bill was fighting a forest fire. The next day, five inches of snow extinguished every fire in the district!

The Big 1970 Fire Bust

To this day, the summer of 1970 is considered one of the biggest seasons in smokejumper history. All the action took place right here at the North Cascade Smokejumper Base. According to Francis Lufkin, for three days this Methow Val-ley airport had more air traffic than the Spokane International Airport. There were 325 takeoffs and landings per day.

So many fires blazed here that hot season that all of North Central Washington filled up with smoke. The smoke got so dense it became hard to fly to the fires and harder still to spot new fires. Seven thousand acres burned in the Boulder Creek area. A fire engulfed Williams Lake near the Twisp River Valley. It was burning up War Creek, South Creek, and Bear Creek above Pearrygin Lake. In all, there were 212 fires here to fight and often resources were spread so thin no one was left to fight them.

The Intercity Airport became a place of frenzied activity. One heard the constant roar of DC-2 and DC-4 airplanes tak-ing off and landing at the base, transporting a total of 4,500 firefighters. Twenty-five helicopters buzzed in and out of the base, while FAA controllers worked 24 hours a day directing air traffic. The National Guard helped out and the mess hall remained open all day and night feeding the hungry troops.

Firefighters and jumpers flew here from all over the US, in-cluding the East Coast and Alaska. Bill Moody remembered

Please send us this card to receive our latest catalog.

☐ Check here if you would like to receive our catalog via e-mail.

INNER TRADITIONS

HEALING ARTS PRESS

DESTINY BOOKS

Park Street Press

E-mail address _____

Name _____ Company _____

Address _____ Phone _____

City _____ State _____ Zip _____ Country _____

Order at 1-800-246-8648 • Fax (802) 767-3726

E-mail: orders@InnerTraditions.com • Web site: www.InnerTraditions.com

Inner Traditions International, Ltd.
P.O. Box 388
Rochester, VT 05767-0388
U.S.A.

309

making his first jump of the season on June first and continuing to jump until November first with no let up. Everyone was fired-up, so to speak; people worked overtime, double time and way beyond normal endurance. Sleep was a luxury; somehow fighters just kept running on adrenaline.

The Future of the North Cascade Smokejumper Base

The North Cascade Smokejumper Base is still active with a healthy contingent of about 30 jumpers assigned to the site. Bill Moody became head of the base after Francis Lufkin retired in 1972. To a great extent, the present strength of the local base is due to Bill's inspired supervision of smoke-jumping activities and his energetic public relations work in support of the base.

Bibliography

Cohen, Stan. *A Pictorial History of Smokejumping.* Pictorial Histories Publishing Co., Missoula, Montana, 1983.
Lufkin, Francis. Phone Interview. Winthrop, Washington, fall 1991.
Mitchell, Roy. "The Story of the Smokejumpers." *Okanogan County Heritage*, Fall 1972.
Moody, William. Phone Interview. Twisp, Washington, fall 1991.
Roe, JoAnn. North Cascade Institute Class. Sun Mountain Lodge, Winthrop, Washington, October 1991.
———. *The North Cascadians.* Madrona Publishers, Seattle, 1980.
Strickland, Ron. *River Pigs and Cayuses: Oral Histories from the Pacific Northwest.* Lexikos, San Francisco, 1984.

From the late 1880s through the 1920s, homesteads flourished in Pipe-stone Canyon before drought discouraged farmers. Photo from the Shafer Museum collection.

Chapter 23

OF FLOODS, SNOWSTORMS AND OTHER WEATHER SEVERITIES

World Class Snows

Historically, too much precipitation in the form of rain or snow, or conversely lack of both, has caused catastrophe in the Methow.

One of the earliest Winthrop weather observers, Anna Greene Stevens, at age 13 witnessed the severe winter of 1892-93. Anna claimed it was one of the worst winters the area had known, rivaling the infamous Methow winter of 1889 (discussed in the chapter on pioneers). She described a miserable outing she had in a blizzard that season.

> Temperatures went down to 36 degrees below zero and stayed there for days at a time. The blizzard continued for days until there was 4 feet of snow on the level. With snow falling hard I set out on horseback on one of my daily chores which was to ride three miles downvalley to Bear Creek to pick up a can of milk. It was bitter cold and I was wrapped in a blanket on my saddle. On the way home the milk froze and popped the top off the can.
>
> —*Okanogan County Heritage*, June 1970.

During this storm, snow drifted over housetops and buried barns and outbuildings. For months all communication with the outside world was severed. Food became scarce for people, but even more scarce for stock animals. A neighbor of Anna's owned some fine horses that were dying of starvation. Lacking feed, the horses had chewed off all the pine branches within reach, then resorted to eating each other's manes and tails.

Local pioneers weathered another memorable storm in 1916 when one of the heaviest snowfalls in history fell in the Methow Valley. Clara L. Williams well remembered that big storm because the night it hit she gave birth to her first baby. It snowed 6 inches per hour all night. "By morning it had climbed clear up to the eaves of the house," she recalled. Packed snow levels reached 5 feet that winter.

In 1935 once again a record snowstorm bombarded the valley. Within 24 hours, 53 inches of snow piled up. When 4-foot-11-inch Prudie Imes tromped out to the chicken house during that storm, she found herself literally up to her neck in snow. Looking back, she couldn't even see where she had walked. Methow Valley schools closed for a prolonged period due to the enormous snowfall that season.

Sometimes it wasn't snow volume that wreaked havoc but freezing temperatures. Clara Williams remembered a very hard freeze in 1920 when all the apples froze solid—yet no snow covered the ground near Carlton at the time. The 1968 freeze, with temperatures 50 degrees below zero, killed most of the apple trees in the upper valley and sent the valley's economy into a tailspin.

The record winter of 1915-16 on the main street in Twisp. Photo from the Dick Webb collection.

A Winter of Calamities

A series of massive Pacific weather systems smashed into Washington during the winter of 1996-97, piling up record amounts of snow in the Methow Valley and throughout the state. Storms closed all major passes leading to the valley for days at a time during the holiday season and beyond. Snowstorm followed snowstorm until much of the state became paralyzed.

Economically the winter was a disaster. At Christmas and New Year's, recreationists from the Puget Sound area usually flock to the Methow. That year many never made it here; they were snowbound in their homes on the Coast. Some travelers who did manage to drive here became marooned when avalanches blocking highways prevented access out of the valley. Lodges suffered cancellations up to 50 percent or more.

Valley residents were awestruck by the accumulation of snow. No sooner had people hand-shoveled out their walks and driveways than a new 3-foot dump nullified all their back-breaking labor. Some people waited all day for a truck to plow out their driveways, only to have another storm cover all traces of the work. As storms relentlessly succeeded one another, locals often had to hire a front-end loader to barge snow away from their homes. Residents' snow removal costs were astronomical.

Once locals managed to get out of their driveways, there was no guarantee they could get any farther. New Year's Day greeted Mazama residents with a mile of road blocked by seven avalanches which had plummeted down from Goat Wall. The slides stranded all residents and visitors in the upper Mazama area.

Roy Kumm, Winthrop, who had kept records for 61 years, reported 8.5 feet of snow for October through December—the most snow he'd ever seen that early in the season. And there were still three more months of winter to go!

Returning to classes after vacation, students at the new Liberty Bell High School had to dodge buckets and trash cans set out to catch leaking water from the roof. Water dripping into light fixtures had stained 392 ceiling tiles. Heaving sidewalks prevented 90 percent of the doors leading outside from fully opening. Parents worried whether their kids could safely evacuate the building. Afraid of roofs collapsing, the school district hired every available worker to shovel snow off of the elementary and high school roofs.

The threat of roofs caving in from snow load was real. In the middle of Winthrop's main street a flattened gas station garage warned everyone of the winter's unbearable snow load.

Winthrop Motors' clock had frozen at 5:20 p.m., December 29, 1996, when the roof of the garage portion of the building crashed to the ground. "It went boom and the whole front flew out like Mt. St. Helens," said owner Jerry Petersen. He heard the sound seconds after leaving the scene to get a screwdriver from another part of the building. The accident damaged a new tow truck and squashed seven customer cars but Jerry felt lucky to be alive.

After Winthrop Motors collapsed, everyone crawled up on their own roof and began to shovel. Some didn't arrive in time. The Twisp River Lodge housing five businesses caved in. Craig Boesel's 2-year-old barn collapsed, making so much noise prior to falling that nearly all the 100 animals housed in the building escaped. Fifteen barns and haysheds in the Methow Valley collapsed. But winter wasn't done with the Methow yet. Ten days after snow destroyed Winthrop Motors' garage, the Outdoorsman store down the street blew up.

One witness said it sounded like a bomb had gone off. Ammunition exploded like fireworks. A mounted moose head in the Outdoorsman blew out of the window and across the street into the toy store. Businesses on both sides blackened and burned. Windows from six shops across the street blew out. Residents felt and heard the blast five miles away and sky-blown roofing debris landed two blocks from the scene.

Investigators determined a leaking propane line outside the store caused the blast. The winter's exceptionally heavy snow cracked an unsupported pipe which then leaked gas through a crack in the concrete wall between the Outdoorsman and Three-Fingered Jacks next door. When electric heaters kicked on in the store the gas ignited.

As in the collapse of Winthrop Motors, it seemed a miracle no one was seriously injured in the disaster. Yet someone could have been. Noel Simmons, waitress at Sams Place across the street, tells her story:

> It was within five minutes of 9 o'clock. I had
> gone out to deposit my bag at the bank. I came back
> in the front door and as soon as I went around to the
> window it (the explosion) came at me from behind
> and knocked me over. I fell down and hit my head.

Winthrop Motors' roof collapses under the weight of winter's snow. Photo from the Methow Valley News.

Five seconds earlier and I would have been on the
other side of that window.
The Wenatchee World, January 9, 1997

If Noel had been outside Sams Place when the explosion occurred, the outcome could have been tragic. Winthrop merchant
Robert Hult summed up the story, "Now they're calling Winthrop
a *boom* town. But at least it's not a *ghost* town."

316

The Methow's Two Great Floods

The two great Methow floods of 1894 and 1948 caused more local destruction than any other weather disturbance on record.

In comparing the two floods, the Army Corps of Engineers classed the 1894 torrent as a 92-year flood, one that on the average would occur once every 92 years. The 1948 flood got a more moderate 30-year flood rating. The later flood received more press, however, because the valley's population had ballooned since the early inundation; there were more buildings to destroy and more land under cultivation to disrupt.

The first flood (1894) caused a singular catastrophe. It washed a Methow town clear off the map. Here's what happened. The temperatures had been so cool for several summers according to U.E. Fries, Methow historian, that the snow never completely melted in the Sawtooth Mountains. Belated hot weather hit in May, followed by warm rains which saturated the soil. These conditions created the flood which Fries said "changed the face of the entire county along the watercourses." It tore out all the bridges in the Methow, scooped up the town of Silver south of Twisp, and sailed its domiciles downstream. One resident of Silver fell into the swift floodwaters and drowned.

The flood of 1948 caused much more damage to this valley than the 1894 flood, claimed local Vernon LaMotte, which is not surprising since the valley had become so developed in the 54-year interval since the first deluge. More curious is Vernon's evidence that shows the latter flood to be the bigger one, refuting government reports to the contrary.

Vernon's great uncle, Bill LaMotte, showed his nephew the high-water marks of both floods in his backyard near the mouth of Beaver Creek. The 1948 flood left a line 4 feet above the 1894 mark. Lifetime Methow resident Ken White figured a flood of such magnitude hadn't occurred for two centuries because 200-year-old trees grew along the Methow River before the raging flood waters of 1948 uprooted and washed them away.

Vernon LaMotte's final analysis makes even greater claims for the flood's immensity.

> My basic study of geology, including the making
> of valleys by water erosion, leads me to believe
> that no greater flow of water came down the

The 1948 floodwaters rip out the second bridge above Pateros. Photo from the Elinore Drake collection.

Methow since the glacier receded from our valley around 10,000 years ago.

    —*Okanogan County Heritage*, Spring 1988.

Old timers who lived through both floods said the spring preceding the 1948 disaster reminded them of the spring of 1894. Dick Webb related the warning weather signs of the later deluge.

> I remember a cold spring that broke on the twenty-third of May. Daytime brought soaring temperatures and nighttime brought thunder and lightning with torrential rains. The daytime temperatures and nighttime rains exchanged places with daylight and darkness like acts in a play. After three days and nights every creek became a river and every river a torrent. In our minds we knew that it would break and start to recede at any moment. But it didn't.
>
>   —*Ibid.*

Four times the normal amount of precipitation fell in April, said Edith Nelson, but it stayed cold, dropping snow in the mountains, while rain poured in the valleys. Suddenly the weather changed. Rain continued, but now it was warm snow-thawing rain. On May 28 when the thermometer peaked in the high 80s, the Methow's floodgates were thrown open.

While the 1948 flood inundated the entire county and devastated many areas of Eastern Washington, it appeared to unleash its worst fury in the Methow Valley. Here's how Edith Nelson saw the situation:

> There was a difference between what was happening in the Methow Valley and elsewhere. Here it was primal erosion by elemental forces tearing away what had been sea floor eons ago, being torn away now by running water, not a creeping up to engulf everything like in the other valleys.
>
> —*Ibid.*

Anxious about the safety of friends living on the swollen banks of the Twisp River, Edith hired a six-seater airplane to check out the Methow on May 29. Edith's pilot flew low over spots where the Methow's gravel banks were melting like sugar spilling into the river. Three miles below Gold Creek, erosion had stolen half an orchard on a bluff. Gravel rolling downslope undercut the trees which would then topple over and slide into the river.

Beulah LaMotte nervously eyed the rising waters from her riverside home near Carlton.

The flood of 1948. Photo from the Nedra Horn collection.

After the '48 flood, the LaMottes' house teetered on the brink where the river had scoured out its banks. Photo from the Okanogan County Historical Society.

> Big trees, debris and parts of buildings rode swiftly down the river. Boulders rolled and crashed into the river making the nearby bank shake. It sounded as if a dozen freight trains were going past and you couldn't hear anything else when you were near the banks.
>
> *—Ibid.*

Her husband, Vernon, said at the peak of the flood stage the river waves looked like huge ocean swells with caps about 40 feet apart. The LaMottes felt secure with their house 20 feet above the river, but they hadn't dreamed of a flood with the power this one packed. When the storm abated, they still had a house, but it teetered on the brink where the river had undercut its banks. Before the house careened into the swift current, the couple moved it to higher ground.

After the Flood

When the flood damage tally was taken, a great deal of property appeared lost or battered but no one was killed. In Winthrop, an entire row of Heckendorn houses had washed away. The flood had taken out nearly all the bridges from Pateros to Winthrop.

The bridge crossing the Twisp River at the north end of Twisp hung on and LaMotte reported the Carlton bridge still usable, despite the huge pines piled up against the structure and the bridge's violent shaking as Vernon made an experimental crossing.

After two sections of the Winthrop bridge collapsed, locals Keith Johnson and his son Kay Johnson immediately rigged up cables and a cage to transport people and supplies across the river. To do this the ingenious duo shot an arrow across the river with a fish line attached. They had tied the twine to a rope which was connected to the cables which held the cage conveyance.

Phone service was cut for days and the entire Methow Valley lost power. Grocers handed out free perishable meat when their emergency generators failed. Kids discovered the storm had a silver lining when they received free ice cream that began melting in the stores.

For some days the only passable road into the Methow Valley was the old pioneer stage route from Brewster over Paradise Hill along Benson Creek. Many people found themselves marooned by road washouts. The LaMottes, for example, discovered three sections of county road gone between their home and Twisp and two sections gone below them and opposite Carlton.

When the combined Chewuch and Methow rivers flowed over the Winthrop Fish Hatchery 310,000 blueback salmon swam to freedom. Adrian Bernier, the hatchery manager, was unperturbed. "Everything's fine," he said. "They've just been released a little earlier than planned."

In contrast to Mr. Bernier's insouciant view, outdoorsman Ken White feared the flood devastated the Methow fish population. According to Ken, before the '48 flood gigantic logjams 30 feet deep and half a mile long had over time built up in certain places on the river. Underneath these river obstructions water currents had formed spawning pools. When floodwaters came, they picked up the logjams like a pile of sticks and in doing so destroyed the spawning beds. New pools might have formed as uprooted trees hung up on newly created gravel bars, but the Army Corps of Engineers burned all the drift-wood. Their purpose was to prevent the logs from pushing out bridges in future floods, but unfortunately they also prevented new spawning pools from forming.

Drought: The Slow Disaster

In the Methow, water is the limiting resource and drought can mean slow death. No snow stored in the mountains and no valley rain in the spring equals poor crops, dry wells, and fire-prone forests and fields. The Methow has suffered through recent droughts. In 1976-77, no snow fell in the valley and only a small amount covered the surrounding Cascade Mountains. The 1980s were all low-snow years in the valley. Thankfully, throughout this drier decade, the Cascade Mountains captured and stored enough precipitation to run irrigation every summer. Without that mountain reservoir of moisture, the Methow might have been in trouble.

When the original pioneers arrived, copious amounts of water flowed through the hillsides and down the valley. One could carve out a homestead on what are now crispy-dry hills. From the late 1880s through the 1920s homesteads joined homesteads in every direction in the Pipestone Canyon area, a high, dry, hilly place five miles northeast of Twisp, now Washington Department of Wildlife land. People homesteaded all along the canyon floor, even on hilltops surrounding the canyon. Several schools were started to service all the families living there. One school, located on a bench at the mouth of the canyon, was named Balky Hill School because the climb up to it was so steep horses balked on the way. Now weedy vegetation like barnaby thistle and cheat grass dominates the landscape in Pipestone Canyon with only patches of alfalfa growing in wetter spots of old fields.

"The drought pulled the rug out from all the ranchers living up every draw with a hog or two and four or five cows," declared Clarence Heckendorn. "Some had to leave the valley a lot poorer than when they arrived." Pioneer Mary Thurlow Kerr recalled, "A farmer might leave his frame house to the pack rats, his yellow rosebushes to go wild and fruit jars to purple in the sun."

The people who had water through luck or foresight often

322

had to fight to keep it. As Mary Kerr remembered it:
> Neighbor turned against neighbor as the dry
> years progressed. The raising or lowering of a
> headgate (irrigation) at night would sever a friend-
> ship. A gopher hole in an irrigation ditch bank
> was regarded suspiciously until its origin could be
> proved.
> —*Okanogan County Heritage.* June 1963.

Water was vital to life in the valley and people became para-
noid and competitive as they watched this precious resource
dry up.

Lightning-Sparked Fire Storms

To comprehend how the Methow forest fires of 1994 affected
locals' activities and psyches, one must consider the entire fire
scene in North Central Washington that summer.

In the Methow, some people were told to evacuate. Smoke enshrouded the valley for days at a time. Fires burned in several
valley locations; but in neighboring cities—Chelan, Entiat, Wenatchee and Leavenworth—the fire created a holocaust. From late
July until late August, when all the fires were finally controlled,
everyone's lives in these towns revolved around wildfires.

It all began innocently enough. A lightning storm hit the area
July 24, 1994, touching off a series of small fires in North Central Washington. The lightning arrived on the heels of an oven-
hot stretch of weather and when winds suddenly whipped up to
35 mph, fire exploded through crackly-dry timber.

Overnight all the world seemed to be burning. "OUT OF
CONTROL" read *The Wenatchee World* headlines as the Tyee
fire torched the Entiat Valley. This fire incinerated 21 homes,
75 barns and outbuildings, and 106,000 acres of land. After the
Tyee scorched Chelan Butte and began to gnaw on the south
side of Lake Chelan, residents prepared to evacuate. Tourists
panicked and checked out of hotels.

Meanwhile, 30 mph winds blew up the Rat Creek fire which
seared Icicle Canyon and caused hundreds of people living near
Leavenworth to evacuate. One fire officer from Leavenworth
perfectly summed up the outlook: "It's going nuts here, there's
fire everywhere; it's the most incredible thing I've ever seen."

In the Methow Valley near Twisp, Poorman Creek residents,
whose houses lay in the path of a fire, watched in awe as flames

Smokejumper fighting the fires of 1994. Photo from the Methow Valley News.

uprooted huge trees hurling them like toothpicks into the air. Fanned by a powder keg of wood fuel the Poorman Creek fire burned 800 acres before a force of 200 firefighters, two helicopters, three fire engines and two bulldozers controlled it.

Frank Carroll, Forest Service public information officer, explained why the fire had spread so fast. According to Carroll, since we don't allow fuel (timber) to burn regularly on the Okanogan National Forest as nature intended, there are now many more trees per acre. The newer trees are mostly fir that can't tolerate fire like the larger pines that once predominated on the hills surrounding Poorman Creek. Fire normally would burn through the area every decade with no problem. Now when the forest finally does catch fire, the fuel overload leads to dangerous fire storms.

Besides Poorman Creek, fires burned at War Creek (14 miles west of Twisp), Thunder Mountain (12 miles north of Winthrop), the Burnt Saw area (8 miles southwest of Winthrop), Gold Creek near Carlton and along the west fork of the Pasayten River (30 miles northwest of Winthrop).

The War Creek fire burning in sheer alpine wilderness at 7,000 feet and higher presented a dangerous challenge to firefighters. "The terrain it's in you'd have to tie yourself to the side of the mountain to be in there," one fire officer said. "It's too steep for mountain goats." Plus, firefighters had no escape routes in the area to survive a sudden fire storm.

Despite the risky nature of the terrain, hot-shot crews from Arizona, Oregon and New Mexico began an all-out attack on the blaze which had expanded to 1,300 acres and was still growing. To help douse the fire one of the world's largest helicopters, a Sikorsky S-64, flew in to drop water from its 2,000-gallon bucket.

North of Winthrop, the Thunder Mountain fire burning in lodgepole pine began sending tentacles in many different directions. Sixteen 20-person crews along with bulldozers arrived to punch fire lines around the blaze when it grew from 1,300 acres to 4,780 acres. One day, crews were forced to flee when smoke got so thick it was too dangerous to work.

Called in to aid regional firefighting leaders, national fire commander Mike Monahan sized up the situation in the Okanogan Complex which included all the Methow Valley fires. Referring to all the uncontrolled fires he said:

> It's like a wrestling match ... you keep fighting, looking for holds, trying all your best moves to pin your opponent. Those opponents have a lot of tough moves of their own, but firefighters are winning.
> —*Methow Valley News*, August 8, 1994

Then just when everyone thought the worst was over, the White Face fire broke near Mazama. It ignited August 4, 1994, when an intense lightning storm rolled through the upper Methow. Gusty winds spread the 30-acre fire to 2,500 acres in one afternoon. For miles, residents could see the huge plume from the fire. It looked like a megaton bomb had exploded.

By August 8 the fire had burned 4,200 acres on the west side of Goat Creek. More than 550 firefighters, 10 engines and five bulldozers came to the rescue. But it wasn't enough. The National Guard had to be called to relieve tired firefighters stretched to the brink of collapse.

The Guard brought their helicopters, trucks and jeeps. They built an enormous fire camp at the Mazama and Highway 20 junction which operated like a small town. There was a medical center, bank, restaurants (mess tents), army-style tent residences and stores.

Oddly enough a festive atmosphere arose around Mazama. People felt like they had a front-row seat in a war zone where everyone was united against a common foe. Residents got out their lawn chairs to watch helicopters load up buckets of water. People donated books and magazines to entertain the troops. The Mazama Store was awash in camouflaged customers and Humvees packed the parking lot.

Mazama residents moved out of their homes when told the fire was heading toward the Edelweiss development and to be ready to evacuate within 15 minutes' notice. Some of the same evacuees turned up at Bob Spiwak's annual golf tournament at the former Whispering Rattlesnakes Golf and Flubber's Club, their trucks loaded to the brim with their worldly goods. Of course they were correct to show such unconcern regarding the fire's encroachment, since the warning had been a false alarm. Apparently a firefighter had placed the blaze one ridge over from its true location, so Edelweiss had been less threatened than originally thought.

Eventually, the weather cooperated and firefighters extinguished all the blazes. Everyone welcomed back-to-normal conditions and a return to every day concerns. Yet sometimes the status quo seemed too tame after living at the center of such turmoil. One resident summed it up: "I don't know how to describe what it felt like. There's fear but there's also a sense of excitement and beauty in the whole thing."

Bibliography

Blackburn, Judy. *Methow Valley News*, August 4, 1994.

Carey, Joy. *Methow Valley News*, August 18, 1994.

Duffy, Barbara and Marjory White. "Winthrop History." January 1990.

Hicks, Lee. *Methow Valley News*, January 2, 1997, and January 19, 1997.

Hottell, Diana. "Clara Williams." *Methow Valley News*, September 29, 1977.

——. "Oldest Pioneer Resident: Prudie Imes." *Methow Valley News*, Souvenir Issue, Summer 1977.

——. "Jean Carroll Hansen: A Strong Outspoken Woman." *Methow Valley News*, September 1, 1977.

——. "Clarence Heckendorn: He's Done a Little Bit of Everything." *Methow Valley News*, August 20, 1981.

Kerr, Mary Thurlow. "I Remember." *Okanogan County Heritage*, June 1963.

Kikendall, Hazel. Letter describing her personal history in the Methow Valley. Twisp, Washington, summer 1990.

LaMotte, Beulah. "The Flood of 1948 at Our Home in the Methow

326

Valley." *Okanogan County Heritage*, Spring 1988.

LaMotte, Vernon. "The 1948 Flood." *Okanogan County Heritage*, Spring 1988.

Majors, Henry M. *Exploring Washington*. Van Winkle Publishing Co., Holland, Michigan, 1975.

McKinney, John. "His Name Was John McKinney." From his diary, *Okanogan County Heritage*, March 1964.

Mehaffey, K.C. *The Wenatchee World*, January 8, 1997, January 9, 1997, January 22, 1997.

Methow Valley News. August 11, 1994, and August 25, 1994.

Nelson, Edith. "Flood! Flood! Flood! Flood!" *Okanogan County Heritage*, Spring 1988.

Olling, Velma Batie, Jessie Schmidt, Olive Wolfe Doan and Helen Wolfe Swenson. "Pipestone Canyon: The Homesteaders, the Families, the Schools," *Okanogan County Heritage*, Fall 1984.

Partridge, Michelle. *The Wenatchee World*, July 27, 1994, and July 31, 1994.

Siderius, Charles. *The Wenatchee World*, July 28, 1994, July 29, 1994, and August 7, 1994.

Stevens, Anna Green. "Life in the Okanogan." *Okanogan County Heritage*, June 1970.

White, Ken. Interview. Winthrop, Washington, summer 1990.

Wilson, Bruce. *The Late Frontier*. Okanogan County Historical Society, 1990.

Chapter 24

THE SUN MOUNTAIN STORY

The Sunny M Ranch

With its wood, western-style buildings freshly painted barn red, and its grounds landscaped and planted with flowers, the Sunny M Ranch on Wolf Creek Road has become a lovely Methow Valley landmark. The Sunny M is Sun Mountain Lodge's predecessor—the place where Jack Barron first began to dream of building a mountaintop resort. From the Sunny M one can see Sun Mountain Lodge perched high above on a hill. Beyond the lodge, 9,000-foot Gardner Mountain provides a stunning backdrop.

The ranch land is woven with clear creeks and ponds, where ducks and geese, blackbirds and beaver share a residence. Tall, shady, black cottonwoods frame the dwellings. Alfalfa grows rich and green in surrounding fields. The Sunny M is a classic Methow landscape deserving of the protective status awarded it by its present owners, Erivan and Helga Haub.

Clint Shulenburger, a bachelor living in the Wolf Creek area, homesteaded the Sunny M lands. He raised the first Jersey cow herd in the valley and helped build the first irrigation ditch from Wolf Creek.

E.F. (Elmer Fisk) Banker, a state representative for seven years, developed the Sunny M into a big cattle ranch. Banker brought some of the first purebred cattle to this area. For a

long time locals called the Sunny M environs the Banker Place.
In the 1930s, Dr. O. J. Blende, a Winthrop physician, bought
the Banker place and converted it to a dude ranch.

The next owner, Seattlite Manson Backus, ran the Sunny M
as a dude ranch and a successful cattle ranch as well, according to Winthrop resident Archie Eiffert, who worked for
Backus when Archie was a young man. During Backus' time,
the guest ranch consisted of a main lodge with six bedrooms
and eight cabins, recalled Archie. The large, gracious ranch

Sunny M wrangler Archie Eiffert takes a spill. Photo by Dick Webb.

house on the present Sunny M Ranch originally served as the
old main lodge. There was a big, white house that later burned,
a bunkhouse and a swimming pool.

Backus' ranch encompassed a huge area. It included the site
of the present Sun Mountain Lodge which wranglers then
called the "Horse Pasture." The Pine Forest development south
of Sun Mountain was part of the ranch, as well as most of
the land around Patterson Lake and land on the north side of
Thompson Ridge.

Under the skilled management of Foss Creveling, Archie
Eiffert worked as wrangler and general ranch help during the
summers from 1950 to 1953. "We were young, dashing cowboys," said Archie. "With Swede Miller, Les Taylor and Paul
Berganholtz, we'd take people on overnights and two-night
trips into the Wolf Creek area and Gardner Meadows, or ride
around the Sun Mountain area. City girls from Seattle thought
we were terrific. We'd work all day and play all night."

Archie earned $200 a month and received room and board
but spent every penny he earned entertaining female admirers.
The girls loved the attention, according to Edna Creveling,
who helped her husband, Foss, run the ranch. "All the guests
insisted on eating with the wranglers," remembered Edna, "because those boys told more stories than the law allows!"

Every Sunday the Sunny M held a rodeo, well-attended by
both cow-puncher participants and city-slicker spectators.
Archie'd visit neighbor Ray Thompson, who kept wild horses
for pleasure, and trade a fifth of whiskey to use Ray's horses
for rodeo riding. "Wild" cattle were supplied by any animals
that got lost and wandered out of their own range onto Sunny
M land. Under the pretext of bringing them to the Sunny M to
alert their owner, the boys would just "borrow" the heifers for
rodeo riding. "After all," chuckled Archie, "wouldn't want to
burn calories off our own cows!"

Foss Creveling managed the ranch for two years while
Backus owned it. The total operation of the ranch rested on
Foss' shoulders. He irrigated the fields, raised feed for the
animals and kept all the guests happy. "He was good at it all,"
said Edna.

Foss had a special way with people and they loved to hear
him tell his stories. His charm helped build up the ranch's
clientele, and guests kept returning even when they could get

better prices elsewhere. Edna reminisced, "Foss met people and always remembered them, their names and faces, plus some little thing about them to make the reacquaintance nice and interesting." If he were lost in a crowd, Edna just had to look for the man with a circle of women around him, listening to his stories.

Foss charmed horses as well. "You could tell he was a super rider just by watching Foss, he was so in tune with the horse he rode," said Edna. She remembered only one time when a horse bucked him off. "And that one time his head was completely in the dust. Usually he knew just when to jump off before the horse bucked. He could just feel it. Foss rode horses from the time he was a little kid until he died."

The Barrons Buy the Sunny M Ranch

In the early 1950s Joe Barron bought the Sunny M Ranch. A native of Washington, Joe was a financial wizard who lost all his money in the Depression, then gained it all back later. He bought old hotels and real estate in downtown Seattle before becoming owner of the Inglewood Golf and Country Club.

The Methow Valley always appealed to Joe because his family originated here, and because of his great-uncle Alex Barron's discovery of the "Eureka lode" that launched the 1890s gold rush in the Slate Creek area. Miners named the town that sprouted at the site of the discovery "Barron" after Joe's famous relative. Joe's interest in the Methow inspired him in 1950 to trade several parcels of land on the west side of the state for the Sunny M Ranch in Winthrop.

The following story of the Sunny M Ranch during Joe Barron's and later son Jack Barron's ownership is excerpted from a letter written by Mark Barron, Joe's son. Mark's "Sunny M History" is a personal recollection of the times his family spent at the ranch.

> My dad owned the ranch from 1950 to about 1965. During that time the Sunny M consisted of a main ranch house and some small cabins. The cabins were later remodeled and relocated at Patterson Lake Resort. Family and guests swam in a cold-water swimming pool and played horseshoes and badminton behind the main house. Fifty people filled cabins and the main ranch house to capacity at this time.

Foss and Edna Creveling at the Sunny M. Photo courtesy of Edna Creveling.

Of all the activities offered at the Sunny M, people loved horseback riding the most. Wranglers guided guests on scheduled rides every day, plus led evening cookout rides to the old Hough Homestead. From the Sunny M Ranch, we'd trot up a winding trail, finally entering the old road at the north end of Patterson Lake. Ruth, my dad's wife, would be waiting in her red jeep wagon with cool drinks and a savory meal all laid out for the riders.

Everyone looked forward to the family-style meals served at the ranch house which were always lively and fun. Often, someone played the piano and stirred up a real cowboy atmosphere. My dad had learned to be a superb meat cook while living on an Iowa farm, so every Sunday night he cooked a huge standing rib roast which he proudly carved for the guests.

Adjacent to the ranch house stood my father's

The Sunny M Ranch in 1992. Photo by Don Portman.

bird pens. Dad loved exotic birds, loved to collect
them. He had a working relationship with the
Woodland Park Zoo in Seattle, where he traded
peacocks for pheasants or other birds of plumage
he believed Sunny M guests might enjoy seeing.
Birds of every color could be found roaming the
property any time of the day.

Some colorful wranglers and cowboys led trail
rides when my dad owned the Sunny M. One
young lady of great personality was Nancy Bell.
She was a Methow Valley girl who grew up on a
horse, and she was extremely popular with guests.
They would come back each year just to be around
Nancy, to listen to her lingo and be entertained by
her cowgirl mannerisms. She was the real McCoy.

Some true-blue cowboys just like in the movies
worked in the valley during the '50s and '60s.
One particular event was amusing. A couple of
rather proper female guests from the Sunny M
were about to take a drink in a stream off the trail
when all of a sudden a cloud of dust arose and
two cowboys rode up and said, "Pardon me,
ma'am, but you'd better drink above the manure."

Joe's son, Jack Barron, took over management
of the Sunny M around 1965. Jack surrounded
himself with a passel of cowboys during his first

few years. One memorable lady was a little
wizened person named Babe, who had a terrific
personality just like Nancy Bell. Babe herded
horses and cattle in addition to wrangling and of
course spent her share of time shooting the breeze.
She spoke in her own unique style—all one-liners.

Babe and many other Sunny M employees became tremendously loyal to Jack. Jack had a gift
of asking people to do things in a way that gave
them a sense of importance and self-respect. They
were all family to him.

The Haubs Buy the Sunny M Ranch

When Erivan and Helga Haub bought the Sunny M in the
late 1980s, they knew it needed to be spruced up. They decided
to restore and preserve the ranch both for historic and environmental reasons. They wanted local people to be proud the
ranch was a part of the Methow community.

With these goals in mind the Haubs approved the Sunny M
upgrade plan. Under this plan, 300 acres of weedy, neglected
ranch land has been replanted with alfalfa and grain crops.
The Haubs restored the irrigation system from Wolf Creek,
and introduced a new pivot irrigation system at Patterson Lake.
To control weeds, the new owners chose the cultivation method
—disk, plow, disk and replow—over herbicide spraying whenever possible.

Over half of the total property bought by the Haubs is designated as open space. No big development plans exist. In the
future, the ranch and its environs will conform to the Haubs'
stated goal which is "preservation of the Methow environment."

Jack Barron

Jack Barron was the original builder and owner of Sun
Mountain Lodge, the Methow Valley's first, largest, and most
famous four-season resort. Tall, handsome, an accomplished
businessman, considered wealthy and powerful, Jack cut a romantic figure dashing up to his beautiful lodge in his 1966
Buick convertible. He'd stay a day or so for a whirlwind series
of business meetings, then pilot his twin-engine Cessna back to
Seattle where more commitments awaited him.

Jack appeared to many people like a figure from the Court of

Camelot. Yet when you knew him on a personal basis, he seemed thoughtful, shy, a man who loved the quiet and solitude found at his Methow retreat and the company of the native and exotic birds he raised there.

Jack Barron's introduction to the Methow Valley came when his father bought the Sunny M Ranch. He immediately felt at home here and with his family he began to spend a great deal of time on the east side of the mountains.

When Joe Barron needed someone to run the ranch, Jack stepped in. Once Jack became manager, the Sunny M changed from being a dude ranch to a smaller, intimate resort. At the same time, Jack got involved in local real estate.

Familiarity with the territory boosted Jack's Methow real estate business. During the many years Jack had been a Sunny M wrangler, he'd explored every inch of ground around the ranch. While most of the land surrounding the Sunny M turned out to be national forest, Jack discovered a great deal of private land as well. In the mid-'60s Jack started purchasing large parcels of property adjacent to the ranch, eventually acquiring 4,000 acres.

While acquiring land, Jack began to dream about the biggest project of his life—the building of Sun Mountain Lodge. According to Jack's brother, Mark, Jack chose the future lodge's location high above the Sunny M Ranch. Mark remembered, "He viewed this ridge from the back window of the ranch and thought it was the perfect location for a resort."

Jack Barron's dream of a lodge overlooking the Methow Valley appeared more plausible in the 1960s when plans for opening the North Cascades Highway became definite. Financing his grandiose scheme then became Jack's quest. He gained the support of Congressman Tom Foley, who helped secure federal financing. Frank Buell, his ally at the local Farmers State Bank, also provided a great deal of expertise and financial backing.

Jack Barron succeeded in building his hilltop resort—a massive undertaking considering the location, the lack of road access and the difficulty of providing utilities. He named the resort Sun Mountain Lodge. Was he pleased with his creation? Brother Mark said, "Jack loved his Sun Mountain. Whenever he flew in from the coast he would circle the lodge and dip his wings in salute before landing."

Jack Barron: owner and builder of the original Sun Mountain Lodge. Photo by Josef Scaylea.

Jack ran the lodge more as a hobby than a financial investment, often basing management decisions on personal ideals rather than economic pressures. Hence, Sun Mountain remained a special place for Jack but it never produced much profit. When the costs of maintenance rose and need for rehabilitation became imperative, Jack began talking to Henry Van Baalen of the Haub Trust about a joint investment program. Nothing was finalized and the Haubs became seriously involved with Sun Mountain only after Jack's death.

Jack will be remembered mostly for his stunning Sun Mountain Lodge development, but he had another side that people close to him remember just as well. Like his father Joe, Jack was a bird fancier, well known in the "bird world" for his breeding of exotic species. He loved both wild and captive birds,

The original Sun Mountain Lodge. Photo by Don Portman.

his favorites being ducks, geese, and swans, and he raised many species of land and water birds at the Sunny M.

Come summer, fishermen and guests at Patterson Lake Resort delighted in seeing Jack's best waterfowl set free on Patterson Lake where he had had a small island built to shelter the birds. "His mute and black swans were a grand sight there," said Jack's companion birder, Ken White. "With the skilled help of his trusty ranch hand, Pat Meadows, Jack put up many nesting sites in the area for wood ducks."

Ken remembered Jack's kind and gentle treatment of the birds he raised, as well as his consideration for wild bird life. When employees caught a flicker drilling holes in the walls of Sun Mountain Lodge, Jack searched for a means to deter the culprit without harming it. The snags in Patterson Lake were saved because of Jack's insistence the trees be kept for wildlife habitation.

Mark Barron said of his brother:

> Jack Barron was a doer. He was forever on the go, always immersed in a project. All his life he never stopped working because he had dreams he wanted to make happen. And he succeeded. Jack transformed his vision into reality.

The Original Sun Mountain Lodge

To Jack Barron, the incredible difficulties in building a resort on top of a dry hill, nine miles away from the nearest town and 1,000 feet above it seemed insignificant compared to the one incredible benefit of building there: the view! After combing the area on horseback for years, Jack discovered the Sun Mountain site had the best view of mountains and valley. From the lodge one can almost reach out and touch craggy Gardner Mountain, snow-clad through early summer. Robinson Mountain and Last Chance Point, gateways to the Pasayten Wilderness, rise to the northwest. Striking Goat Peak and the sheer face of Goat Wall enclose the head of the valley, while tiers upon tiers of North Cascade peaks march to the west.

From the Sun Mountain summit one views the glacier-carved Methow Valley stretching north toward Mazama. Down the center of the valley the Methow River weaves a pattern of green life. At night Winthrop appears to be an enchanted village with its town lights twinkling below the stars.

Because the Methow Valley was economically depressed in the mid-1960s, it proved the perfect time to introduce a project like Sun Mountain Lodge. The Economic Development Administration conducted a feasibility study to see if tourism and recreation would sustain the new resort facility. Agriculture, mining and cattle ranching appeared less economically important than in the past, reported the federal agency, and they saw the Sunny M Complex (the new Sun Mountain Lodge) as a stimulant to the local economy. They estimated that the new "ranch" would provide 45 seasonal jobs with a payroll of $83,000 the first year and $100,000 the second year.

Convinced that the Methow needed the lodge and that future tourism could support the development, the Economic Development Administration elected to lend the developers $495,000 of the $700,000 estimated cost of the resort. The owners provided $188,000, Seattle First National Bank and the Commercial Bank of Washington lent $48,000 and Central Cascade Development Corporation supplied $43,000.

More than money had to be obtained before the ground breaking began. Forty-one state, county and federal agencies were required to review and approve the lodge project. Obtaining all the necessary permits took three years.

Construction of the Methow Valley's first complete recreation and convention facility began in the spring of 1966—three years after loan applications had been made. It took a mere two years to build Sun Mountain Lodge which opened May 1968.

The original Sun Mountain had 50 guest rooms in two large motel units and a main lodge with lobby, restaurant, lounge and meeting rooms. For recreation it offered two pools, two tournament-grade tennis courts, and miles of inviting trails for hiking and horseback riding.

From the valley floor, one could see the first Sun Mountain Lodge—but just barely, so well did the structure blend into the site. Roland Terry, internationally famous Seattle architect, designed the original lodge, taking advantage of large natural rock promontories and variations in terrain to camouflage the buildings.

Terry's design called for all natural materials to be used in construction. Native stone, some with marine fossils embedded, and peeled logs framed the structure. On the inside the lodge had a rustic western appeal with big, 24-inch-diameter exposed timbers, aggregate floors edged in grainy, varnished wood, and weathered boards from five local barns lining interior walls of the lobby, cocktail lounge and dining room. The mammoth 8-foot-high main entrance door came from the side of a barn. Floor to ceiling windows merged the outside beauty with the inside and captured views in every direction.

A very special work of art that hung in the original resort can still be seen at the new Sun Mountain Lodge—a four-tiered farm implement chandelier designed by Seattle artist Irene McGowan. To create her unique lamp, McGowan scoured fields and ranches to find unusual and beautiful antique machinery parts. The light is suspended from the ceiling by a chain drive belt and one can see the teeth of an ancient hay rake integrated within the work.

The Haubs Buy Sun Mountain

By the mid-1980s Sun Mountain desperately needed major repairs and renovation if the resort were to survive. It was still an attractive structure but what originally was touted as rustic now simply appeared shabby. Jack Barron had passed away. No one else seemed to have the energy or resources to rescue the place.

Fortunately, at this point promising agents of change arrived

Helga and Erivan Haub, owners of Sun Mountain Lodge. Photo by John Barline.

on the scene in the guise of long-time Methow Valley admirers, Erivan and Helga Haub. Eager to pay back some of the joy the Methow Valley and its people had brought them, the Haubs decided to restore the unique mountaintop resort.

In 1989 the Haubs bought Sun Mountain Lodge, the Sunny M Ranch and 2,000 acres of Jack Barron's property for the bargain price of $2.5 million. In renovating Sun Mountain, the Haubs planned to give the Methow economy a boost by offering well-paid construction jobs to local workers and by ordering local materials. They hired nearly every available valley carpenter.

Who were these benefactors to appear suddenly on the Sun Mountain horizon? The Haubs hail from Wiesbaden, a pretty town in central Germany near Frankfurt. They own food markets in Germany, Austria, Holland, Italy and Hungary. Their Wissoll Candy Company produces Gummi Bears. In the United States the Haubs have a 53 percent interest in the oldest grocery chain in the states—A and P.

Friends of the Haubs, Warder and Annaliese Stoaks of Fox Island, Washington, first introduced the couple to the Methow Valley. Soon after the North Cascades Highway opened, the Stoaks had driven over and landed at Elsie and Jack Wilsons' Early Winters Resort. Exhausted, hungry, wanting to cook dinner, but with no grocery store for miles, the Stoaks were blessed that evening with the generosity of Elsie Wilson, who gladly produced a sumptuous feast for her guests. Wishing to share their great getaway discovery the Stoaks invited the Haubs to accompany them on their next trip to the Wilsons' resort.

Once at the Wilsons', the Haubs rode horseback into the wilderness, ate cowboy dinners, fished in pristine lakes and slept under the stars. The whole family went—Erivan, Helga and their three teenagers, Charlie, Georgie and Christian. After that first time, they returned every year for 10 years—backpacking with their "beloved and admired friend, Jack Wilson," said Helga. On fishing trips into the backcountry, he taught the Haubs' sons natural history and survival skills. "Jack the Cowboy," the kids called him.

It was through Jack Wilson that the Haubs met Kay Wagner and found for themselves a Methow home. Jack was a friend of Mrs. Wagner's and had built her home. The Haubs wished to buy a residence in the Methow and they couldn't imagine a more gracious place than the Wagner Ranch. "So when Kay Wagner moved to town, we bought her beautiful ranch on the Chewuch River," said Helga.

Jack Wilson also introduced the Haubs to Jack Barron, who told them his hopes and dreams for the future of Sun Mountain, according to Helga. When the Haubs first heard that Jack needed to sell Sun Mountain, it kindled their interest. After Jack died several years later, the Haubs resolved to buy the Sun Mountain property to "save it and the land for the community," said Helga.

The New Sun Mountain Lodge

The Haubs hired Seattle's NBBJ Group (Naramore, Bain, Brady, Johanson) to design the new Sun Mountain Lodge, not only because of the firm's fame and good reputation, but because they could plan every facet of the construction. In addition to the overall concept and architecture of the building,

The new Sun Mountain Lodge, 1992. Photo by Don Portman.

NBBJ could plan the plumbing and electrical systems, even the interior design.

Elegant but rustic, that's how new owners Erivan and Helga Haub envisioned the renovated lodge. They wanted it to have the same look and ambiance as the original lodge Jack Barron had built but on a larger scale. With the Haubs' expectations foremost in their minds, the architects created a "grand old lodge of the future." It imitates the heavy-timbered, rock-masonry style of the classic national park architecture of Yellowstone and Yosemite but with modern, clean lines and a lighter touch. The exterior and interior wood is lighter in color than the park lodges and the wood is less massive. The new Sun Mountain has a cornucopia of windows oriented to feature every conceivable view and to bring the sun warmth and sky light inside.

The three-story renovated and expanded main lodge has a gray-board exterior designed to blend the structure into the landscape. It houses a spacious lobby, a restaurant, a library, gift shop, recreation center/ski shop, an exercise room, game room, meeting rooms, and guest rooms. Guest rooms in the separate, renovated, Gardner unit offer suites with fireplaces and private decks overlooking the North Cascades. The project cost $22 million.

In December of 1996 the resort completed the 24-room

Mount Robinson building giving the lodge a total of 102 rooms. The newer unit offers some of the most beautiful views and rooms at the lodge.

Arriving at Sun Mountain Lodge, one enters a soaring two-story lobby framed by massive log beams. An entire south-facing wall of glass offers a view of Gardner and Storey peaks. The floor is polished rock aggregate. An enormous lava rock fireplace at each end of the lobby is the focal point for a friendly circle of overstuffed chairs. Local mason Dave Christiansen completed all the new stonework.

NBBJ Group has its own interior design department headed by Chris Larson, who chose all the interior colors and furniture. Larson ordered new lodge furniture from the Chicken and Egg Company, a non-profit group whose proceeds help abused children. The furniture features lots of willow bent into

The lobby at the new Sun Mountain Lodge. Photo courtesy of Sun Mountain Lodge.

Artist Richard Beyer with front desk carving. Photo by Mike Irwin,
The Wenatchee World.

graceful shapes and softened with cushions and pillows in
muted shades.

As soon as construction of the lodge was completed, Dave
Sabold, owner of the local Gardner Gardens, applied his artis-
tic talent to the task of landscaping. Dave intended to blend the
small-scale landscaping with the natural environment. For the
larger area disturbed by lodge construction, he hoped through
his efforts the land would someday look untouched.

Dave planted hardy native vegetation to camouflage scars left
by buried sewer and water lines. Around the lodge he installed
a lush carpet of lawn, planted a variety of trees, and arranged
small gardens of brilliant flowers which accent the scene like
colorful swatches in a patchwork quilt.

Sun Mountain builders needed to obtain 22 permits for
reconstruction and expansion of the lodge. The agencies involved in the process were the Okanogan County government,
state Department of Ecology, state Department of Health, state
Department of Fish and Wildlife, US Forest Service, the town
of Winthrop and the Wolf Creek Reclamation District.

When Sun Mountain tackled its sewage permit, the town of

344

Winthrop simultaneously found itself out of sewage capacity with no way to fund a costly expansion. Sun Mountain and Winthrop then became instant allies in a waste-disposal project. The lodge agreed to subsidize a new, improved Winthrop sewage system that could handle additional town hookups as well as increased input piped down from Sun Mountain.

Art at the New Sun Mountain

Sara Borgerson and Joni Schade Hager took on the challenge of choosing art for the renovated lodge. The simpatico pair became collaborators by coincidence.

Sara, founding Executive Director of the Confluence Gallery, was contacted by Sun Mountain's Rob Thorlakson. Joni, a founding board member of the gallery and accomplished artist, called Sun Mountain because of her interest in fabric art. Both agreed that joining forces would be practical and exciting.

With their extensive connections in the art world, the two commissioned 90 art pieces, or 85 percent of the total lodge collection. They chose the remaining 15 percent from pieces already completed.

Sara Borgerson (left) and Joni Schade Hager with woven hanging by Hager at Sun Mountain Lodge. Photo by Mike Irwin, The Wenatchee World.

Sara and Joni enlisted 47 North Central Washington artists to produce paintings, ceramics, woven works, quilts, photographs, iron sculptures, and wood carvings to add interest and beauty to the lodge interior. It took the women two years to fill the lodge with local creations and their project is still in progress. New art is added and displays are changed. "It's an ongoing project," said Sara.

No primary colors, no vistas, no abstracts—these were the guidelines Joni and Sara set for themselves. "We wanted a glimpse of what it's like to live here," explained Sara. "To show the color, feelings, seasons and history of the Methow were our goals. We chose intimate and private art to counterbalance the grand views from the lodge."

With this concept in mind, they chose three art pieces for each guest room. Pieces in the sleeping/sitting rooms included photos, prints, drawings, watercolors, crocheted pieces and woven pieces for the walls, along with dried-flower arrangements or handwoven baskets for the dressers. Freeform handwoven willow pieces adorn the bathrooms.

Richard Beyer, famous for his outdoor sculpture "Waiting for the Interurban" in Seattle's Fremont District, carved the relief in Sun Mountain's massive front desk. The artist's tumbling woodland creatures and sasquatch chiseled from the desk's blond-colored wood give the piece a lively, whimsical look.

Local master craftsman Dick Ewing built the concierge desk opposite the front desk. Richard Beyer carved the dramatic relief of natural forms which wraps around the desk.

Beyer's relief tells the allegorical tale of coyote who watches the weather on television while all the other Methow animals are outside immersed in changing weather events. He depicts a cougar that represents hot days, a deer in gentler weather, birds that "sing the rain," a bear that makes the river flood, a mountain goat pouring snow on the land, a stormbird, a windsnake and a pack of pikas bending a rainbow. Coyote gets the message: Turn off the TV; experience the outdoors for yourself!

A magnificent oil painting by C.E. Ottman graces the lobby. The artist captures the essence of the Methow Valley landscape near the lodge.

Local sculptor Bruce Morrison carved the two life-sized bighorn sheep heads in the lodge library's mantlepiece. Jill Sabella's hand-tinted historical photos of the Methow Valley line the main hallway.

Regional works may also be viewed in Sun Mountain's private gallery. Some past exhibits include Rod Weagant's impressionistic landscape oil paintings and Laurie Fry's watercolors of local landscapes. The cover of this book is an example of Laurie's talent.

Bibliography

Barron, Mark. Letters. Bothell, Washington, 1990 and 1991.

Borgerson, Sara. Interview. Winthrop, Washington, spring 1990.

Charlton, Brian, manager of Sun Mountain. Interview. Winthrop, Washington, summer 1990.

Creveling, Edna. Interview. Twisp, Washington, spring 1990.

Eiffert, Archie. Interview. Winthrop, Washington, spring 1990.

Geniesse, Gael Barron. Letters and phone conversations. Bainbridge Island, Washington, spring and summer 1990.

Haub, Helga. Letter. Wiesbaden, Germany, July 5, 1990.

Irwin, Mike. "Resort Goes for the Top." *The Wenatchee World*, April 8, 1990.

——. "No Ugly Motel Art at Sun Mountain." *The Wenatchee World*, July 5, 1990.

Johnson, Abbie Williams. "Life in the Upper Methow." *Okanogan County Heritage*, March 1968.

King, Jim. Phone interview. Omak, Washington, fall 1990.

Methow Valley News. May 1968.

——. April 21, 1966.

Okanogan County Outlook. June 1967.

Pidcock, Emma Rader. "Pioneer Life in the Methow Valley." *Okanogan County Heritage*, March 1969.

Stark, Diane. Phone Interview. Winthrop, Washington, fall 1990.

Van Baalen, Henry. Interview. Winthrop, Washington, summer 1990.

White, Ken. Interviews and notes written by Mr. White. Winthrop, Washington, spring and summer 1990.

Chapter 25

THE PERFECT PLACE TO SKI TOUR

The Methow Valley offers perfect ski touring terrain and perfect scenery for the skier to enjoy. Ancient glaciers created this ideal touring topography. Over 10,000 years ago, a giant sheet of ice plowed down the Methow, gouged out the river valley, sculptured terraces and scooped out tear-drop lakes. Melting back, the glacier unveiled an unparalleled landscape for skiers. Smoothed-over hills descend like a staircase from the high country to the level land along the river. It is a forever undulating, varied country, in every direction offering a new vista and new discovery on skis.

The earliest Methow pioneers were quick to experiment with skiing for transportation and entertainment. However, the very first winters the pioneers spent here were mild with little snow —hardly conducive to skiing. Then the winter of 1889-90 hit the valley and suddenly everyone needed slats to skim atop the deep snow. You couldn't buy skis here at that time, so people fashioned their own unique varieties. J.L. Fulton, for example, chopped down a straight-grained green quaking aspen tree, split it in half, and made himself a pair of sliders, each 6 inches wide.

According to Fulton:

> Our skis worked very well when it was very
> cold and the snow dry, but when the snow was

348

wet it was different. More than once that winter,
I would have to put my skis on my shoulders and
flounder through the snow as best I could to reach
home. And this was the experience of many, especially when the sun got warm enough to melt
the snow.

J. Lee Fulton, from
Tales of the Trail

Which goes to show ski technology hasn't progressed *that* far
since we experience the same problems today!

"Dad made skis for us," said Nedra Horn. "He soaked
boards in hot water until the ends turned up. Then he cut
leather straps to secure the feet." On bright moonlit nights
Nedra and friends loved taking romantic ski jaunts.

Clara Williams recalled a ski game her kids played in pioneer times:

Our kids used to entertain themselves in the
wintertime by putting on their skis and tying a
rope to a horse. Then they would make the horse
pull them at a gallop through the snow. I think
they used to call it ski-jarring.

—*Methow Valley News*, September 29, 1977.

The Methow Valley's Original Ski School Program

Frank Johnson was one of the most enthusiastic and skilled
of early-day Methow skiers. Frank recalled that everyone
telemark-turned in the early days because of the old-fashioned
equipment technology. Bindings attached to one's toes, nothing
secured your heels, so the split-leg curtsy of the telemark position gave the best balance for turning on skis. "People ridiculed
our telemarking," said Frank, "but it worked."

Frank remembered when physical education teacher Victor
Kovac arrived here in 1938. Kovac took one look at the
Methow's telemark turners and decided a local revolution in
ski technique was in order. Victor had mastered the modern
Arlberg ski method from Austrian ski instructor Otto Lang.
Instead of the Norwegian telemark turn, Arlberg instructors
taught snowplows, christies and parallel turns.

The local school superintendent gave Kovac the go-ahead to
teach skiing to Methow kids. With characteristic zeal Victor
launched an Arlberg-technique ski program in the Methow
Valley schools. This was a radical departure from the usual

course selection. In fact, the Methow Valley was the only known district in Washington state at the time where skiing was part of the curriculum.

Suddenly in the Methow skiing became more than a mode of transport and form of snow play. It became a sport. Kovac's enthusiasm was contagious; it seemed everyone in the valley got excited about skiing. Sixty grade school students, 39 high school classmates, and seven of the valley's 10 teachers eagerly joined the program. Skis were relatively expensive then, about $15 a pair in the late '30s; nevertheless, all the kids who could raise the money bought their own equipment.

Students took lessons right on the school grounds near Winthrop. The CCC (Civilian Conservation Corps) contributed by building some ski trails near town. Expert skier Frank Johnson helped teach ski classes at the school.

Level terrain makes skiing easy in Mazama. Photo by Don Portman.

After mastering the basics down on the flats, the students were ready to tackle the hills. Program promoters outfitted the school buses with racks to ferry the children's skis to nearby slopes. On weekends the advanced skiers headed to Lewis Butte in the Rendezvous area. Lifts were an unaffordable luxury, so the kids got fit side stepping and herringboning up the hills.

Skiers competed in downhill races at Lewis Butte and at the Nagley place, recalled Frank Johnson. The Nagleys lived on the northeast hills of Moccasin Lake Ranch near Dibble Lake and Twin Lakes. Mr. Nagley, a farmer, offered his land for use at no charge. According to Howard Brewer, another ace skier, Mr. Nagley's generosity was typical of Methow landowners in those days. "Everybody respected everyone else. Everyone trusted people not to damage their property," said Brewer. "The Methow was very community-minded."

People either walked up the Nagley hill, or skied up on deerhide climbing skins. Howard remembered huffing and puffing up the hill on his custom-made, 9-foot-long, 6-inch-wide skis. His skis sported an innovative binding consisting of a toe strap and a screen door spring connected to the heel like a prototype cable binding. The contraption conferred some support, reported Howard, but possibly not enough, since Howard earned the nickname "Windmill Tilly," due to the wild flailing of his arms and poles on screaming descents.

Around the Nagley place plenty of snow coated the hills in earlier times, claimed Howard. One night it snowed 5 feet at his home on Route 20 near the original ski hill. People came from as far as Wenatchee to ski the great snow and slopes at the Nagley ski area.

The Methow's most deluxe early-day ski site was located on the steep terrain above the western edge of Patterson Lake. Howard Brewer remembered clearly the attributes of this historical ski "resort" which operated in the early 1940s. Instead of self-propulsion, skiers gained the summit by way of a rope tow custom-made by inventive skier/engineers. The ropes of the tow climbed over car wheels set in the trees at regular intervals. A skier held the bottom loop of the rope while a car motor powered the tow to the top. The final luxury supplied by the automotive industry was car headlights placed in trees and aimed down at the slope to permit night skiing.

The entire operation cost very little, since volunteers set up the site, the CCC cleared the slopes of debris, and most of the machinery consisted of old car parts. Everyone skied for free, occasionally chipping in for gas to run the engine.

World War II abruptly ended the Methow's unique ski school program, but failed to curtail the local lust for skiing. After the war, the Methow Athletic Club developed a ski area on some hilly land below Sun Mountain belonging to the Lull family. A well-preserved log cabin built by the pioneer Powers family functioned as the Athletic Club's ski lodge. Winthrop resident Elmer Lull remembered the mouth-watering aroma of the rich, fried bread served sizzling hot at the warming hut.

After taking the rope tow to the top, skiers could glide down the gentle knoll at the site. Many locals still made do with homemade skis, but lucky Elmer Lull managed to purchase a pair of secondhand store-bought beauties from Howard Brewer for $3. "No edges on those skis," said Elmer, "but they were the real McCoy."

The First Skiers At Sun Mountain Lodge

Sun Mountain is the Methow Valley's original cross-country ski resort. Skiing here has always been a popular activity with locals, but because of the developed trail system at Sun Mountain, cross-country skiing in the Methow Valley has become a nationally renowned tourist attraction.

Sun Mountain's fame as a cross-country mecca grew mainly because of the area's natural assets. The rolling terrain, the captivating combination of aspen groves and conifer forests, and the wealth of stunning mountain scenery have inspired journalists to call it a "ski tourer's paradise," likening the trail system to that found in Norway. Now Sun Mountain is known throughout the Northwest as one of the finest places to ski, but before the trails were groomed, before the fame, the place first had to be discovered.

In the early 1970s Jack Barron, owner of the recently opened Sun Mountain Lodge, had a brainstorm. Winter brought the doldrums to the lodge, and he wanted to drum up some business in the snowy season. The sport of cross-country skiing was just experiencing a revival and Jack, well aware of the potential touring terrain surrounding his lodge, decided to acquire cross-country ski rentals for lodge guests.

To promote his idea Jack sought help from Dave Chantler, a Seattle REI (Recreational Equipment Inc.) store ski buyer and probably one of the all-time great advocates of the sport of cross-country skiing. Dave promptly arranged for three ski weekend getaways here that included lodging and meals at Sun Mountain Lodge. Before the first troop of city slickers descended, Chantler did some homework scouting out the deer and stock paths that could best double as ski trails.

In January 1974, the first bus left rainy Seattle bound for the Methow's snowy playground. And it had snowed here—tons of snow had fallen. Then it had frozen, which resulted in breakable crust—absolutely the worst possible skiing conditions. Because of treacherous, slick roads, the bus arrived at 3 a.m. and promptly slipped off the original, snaky Sun Mountain road.

Considering the weather, skiing conditions and the driving debacle, it appeared that the first contingent of customers were chosen to be guinea pigs rather than guests. But the story ended quite differently than it began. In fact the first tourers fell in love with the Methow Valley. They raved about the ski terrain, the scenic beauty, the gracious lodge, the joy of touring on trails, which at that point were few and neither groomed nor marked. The whole group signed up for the next, identical trip.

The success of the first getaway convinced Jack Barron that cross-country skiing could pay its way and that the lodge could stay open in the winter. Chantler marked a few trails and Sun Mountain bought a Yamaha snowmobile to pack and track trails for skiers. The ski touring potential appeared so great, Sun Mountain decided to hire a ski professional to run the show. Recently certified cross-country instructor, examiner, and guide Don Portman was hired to organize a complete cross-country program the winter of 1976-77. That was the very winter no snow fell in the valley.

Portman ignored the snowless season, bought more rental gear and bused skiers from the lodge to Washington Pass. The next year, when the snow came on schedule, he was ready with a snowmobile and track setter to groom Sun Mountain trails. He hand painted signs and brushed out trails with hand tools. After grooming trails since dawn, he'd return to the ski shop smelling of oil and exhaust, throw off his snowmobile garb, and don a svelt one-piece ski suit to teach lessons. It

Skiing Sun Mountain's hill-and-dale terrain. Photo by Don Portman.

was practically a one-man show.

At first Sun Mountain maintained 30 kilometers of ski trails, though some were just signed and skied in periodically, instead of being machine-set. By the year 2000, 50 kilometers of immaculately groomed trails honeycombed the Sun Mountain area.

The Rise of the MVSTA

In the winter, the Methow Valley Sport Trails Association

(MVSTA) grooms 180 kilometers of trails—that's over 100 miles of machine-set cross-country ski trails, one of the largest systems in the USA.

Before MVSTA was established, individuals in different areas of the valley had already begun to develop ski trail systems. Sun Mountain's system under the tutelage of Don Portman has already been described. Doug Devin, Bob and Martha Cram, and many friends founded the Mazama Ski Club and created the Methow Trail and Jack's Trail—a 6-mile circle tour of the upper valley. Jack's Trail was named after Jack Wilson, one of the original ski trail groomers in Mazama.

North Cascades Basecamp owners Dick and Sue Roberts added trails to the original Mazama Ski Club system and assumed grooming responsibilities in the area. At the same time, Jay Lucas had been busy laying out and grooming a separate trail system at the nearby Mazama Country Inn, while Enoch Kraft groomed trails in the Rendezvous area and initiated a hut-to-hut skiing operation.

Some of these ski trail developers plus other local ski enthusiasts gathered to form MVSTA's predecessor called the Methow Valley Sports Club. In 1980 when the sports club evolved into the Methow Valley Ski Touring Association, cross-country skiing in the Methow Valley became a serious business. MVSTA obtained special-use permits from the Forest Service along with legal rights-of-way through private properties. The organization collected fees for trail use, upgraded grooming equipment and began to pay groomers who had previously worked for free.

The MVSTA continues to evolve. In 1991 it changed its name to the Methow Valley Sport Trails Association. In addition to ski touring, the organization enthusiastically encourages mountain biking, largely because local ski trails function perfectly as fat-tire bike trails.

The MVSTA's purpose is first and foremost to groom the numerous ski trails in the valley. Dedicated groomers driving expensive high-tech machinery strive to keep the trails constantly buffed to a perfect finish with clean, sharp tracks for diagonal skiers and firm corduroy texture for skate skiers.

To celebrate the valley trails, MVSTA sponsors ski races, ski swaps, ski clinics, and a mountain bike festival. Members produce maps of the local ski areas and informative brochures,

The magnificent, 250-foot Tawlks-Foster Bridge on the Methow Community Trail. Photo by Don Portman.

and churn out daily ski reports for radio and on the internet (mvsta.com).

Ski Areas to Suit Every Taste and Ability

Today one organization, the MVSTA, maintains all the trails in the Methow Valley. But each area—Mazama, Rendezvous, and Sun Mountain—has its own character.

The Mazama area is mercifully flat, so beginners will enjoy a wonderful first day on this terrain. A skier of any ability, though, could not help but love the fun of these easy trails and the stunning scenery of the upper valley. Trails traipse over and around the Methow River, through gentle meadows and open forests featuring views of Goat Wall cliffs, Gardner Mountain and other North Cascade peaks.

The extensive Rendezvous area offers a unique experience. One can ski on expertly groomed trails to fully equipped backcountry huts. A gradual climb by way of a Forest Service road to Rendezvous Pass leads skiers to some of the best views of Silver Star, The Needles, and Gardner Mountain.

356

Skiers who start their tour right at Sun Mountain Lodge are treated to a 360-degree view of both the Methow Valley and the Cascade range. Beginners feel confident skiing through aspen groves on the level Beaver Pond Trail, where there's the added attraction of a well-engineered beaver dam and pond.

The 16-kilometer Thompson Ridge/Meadowlark loop at Sun Mountain features all the best ingredients of a Methow day tour—a good workout in the shade of cool conifers, sunshine in meadowland, up-and-down always interesting terrain, and views of white-capped Pasayten Wilderness peaks.

The popular 25-kilometer Methow Valley Community Trail links the three ski areas together. Skiers can glide from Winthrop to Sun Mountain or to Mazama and on to the Rendezvous on one continuous trail ... if they have the energy!

Before the trail could be built local planner John Hayes, working through the Methow Institute Foundation (MIF), along with lawyer John Sunderland, obtained easements and covenants from over 82 separate landowners. MIF applied for and received a state grant to help fund the project.

A source of community pride and endless enjoyment, the trail follows a mostly easy route (with some challenging exceptions) on the valley floor. It travels along the river, through farmlands, woods and meadows with grand views of surrounding peaks. A highlight of the trail is the magnificent 250-foot suspension bridge three miles south of Mazama used to convey skiers—and in the summer, other non-motorized recreationists —over the river.

Bibliography

Brewer, Howard. Phone Interview. Twisp, Washington, fall 1991.
Chantler, Dave. Interview. Winthrop, Washington, spring 1990.
Duffy, Barbara. Notes from Wenatchee Valley College Class on Methow Valley History. Winthrop, Washington.
Horn, Nedra. Interview. Winthrop, Washington, summer 1990.
Hottell, Diana. "Virgil Webb." *Methow Valley News*, October 13, 1977.
——. "Clara Williams." *Methow Valley News*, September 29, 1977.
Johnson, Frank. Phone Interview. Winthrop, Washington, fall 1991.
Lull, Elmer. Phone Interview. Winthrop, Washington, fall 1991.
Portman, Don. Interviews. Winthrop, Washington, summers 1991 and 1992.
Quarnstrom, Joni. "Mazama Panorama." *Methow Valley News*, January 23, 1992.

Chapter 26

THE JOY
OF METHOW WILDLIFE

The Methow Valley is blessed with a rich and diverse wild-life population. Steelhead salmon spawn in the Methow River. The largest mule deer herd in Washington migrates through the valley. Black bears inhabit the lowlands as well as the Cascade backcountry. Cougars are seldom encountered, but one may come across their big cat tracks in the winter snow. The many ponds created by beavers provide choice real estate for colorful waterfowl and songbirds. Bald eagles view the Methow scene from favorite snags along the river, while red-tailed hawks soar on updrafts and circle over alfalfa fields.

Every day the wild creatures give joy to the people who live here. A friend reflects on the grace of tundra swans gliding on a lake near his home. Another friend spies a bobcat in her back-yard. On most summer evenings in the author's backyard, a family of deer convenes. They nibble low branches, sample some flowers, then settle down like statues spread among the trees.

The Waxing and Waning of Methow Mule Deer Herds

Today the Methow Valley has the most famous mule deer population in Washington. Deer are so visible here it's easy to assume that there have always been healthy herds and that deer will always be abundant. But historical records challenge this assumption. From the time the first pioneers arrived in Okan-

ogan County, the size of the local deer population has fluctu-
ated tremendously.

The early 19th-century Fort Okanogan fur traders mention
deer in their records, but since they ate a regular diet of horsemeat all winter, historians believe deer must have been scarce
at the time. In the mid-19th century deer became more abundant, and by the end of the century homesteaders depended on
deer as an important protein source.

While traveling in Okanogan County in 1884, Guy Waring
claimed he saw "herds amounting to 200 head in all in the
course of a day's travel." Later in that decade, Harvey Nickell
and his brother counted 1,000 Methow deer in one drove.

The record winter of 1889-90 decimated the Methow deer
population and for the next 40 years the animals remained
scarce. Pioneers, desperate for meat, would follow any track
until they found the deer. Ellis Peters remembered during his
childhood in the early 1910s his family saw very few deer in
the valley. "Dad would sometimes hunt for more than a week
before he'd find one to bring home," said Ellis.

When a local newspaper at the time reported that someone
had seen a small herd of deer around Poplar Flats on the
Twisp River, local people rushed to hunt the rare commodity.
A Forest Service report claimed that in 1911 only 50 deer inhabited the entire lower Methow from Twisp to Pateros.

Hoping to remedy the situation, the state Supervisor of Game
closed the 1923 and 1924 deer seasons in Okanogan County.
However, local historians say this failed to halt hunting in the
valley. Venison was essential to the survival of some valleyites,
so they hunted, knowing it was illegal. A soft-hearted game
warden would not always report poachers when he knew the
deer were needed for food. If the game warden *did* report the
poacher, the latter might appeal to the local justice of the
peace, who was frequently lenient when levying fines on
poverty-stricken families.

The recovery of local deer herds in the 1930s followed a period of heavy domestic stock grazing in the valley. Wildlife biologists say the two trends are related because overgrazing kills
grass while promoting bitterbrush, the deer's favorite winter
fare. By the late 1930s a rich crop of bitterbrush had grown up
on overgrazed land.

In addition to winter feed becoming plentiful, Methow winters became milder, the two trends combining to send the deer population pendulum too far the other way. As a result, the deer herds once considered so vulnerable and valuable became a menace, gorging like locusts in farmers' fields. Ellis Peters recalled the deer would quickly dispatch an entire hay crop. Already contending with drought, the rancher now had to fend off famished deer. Local Department of Wildlife official Jim Mountjoy claimed, "Deer were running people out of the country then."

Methow mule deer. Photo by Steve Barnett.

The state Game Department (now the Washington Department of Wildlife) watched with growing alarm as deer herds expanded and crop damage increased. No state damage control plan existed, yet immediate action had to be taken. The choice seemed clear: Either eliminate some deer or create a reservation for the burgeoning herds.

Authorizing the kinder option in 1940, the state Game Department established the Land Acquisition Project which set aside 15,210 acres of land for deer habitat. The state chose an opportune time to purchase wildlife protection areas in the Methow. Dryland farms were failing. Farmers wanted to sell fast, so they sold cheap. Some land went for only $1 an acre.

Since 1970 substantial purchases like the Big Buck Ranch between Moccasin Lake Ranch and the Twisp River Road have added protective status to more acres. In the fall of 1991 the Washington Wildlife and Recreation Coalition, a group of private citizens, orchestrated the purchase of the 845-acre Big Valley Ranch for wildlife habitat. The ranch, located 4 miles northwest of Winthrop, is one of the last large holdings of undivided property in the Methow. It's a pastoral, picturesque piece of landscape which includes over 3 miles of streamside and 35 acres of wetland. In winter large numbers of mule deer and whitetail deer migrate through the area. In the Methow Valley in 1997, there are approximately 26,000 acres set aside for wildlife habitat.

During the '40s along with land purchases to protect habitat, the department financed fences to protect the farmer. A cooperative program began whereby the state furnished materials and the landowner built deer barricades.

Twice during the 1940s, the state allowed special hunting seasons with no permit required to mitigate deer damage to fields and orchards. Pioneer Marie Risley remembered one season in the late 1940s she labeled "the slaughter." One particular day the state declared an open season on everything—bucks, does, and fawns. Marie saw entire families with all the kids out hunting in the hills. "In every little nook and valley there were people cleaning their deer," Marie said.

Deer numbers remained high in the '50s and '60s despite liberal hunting seasons. State Wildlife Biologist Jerry King believes the highest peak ever in the local deer population occurred in 1967 and 1968. This all-time-record deer population soon faced one of the Methow's all-time-record winters—that of 1968-69. Many, many deer starved during that severe season.

Since the 1970s deer numbers have remained fairly stable. Biologists estimate that 19,000 (plus or minus 6,000) deer inhabit the Methow Valley. The wide range for error comes from counting deer from a helicopter—not a very precise business.

Although weather controls population numbers more than any other factor, Bob Naney, Forest Service wildlife biologist, says that the loss of habitat now exerts more and more pressure on Methow deer. When humans landscape and farm they lower plant diversity, hence, unknowingly, they limit the deer's diet, Naney explained. Noisy, human machinery and dogs both scare deer, which raises the animal's stress level and burns valuable fat reserves.

Population growth in the Methow Valley is inevitable, many people believe. Wildlife habitat is bound to be lost. Time will tell whether the Methow deer population will diminish as a result.

Moose

Local biologists believe moose numbers may be increasing in the Methow since more sightings have been reported in recent years. Several moose have been seen in the Chelan-Sawtooth Wilderness and in the upper Chewuch River district. Department of Wildlife agent Sig Bakke estimated that six to 12 moose live in the valley full-time.

Much to the surprise and delight of local townspeople a moose wandered nonchalantly through downtown Winthrop in September 1996. A year later, people sighted a moose at the fish hatchery near Winthrop.

Beavers

The beaver population appears to be on the upsurge in the valley. At one time, however, the toothy tree cutters were over-trapped throughout the Northwest.

Ken White remembered when he was a child beaver numbers had dwindled so low that the state decided to close many local areas to trapping. By the time Ken turned 6 in 1926, beaver trapping had become illegal. If beavers interfered with a farmer's operation, a game department official had to be called to trap the animals and release them elsewhere.

As a result of this protectionist policy and the animal's natural reproductive success, the beaver population exploded in the Methow. They became a bane to farmers by clogging irrigation pipes and cutting trees at the edges of orchards. The solution? Allow trapping again. The price of beaver pelts had fallen so low by this point, however, that few trappers found the invitation appealing.

The beaver pond a mile south of Sun Mountain Lodge offers a good case history. The first beavers to arrive at the site dammed the stream flowing in the valley below Sun Mountain, thereby creating the scenic pond. The environment nurtured the beavers and their numbers increased. However, trappers, who came regularly to the area, kept the beaver population under control.

When fur prices declined and the Sun Mountain area began to be managed as a resort, trappers abandoned the beaver pond. With their numbers left unchecked, beavers gnawed whole groves of trees for food and logged entire aspen arbors to build more

The Methow's prolific beavers. Photo by Steve Barnett.

362

Hozomeen wolf seen in May 1991. Photo by Scott Fitkin, Washington Department of Wildlife.

dams. The dams raised the level of the pond, drowning out some huge old-growth ponderosa pines and black cottonwoods.

Now people may trap beavers in most areas of the Methow. The price of pelts is low, so trapping pressure is low. But every year a certain number of beavers are taken and this limits the population.

Wolves

In May 1990, when biologists reported evidence of a gray wolf inhabiting an area near Hozomeen Mountain at the head of Ross Lake, it made the front page of local papers. Wolves had not been seen or heard in the North Cascades or Methow Valley for a hundred years. Researchers felt so protective of the rare animal that they kept the location of its den a secret.

One day not long after the first discovery, some Methow Valley researchers were heading into the field when two wolf pups dashed in front of their vehicle as if proclaiming their presence to the world. After this fortuitous meeting, the researchers spent hours howling into the night air in the hope of eliciting a response from the illusive canine. They were overjoyed when they heard the answering call of a wolf.

Wolves roamed the wilds of the North Cascades for probably 8,000 years. Their major predator, man, took nearly 16,000 wolf pelts from the mountainous region during a 30-year period in the early to mid-1800s. In the latter 1800s, upper Valley pioneer J.A. Youngs hunted for wolves near Billy Goat Pass every winter. The bounty on wolves provided a source of income when no other work was available.

J.A. Youngs' spine-chilling version of the wolf's seranade

indicates how people viewed the animal in earlier times:

> A death-like silence would spread itself over the
> land and on occasion off in the distance could be
> heard the coarse-throated, long-drawn howl of a
> wolf giving vent to his feelings and a shiver
> would creep up the back of your neck.
>
> —Barbara Duffy's Historical References

Though records show the wolf to be almost nonexistent after the mid-1850s, some Methow pioneers recalled their nightly chorus. The Rader family remembered "evenings (in the 1890s) when quite a band of timber wolves would come out in the open and give a lively serenade." Many old-timers talked about wolves, but they disappeared from the valley a long time ago.

Cougars

Many Methow pioneers remember times when they had the eerie feeling something was following them. They'd glance over their shoulders, hasten the pace, but never actually see a pursuer. Later, when they'd retrace their steps to check out their suspicions, some found cougar tracks on top of their own.

In the history of Okanogan County, there is only one recorded cougar attack on a human being. But this horrifying event became a prolonged nightmare for locals. For a month, stories about the tracking and capturing of the culprit dominated the news media. For weeks, parents kept their children home from school. It took a long time for people to lose their fear of cougars.

The victim of the attack was 13-year-old Jimmy Fehlhaber, from Olema, a town located in the Chiliwhist area of Okanogan County. The tragedy occurred in mid-December 1924. The temperature was 15 below zero the day Jimmy's step-parents' car got stuck. Sent to borrow a neighbor's team of horses to pull the auto out, Jimmy chose to take a short cut through a brushy canyon.

No one will ever know exactly what happened, but reporters constructed a story based on evidence at the site. The cougar waited until Jimmy came within 50 yards. Then, it charged the boy, covering the distance in an instant. Jimmy struggled, lost the fight and was killed by the cougar.

Shortly thereafter, Winthrop farmer/miner Wash Vanderpool shot a 7-foot-long cougar on Blue Buck Mountain, located near Cougar Lake in the Methow Game Range. When experts realized the tracks left by the Vanderpool cat's injured left hind foot matched the prints found in Olema Canyon, they heaved a sigh of relief. The killer cougar had been caught!

People were just beginning to forget the tragedy when two weeks later near Olema, Charles Garrett shot what he believed to be the offending cougar. Grisly evidence of human hair and clothing retrieved from the stomach of the second slain cat seemed proof of its guilt. The incident at this point became so emotionally charged an irate Bill Brinkerhoff wrote in his publication, the *Methow Valley Journal*, that human hands had forced the remains down the cougar's esophagus into its stomach.

No one ever proved beyond a shadow of a doubt which cougar was the real villain. The dispute only added a sad footnote to a tragic event.

A more recent cougar encounter fortunately ended on a positive note. One late April day in 1999, local runner Mark Rhinehart was jogging up a steep hill a few miles up the East Chewuch when he heard rocks rolling down nearby. When he turned around he saw a mountain lion charging straight at him. "It was coming so aggressively, you could tell it was attacking," Mark recalled. Mark yelled, "Hey!" The cat stopped in a crouched position about 15 to 20 feet away. Mark raised his arms, jumped up and down and made deep barking noises. After about 10 seconds the cat jumped onto some rocks but stopped again still quite close to the jogger. Mark picked up a bunch of rocks and threw them at the cougar. Finally the cat turned away but without much haste and without any sign of fear. It seemed as though the cat decided the jogger, while being no threat, was too troublesome a prey.

According to wildlife experts the encounter was a good example of how people should behave in similar circumstances. The rule is—don't run from a cougar. Be big, be noisy and be aggressive.

Because cougars preyed on local stock, there was a bounty on the cat until 1965. After the state axed the bounty system, people could hunt cougars during a one-month open season in winter. The rules allowed each hunter one cougar but set no limit on the number of hunters.

Alarmed by the number of cougars killed during these open seasons, the Department of Wildlife introduced a permit system in the late 1980s. They allotted 35 permits which meant 35 cougars could be taken per season in an area covering all of Okanogan County and part of Ferry County.

New Cougar Laws

Washington state passed an initiative in 1996 that banned cougar hunting with hounds. (A game warden could still use hounds to hunt a problem cougar.) Then in response to increased sightings of cougars in populated areas and a cougar

Cougar. Photo by Dick Wenger.

attack on a 4-year-old boy in Kettle Falls, the state House voted in March 2000 to allow cougar hunters to use dogs in areas where the cats had become a problem.

The first three years after passage of the 1996 law, the Methow saw a marked increase in cougar sightings. In the winter of 2000-01 the number of sightings rose exponentially. For a while during that season, cougar tracks, sightings and encounters became the main topics of conversation among locals.

Wildlife agents attributed the sightings to an increase in the human population encroaching on cougar habitat as well as an increase in the cougar population due to the ban on hunting the cats with hounds. Bob Naney, Forest Service biologist, had a different slant on the situation. Cougars follow the deer, their preferred prey, said Naney, and the deer lived near people during the winter of 2000-01. If deer hang around homes and travel on recreation trails, cougars in search of food will likely do the same.

Lynx

About 15 to 20 lynx, the greatest concentration in the lower 48 states, live near the Methow Valley in the Meadows area of the Okanogan National Forest. The high elevation lodgepole forest of the Meadows provides the type of habitat the lynx require to survive.

Valued for its beautiful, soft and spotted pelt, lynx populations have been decimated in former ranges by trappers, bounty hunters and poachers.

Another reason for the lynx's decline may be its seasonal dependency on a single food source. In winter the lynx preys solely on the snowshoe hare. When the hare population fluctuates, so does the lynx population. A 1986 study revealed only one in eight lynx kittens survived the winter. The cause may be a scarcity of prey for the parents and resultant lack of nourishment for their offspring.

Now listed as a "threatened" species under both the state and federal Endangered Species acts the lynx can no longer be hunted in Washington.

Bighorn Sheep and Mountain Goats

A hundred years ago a healthy population of bighorn sheep inhabited the Gardner Mountain area, Bear Creek area, and Twisp River drainage, according to Ken White. For proof he cited the many antique skulls of the wild sheep he discovered while exploring these places.

In the early 1900s, more bighorn sheep than deer lived in the eastern Pasayten Wilderness, claimed Paul Louden, sheepman and miner. People counted herds of up to 400 sheep in the region at that time. In the 1920s several small herds were still being reported. From the '20s on, however, diseases brought by domestic stock weakened the bighorn sheep and by midcentury the handsome animals had become scarce in the backcountry.

Bighorn sheep still live in Canada and occasionally one will stray into the northern Pasayten near the Canadian-US border.

Mountain goats disappeared from the valley about the same time that bighorn sheep vanished and probably due to the same cause—susceptibility to stock diseases.

Pioneer Ellis Peters observed several herds of more than 10 mountain goats living near Mazama's Goat Wall until the 1920s. As the valley became settled, Ellis watched the goats disappear. Unlike the bighorn sheep, however, mountain goats maintain a respectable population in the backcountry and are often seen by hikers.

The animal now ranges in the Chelan-Sawtooth Wilderness,

Merchants
Basin, several
localities on
both sides of
the Twisp
River drain-
age and in the
Pasayten Wil-
derness.
Along the Pa-
cific Crest
Trail north of
the North
Cascades

A mountain goat high in the North Cascades.
Courtesy of the Okanogan National Forest.

Highway, rather tame goats frequently greet delighted hikers.

Black Bears

Ken White used to worry that hunting pressure threatened the
Methow black bear population. But every year from 1955 to
1985 Ken invariably received about 100 bear skins to tan at
his Winthrop taxidermy shop. Since the number of bears killed
during hunting season varied so little, Ken concluded the local
bear population likewise remained constant over the years.

Land development and the resulting loss of habitat have
possibly a greater potential than hunting to reduce local bear
numbers. So far, however, the animal seems to be holding its
own despite increasing human encroachment on bear territory.
In fact, when Ken was a child, he rarely saw a bear, but in
more recent years often encountered them in the backcountry.

The adaptable nature of bears explains their reproductive
success. Being omnivorous, bears picnic on a broad range of
food choices, including vegetable matter as well as meat. This
gives bears a competitive edge in the animal kingdom. And
bears snooze through the winter months, thereby avoiding the
need to scrounge for food in snow and cold.

Ken believed that past logging in the Methow may have indi-
rectly fostered a healthy bear population. Cutting trees opens
up the forest, allowing the understory plants (bear fare) to receive more sunlight. Thus, eliminating some of the forest
canopy in the valley has increased bear rations.

A 1996 state initiative ending the practice of using bait to attract and kill bears could also have a positive effect on the bear population.

Grizzly Bears

No one knows how many grizzly bears once roamed the wilderness surrounding the Methow Valley. But biologists *do* agree that more grizzlies inhabited the North Cascades region before white settlers arrived.

Methow Indians hunted grizzly bears and paid homage to the animal's strength in religious ceremonies and rites of bravery. According to legend, tribal women sometimes metamorphosed into grizzly bears.

Hudson's Bay Company records document that a good-sized grizzly bear population inhabited North Central Washington in the mid-1800s. The Fort Colville Trading Post received 382 grizzly bear hides in 1849—an astounding number of pelts considering how rare grizzlies are in this region today.

European-American trappers slaughtered so many grizzlies during the mid-1800s that they nearly exterminated the animal in the North Cascades. Later in the century, mining activity contributed to the grizzly's demise in the area. Miners killed bears that threatened their property or personal safety and sometimes shot bears for sport. When stockmen introduced cattle and sheep to ranges on the eastern slope of the mountains, grizzlies attacked and consumed the easy prey, which in turn led sheepherders to hunt and kill the stock thief.

After a bear killed some cattle near Winthrop, government hunter Pete Peterson was hired to track down the predator. On September 20, 1923, *The Methow Valley Journal* reported that Peterson found and shot the cattle attacker at Holman Pass in

Grizzly bears. Photo from the US Fish and Wildlife Service.

the Pasayten Wilderness. Two photos taken of the 1,350-pound animal confirmed it to be a grizzly bear.

In the early 1940s near Smith Lake in the Pasayten's Horseshoe Basin rangeland, a hunter shot a 1,400-pound grizzly known to have massacred many sheep. The animal's paws measured 9½ inches by 11 inches.

Rocky Wilson bagged a grizzly bear in 1967 on Fisher Creek —the last grizzly legally killed here. In 1969 grizzlies received legal protection in this region.

Although human activity nearly eliminated the grizzly from the North Cascade ecosystem, biologists claim recent sightings of *Ursus arctos* prove the presence of a "resident, remnant population of possibly 20 to 30 grizzlies." Researchers believe that the huge habitat found in the very heart of the North Cascades has remained fairly unscathed, and it is in this interior wilderness, where few people set foot, that the grizzly still lives.

In the mid-1980s Jon Almack, a grizzly bear biologist for the Washington Department of Wildlife, discovered a buried deer carcass in the Hozomeen area which he identified as a grizzly bear food cache. He also identified a grizzly bear track in Toats Coulee near Loomis.

In 1992, officials from the US Fish and Wildlife Service and the state Department of Fish and Wildlife began work on a plan for recovering a grizzly bear population on 10,000 square miles north of Interstate 90 and south of the Canadian border. The creation of a recovery plan for the grizzly, listed as a threatened species in the lower 48 states and an endangered species in Washington state, are the first steps toward the bear's re-establishment in the area.

Bibliography

Almack, Jon. "North Cascades Grizzly Bear Project." Washington Department of Game, December 1986.

Duffy, Barbara. Notes from Wenatchee Valley College Class on Methow Valley History.

Hanron, John. "Chewuch man has close encounter with big cat." *Methow Valley News*, April 29, 1999.

____. "Cougar Sightings on Rise in Valley." Methow Valley News, January 31, 2001.

Hottell, Diana. "Ellis and Martha Peters: A Mazama Story." *Methow Valley News*, December 14, 1978.

370

——. "Marie Risley ... She is One Who Remembers." *Methow Valley News*, July 11, 1981.

Kenady, Mary. US Forest Service Research notes on Pasayten Wilderness History.

Kerr, Charles C. "Okanogan's Killer Cougar." *Okanogan County Heritage*, December 1964.

King, Jerry. District Wildlife Biologist, Washington Department of Wildlife. Phone Interview. Okanogan, Washington, winter 1992.

Mountjoy, James. Wildlife Area Manager, Washington Department of Wildlife. Phone Interview. Winthrop, Washington, winter 1992.

Naney, Bob. Wildlife Biologist, Forest Service. Interview. Winthrop, Washington, fall and winter 1991 and 1992.

Partridge, Michelle. "State Will Buy Methow Ranch." *The Wenatchee World*, November 17, 1991.

——. "Plan to Save but not Import Grizzlies." *The Wenatchee World*, May 5, 1992.

Roe, JoAnn. *The North Cascadians*. Madrona Publishers, Seattle, 1980.

Schade, Shirley Mantei. "The George Washington Rader Family." *Okanogan County Heritage*, Fall 1984.

Schultz, Lon. Winthrop District Wildlife Biologist, Forest Service. Phone Interview. Winthrop, Washington, winter 1992.

Skatrud, Mark. "Densest Lynx Population in the Nation Threatened: and We are its Nearest Allies." *The Valley Voice*, July/August 1991.

Spohn, Isabelle. "Wolves Return to Washington Via the North Cascades." *The Valley Voice*, September/October 1991.

Sullivan, Paul T. "Preliminary Study of Historic and Recent Reports of Grizzly Bears, *Ursus Arctos*, in the North Cascades Area of Washington." Washington Department of Game, November 26, 1983.

The Wenatchee World. "House votes to allow limited use of hounds to hunt cougars." March 5, 2000.

Washington State Department of Wildlife records received from James Mountjoy. Winthrop, Washington.

White, Ken. Interview. Winthrop, Washington, summer 1990. Also Ken's personal notes on the history of wildlife in the Methow Valley.

Wilson, Bruce. "An Inquiry Into the Occurrence at Olema." Fall 1982, and Winter 1982-83.

Wooten, George. Botanist, Forest Service. Phone Interview. Winthrop, Washington, winter 1992.

Zeigler, Don L. *The Okanogan Mule Deer*. Washington Department of Game in Cooperation with the Okanogan National Forest, August 1978.

Chapter 27

SOME NOTES
ON PLACE NAME ORIGINS

Methow Valley

"Methow" (pronounced Met'-how) is the white man's version of the Indian name for the valley, which was "Smeethhowe." Early 19th-century explorer of the area David Thompson called the tribe he met living between the Methow River and Lake Chelan the "Smeethhowe" tribe.

Some pioneers claimed Methow was the Indian word for sunflower which symbolized the Indians' spring migration to the valley. In ancient times, Indians lived in the Methow year-round, but once they owned horses Indians spent winters in the Columbia Basin and other balmier climes where less snow allowed stock grazing in all seasons. Come springtime, the local tribe returned to the valley, where they'd be greeted by showy, golden sunflowers or balsamroot spread over the hills like a thick layer of butter. Thus, the Indians associated the valley with the beauty of the area's dominant wildflower.

The Yakama Indians believed Methow meant "plenty" or "land of plenty," or "place to have a good time," which referred to the cornucopia of available food sources in the valley. Sunflowers, with their rich, oily seeds, were a mainstay of the Indian diet, so, broadly interpreted, this second definition is similar to the first: Methow is synonymous with sunflower.

Early Winters Creek

Though she never lived here, historical records indicate an admirer of a woman named Ella Winters named the clear, rushing creek in the Mazama area after her. Through usage the original name changed to Early Winters Creek.

Some people believe the obvious—that the creek's name derived from the fact that winter often comes early to the northernmost tip of the Methow Valley through which the stream flows.

War Creek

Natives living on both sides of the Cascades traveled over the mountains to trade with other tribes. Relations between the tribes were usually peaceful but one time a clash occurred between West Coast Indians and East Interior Indians. The large Twisp River tributary at the site of the battle received the name of War Creek.

Pearrygin Lake

The Methow Valley's favorite recreation lake was named for the third person to settle along its shores, Benjamin Franklin Pearrygin. Anna Greene Stevens, Guy Waring's stepdaughter, offered this anecdote describing Mr. Pearrygin:

> A settler named Pearrygin who lived not far from us was one of the most amusing characters in the whole area. He owned a ranch on Pearrygin Lake, one of the lovely ones of the region, and made his living from trapping.
>
> One day he stopped by when Mother was cooking beans. To make conversation, she asked him what his method of cooking beans was. "Why, Mrs. Waring, you can't git 'em too did. The fact is, the doner you git 'em, the better they be."
> —*Okanogan County Heritage*, September 1970.

Gardner Mountain

Winthrop's founder, Guy Waring, named the highest peak in the Methow area, 9,000-foot Gardner Mountain, after East Coast belle Isabella Gardner, the same woman for whom the famous Isabella Stewart Gardner Museum in Boston is named. Waring also named the beautiful series of peaks extending generally north-northwest of Winthrop the Isabella Range, after the same Boston belle.

Tiffany Mountain and Meadows

World famous New York jeweler William Tiffany once visited the valley, camping with his brothers and some wealthy young friends at the base of the mountain and near the meadows named after him. In the winter this peak stands out as a perfectly rounded snow cone on the Methow's northern horizon. In the summer, an easy, scenic day hike to the summit provides 360-degree views.

Pasayten Wilderness

In her historical research on the huge wilderness bordering the Methow to the north, Mary Kenady discovered that Indians called the area the Pasay*teen* rather than Pasay*ten*. "Een" meant water and the rest of the word meant round-topped hills. Hence the full meaning of Pasayten might translate to "water from gentle mountains."

One Forest Service employee thought the name Pasayten might be French rather than Indian. The original name could have been "Pays du Satan," or in English "Land of Satan." This fits with some of the other diabolical place names in the region such as Devil's Park, Devil's Pass, Devil's Dome, Devil's Staircase and Hell's Basin.

Mystery Camp

A site on the banks of the Twisp River where a miner's cabin once stood became known as Mystery Camp after the cabin's two occupants disappeared without a trace—all their worldly belongings left in place.

Liar's Creek

The creek flowing through Moccasin Lake Ranch was named after tall-tale-teller and first settler in that vicinity George L. Thompson. Thompson's legendary sense of humor and story-telling skill inspired pioneers to call the creek meandering through his land Liar's Creek.

Rendezvous Area

In the 1910s locals gave the name Rendezvous, meaning meeting place or gathering place, to the area just north of Winthrop, because cowboys congregated at a cabin and cattle camp in the area where they rounded up stock.

Virginian Ridge and Storey Peak

The round-topped ridge just west of Sun Mountain Lodge received its name from the first western novel, *The Virginian*, written by Owen Wister and published in 1902. Wister, a good friend of Guy Waring's, visited the Methow in 1892 and 1898, gathering information and local color which he later incorporated into his famous novel.

Storey Peak, near Virginian Ridge, also received its name due to Wister's blockbuster novel. Locals liked to believe that Owen Wister based *The Virginian*'s hero on the author's observations of saloonkeeper and colorful character Milton S. Storey, who in the late 1800s worked at Guy Waring's Duck Brand Saloon in Winthrop. Hence locals honored Storey by naming a mountain after him.

Some of Storey's clever words and dashing ways undoubtedly influenced Wister's writing, but his book's main character was probably a composite of people Wister met while traveling throughout the West.

The flamboyant local barkeeper also provided a name for Milton Mountain, a neighbor to both Virginian Ridge and Storey Peak.

Bibliography

Carter, Morris. Isabella Stewart Gardner and Fenway Court. Trustees of Isabella Stewart Gardner Museum, Boston, 1925.

Duffy, Barbara. Phone interview. Winthrop, Washington, winter 1992.

Hitchman, Robert. Place Names of Washington. Washington State Historical Society, 1985.

Jones, Flora Filer. "Origins of Methow Valley Names." Okanogan County Heritage, September 1965.

Majors, Henry. Exploring Washington. Van Winkle Publishing Co., Holland, Michigan, 1975.

Stevens, Anna Greene. "Life in the Okanogan." Okanogan County Heritage. September 1970.

Index

Methow Valley Winter Sports
      Council 228
Miller, Carl 248, 249
Miller, Claude 250–252
Miller, George 248–250
Miller, Rose 248
Miller, William 248
Milner, Enid 127
mining 59–60, 67–80, 81–102,
      211, 300
Molesworth, Jennifer 279
Moody, Bill 307–308
moonshine 299
moose 360
Morley, Thomas 152
Morrison, Bruce 345
mountain goats 366
mule deer 357–360

Naney, Bob 360, 365
National Guard 324
National Marine Fisheries
      Service 276–279
Native Americans. *See* Indians
Nelson, Edith 317, 318
Nickell, G. E. 114, 269
Nickell, Harvey 106, 123, 172
Nickell, Walter 45, 114, 141,
      145, 180, 275, 292, 301
nordic skiing 347–356
North Cascades Basecamp 354
North Cascades Highway 118,
      199, 225, 228, 334
North Cascades National Park
      228

Okanogan Wilderness League
      238–239
orchards 212–214, 267–276
Ottman, C.E. 345

Pacific Crest Trail 90, 367
packing 219, 222, 250
Parker, Glenn 159, 163
Pasayten Wilderness 222, 232,
      284, 296, 303, 366, 369, 373

Patterson Lake 145, 277–278,
      336, 350
Patterson, Sam 145
Pearrygin, Benjamin Franklin
      372
Pearrygin Lake 225
Peters, Ellis 41, 232, 358, 359,
      367
Petersen, Jerry 314
pictographs 23
Pierce, Lieutenant Henry 62, 64–
      65
Portman, Don 352
Prewitt, Claude 164

R.D. Merrill 234–241
Rader, Alice 43, 243
Rader, Emma 128, 130, 139, 271
Rader, George 145, 156, 172
Rader, Jack 149
Rader, Leonard 145, 149
Rader, Pearl 138, 147
Rader, Pleas 131, 156, 172
Randall, Charles 254
Rattlesnake House 220
Rhinehart, Mark 364
Risley, Josh 172
Risley, Marie 360
roads 108–110, 118, 181, 259,
      296
Roberts, Dick and Sue 354
Robinson, Tom and Jim 60, 187,
      268
Robler, Bill 44
Rodman, Samuel 37
Ross, Alexander 56, 177

Sabold, Dave 343
Sandy Butte 228
sawmills 211, 253–262
Schade, Shirley Mantei 171
Schmidt, Jesse 116
schools 155–169
Shafer, Allen 79
Shafer, Dorothy 228

Shafer Museum 99, 203
Shafer, Simon 203
Sharpe, Bessy 299
sheep 281–290
Sherman, Paschal 48
Shulenburger, Clint 327
Sierra Club 233, 238
Silver, town of 71–74, 124, 316
ski area controversy 217, 227–242
ski touring 347–356
Smith, Alfred L. (Parson) 61
Smith, Deke 41, 137, 138, 179
Smith, Helen and Gus 287–289
smokejumping 303–309
Spohn, Isabelle 230, 232
Spurgeon, Esther 196
Squaw Creek, town of 69–71
stagecoaches 107
steamboats 110
Stevens, Anna Greene 104, 111, 136, 188, 207, 311, 372
Stewart, Bill 256, 257
Stewart, John A. 87
Stoaks, Warder and Annaliese 339
stock driveways 283
Stokes, Jay 294
Stone, John Chickamun 71
Stone, Napoleon 106, 123
Storey, Milton 215, 374
Sullivan, James 187, 193
Sun Mountain Lodge 145, 277, 333–346, 351–353
Sunny M Ranch 327–334

Tait, Alma 255
Terry, Roland 338
The Virginian 215, 374
Therriault, Leonard and Paul 113
Thompson, David 54, 371
Thompson, George L. 126, 137, 373
Three Fingered Jacks Saloon 196, 314
Thurlow, Frank 244, 248
Thurlow, Grace 47
Thurlow, Lucille 183, 244
Thurlow, Mason 43, 106, 123, 125, 135, 244, 271
Tingley, Minnie 218
Tonseth, Dale 101, 203
tourism 121, 199, 313, 337
trains 115–116, 181
trapping 53–55, 60, 223
Trust for Public Land 240, 241
Twisp, town of 74, 164, 177–183

US Environmental Protection Agency 232
US Fish and Wildlife Service 276, 369
US Forest Service 195, 226, 228, 231, 233, 246, 276, 282, 294, 304

Ventzke, Fred 263

Wagner, Ernst 260
Wagner, Kathryn 199, 222, 261–262, 340
Wagner, Otto 199, 222, 259–262
Walsh, Ed 257
Wapato, Matilda 47
Wardell, Carol 238
Waring, Guy 74, 104, 135, 178, 187, 203, 207–215, 218, 264, 271, 358, 372
Washington Department of Ecology 232, 239
Washington Department of Fish and Wildlife 364, 369
Washington Environmental Council 233
Washington Pass 224
water rights 127, 239, 245
Weagant, Rod 346
weather 311–325
Webb, Dick 43, 317
Webb, Virgil 40, 107

381

Photo by Don Portman.

SALLY PORTMAN

When Sally Portman and her husband Don moved to the Methow Valley in 1977, they started out much like the Methow pioneers. With a group of friends, the couple raised a one-room cabin miles from town. They drilled a well, watered a garden, and learned they both needed regular jobs to supplement an uncertain sustenance "living off the land."

For many summers Sally worked for Okanogan National Forest as a Wilderness Ranger. In the winter she assists Don with the cross-country ski program at Sun Mountain Lodge. After becoming Winthrop librarian in 1986, she grew fascinated with Methow Valley history.

Sally received a B.A. from Wheaton College in Norton, Massachusetts, and a B.S. from the University of Washington. She is the author of *Ski Touring Methow Style*, *The Wildflowers of Sun Mountain*, and *Birds of Sun Mountain and the Methow Valley*.